W9-BWN-267

ROOTS QUEST

ROOTS QUEST

Inside America's Genealogy Boom

JACKIE HOGAN

ROWMAN & LITTLEFIELD
Lanham • Boulder • New York • London

Published by Rowman & Littlefield
An imprint of The Rowman & Littlefield Publishing Group, Inc.
4501 Forbes Boulevard, Suite 200, Lanham, Maryland 20706
www.rowman.com

6 Tinworth Street, London SE11 5AL, United Kingdom

British Library Cataloguing in Publication Information Available

Library of Congress Cataloging-in-Publication Data

Names: Hogan, Jackie, 1967– author.
Title: Roots quest : inside America's genealogy boom / Jackie Hogan.
Other titles: Understanding America's genealogy boom
Description: Lanham, MD : Rowman & Littlefield, [2018] | Includes index.
Identifiers: LCCN 2018029090 (print) | LCCN 2018033861 (ebook) | ISBN
    9781442274570 (ebook) | ISBN 9781442274563 (hardcover : alk. paper)
Subjects: LCSH: Genealogy—Social aspects—United States. | Genealogy—Study
    and teaching—United States. | United States—Genealogy—History—21st
    century. | Ethnicity—United States—History—21st century. | Group identity
    —United States—History—21st century. | National characteristics, American.
Classification: LCC CS9 (ebook) | LCC CS9 .H64 2018 (print) | DDC
    920.00973—dc23
LC record available at https://lccn.loc.gov/2018029090

∞™ The paper used in this publication meets the minimum requirements of
American National Standard for Information Sciences—Permanence of Paper
for Printed Library Materials, ANSI/NISO Z39.48-1992.

Printed in the United States of America

To Michael and Zoe,
and to the countless grandmothers and grandfathers who made you possible.

CONTENTS

ACKNOWLEDGMENTS

There is nothing like genealogical research to make you aware of both your connections and your debts to others. I wish to thank the many genealogists, archivists, and roots industry professionals who have shared their thoughts and experiences with me over the past five years. Without them, this book would not have been possible. Thanks also to my friends and colleagues who have talked through many aspects of this work with me, particularly Naomi Stover, who provided valuable feedback on my discussion of genetic genealogy. Finally, I wish to thank a group of people who will never read this book—the Czech midwife, the Irish tenant farmer, the Virginia cooper, the Nebraska homesteading mother of six, and all the countless ancestors in my family tree whose perseverance made my life and the lives of my children possible.

1

ROOTS QUESTS

An Introduction

> In all of us there is a hunger, marrow-deep, to know our heritage—to know who we are and where we have come from. Without this enriching knowledge, there is a hollow yearning. No matter what our attainments in life, there is still a vacuum, an emptiness, and the most disquieting loneliness.
>
> —Alex Haley, author of *Roots*[1]

In the basement of a cavernous convention center, a group of eager family historians crowds around one man. In the printed programs they carry, his name is adorned with letters of distinction: CG, FASG, FNGS, FUGA, codes well known to those waiting their turn to speak with him.[2] He is a renowned liberator of ancestors, a professional genealogist, and they have come to unlock the secrets of their past.

If you ask them why they have traveled over wintry roads and paid hundreds of dollars to attend this genealogy conference, they will tell you they are looking for the name of a great-great-great-grandparent, the military service record or baptismal certificate of a distant forebear, a ship's log with traces of an immigrant ancestor, or countless other crucial details to put flesh on the bones of their family histories. But delve a bit deeper and you find that they seek far more than names and dates, places and documents and stories. They seek a sense of belonging—to family, to community, to nation, and to history.

America is in the midst of a genealogy "boom." In 1977, just 29 percent of Americans polled said they were "very interested" in family history. By 1995, that had grown to 45 percent. By 2000, it had jumped to 60 percent; by 2005, to 73 percent; and by 2009, to a remarkable

87 percent.[3] Online genealogy sites have rapidly proliferated in the last decade. The leading subscription service, Ancestry.com, went from being a small genealogical research and publishing firm in the 1990s, to a NASDAQ-listed corporation with 2.6 million subscribers and $850 million in annual revenues.[4] Likewise, the preeminent family history research venue in the United States, the Family History Library in Salt Lake City, hosts in excess of seven hundred thousand visitors each year, and another prominent genealogical library, the Allen County Public Library in Fort Wayne, Indiana, sees more than four hundred thousand genealogists each year.[5] Countless Americans are venturing even further afield in their ancestral quests, with a thriving roots tourism industry expanding to cater to their desire to connect with "Old Country" destinations. Ireland alone hosts almost one million international roots tourists annually (a remarkable figure, given its population of under five million).[6] Amid this bourgeoning interest in ancestry, and no doubt helping to fuel such enthusiasm, several television broadcasters have brought family history series to air, including, most notably, PBS's *Faces of America* (2010), *Finding Your Roots* (2012–17), and *Genealogy Roadshow* (2013–16), and NBC's (now TLC's) *Who Do You Think You Are?* (2010–18).

Many observers have commented on the upsurge of interest in family history and genealogy at the dawn of the twenty-first century. Indeed, *Time* magazine recently ran a commentary titled "How Genealogy Became Almost as Popular as Porn."[7] If, as the piece explains, genealogy websites are now second in popularity only to pornographic websites, then we need to ask ourselves why. Why is genealogy being so enthusiastically embraced at this moment in time? What does genealogy offer its practitioners? What does genealogy in the United States today tell us about our own society and the age in which we live? And, broadening our perspective, what do genealogical practices around the world tell us about any given people's links with their ancestors and with their history? What do our roots quests tell us about what it means to be human? These questions lie at the heart of this book.

Of course, there are simple answers as to why so many Americans (and Canadians, and Brits, and Australians, among others) are pursuing genealogical research these days. Most obviously, increasing numbers of baby boomers are now reaching retirement and finding themselves with time to spare and a keener focus on their legacy. At the same time, rapid improvements to computing and imaging technologies are making genealogical records more readily accessible than ever before. But simple answers seldom tell the whole story. I argue that the growing popularity of genealogy is, in part, a response to some of the large-scale social transformations that define our age—namely, globalization, secularization, the increasingly virtual nature of social life, and the sense of rootlessness these transformations provoke. In short, this book explores the ways our increasingly rootless society fuels the quest for authenticity, for deep history, and for an elemental sense of belonging—for roots.

Let me disclose at the outset that I myself have embarked on a roots quest. While I initially immersed myself in the world of genealogy—websites, conferences, historical societies, research trips, DNA tests, and, yes, graveyards—to better understand the motivations and experiences of genealogists, I soon found myself spending late nights in front of my computer tracking down just one more census record. Then just one more. I discovered a frontier pool hall proprietor in my family tree, a Civil War soldier, a homesteading mother of six, and a religious heritage I'd never suspected. I found that certain cherished family lore could not be supported by evidence. I found scraps of my ancestors' lives scattered from the Czech Republic and Ireland to New York and St. Louis and the prairies of Nebraska. And every snippet, every mossy gravestone, every sepia-colored document pulled me deeper into my quest. When I found a Colonial-era family will in the Family History Library in Salt Lake City, I jumped right out of my chair to the knowing smiles of the seasoned genealogists around me. When I discovered my great-great-grandmother, an Irish famine immigrant, in an archive in Chicago, I was moved to tears. She did not arrive alone, as so many of those desperate refugees did, but rather was surrounded by her family in the ship's manifest. Mother, father, two brothers, a sister. I had not realized until that moment how much I'd wanted her to have the comfort of a family on that grueling journey.

In the course of my research over the past five years, family historians have described genealogy to me as their passion, their hobby, their duty, their favorite never-ending puzzle. But most often they have described genealogy as an obsession. And it is an obsession that I now happily share. It is important to note, therefore, that while I critically examine the many complex forces shaping the current genealogy boom, in no way do I wish to impugn the personal motivations of genealogists or diminish their considerable commitment of time, energy, and resources toward genealogical goals or their impressive skills. Instead, my goal is to better understand this obsession we share and to shed light on its power to enthrall.

Because I believe that we are better able to understand our own behaviors by situating them in the flow of history, chapter 2 provides an overview of American genealogical practices from Colonial times to the present.[8] In this overview, I give particular attention to the character of our current genealogical era and the factors that shape it, principally the following:

- the increasing importance of digital and genetic technologies;
- the secularization of society and a trend toward viewing knowledge and morality in relative terms;
- the increasing saturation of the mass media and the proliferation of virtual forms of social interaction;
- the hypermobility of populations (particularly in wealthy Western nations), and the new ways we are experiencing space and time; and
- the commodification of identities—that is, our increasing tendency to assemble unique identities in large part through our consumption practices.

I argue that such processes are destabilizing our individual and collective identities, prompting us to yearn for "authenticity" and a sense of belonging.[9]

I also believe that we are better able to understand our own behaviors by comparing them with other cultural practices around the world. So, in chapter 3 we go farther afield to consider a broad range of genealogical practices—from the largely documentary practices of American genealogists, to lineage singers in Senegal, to the various forms of ancestor worship that are widespread in East Asia, West Africa, Melanesia, and the Pacific. While some of these practices may strike many Americans as "exotic," I argue that these diverse practices of cultivating links with ancestors actually serve quite similar purposes across cultures. Such "roots work" gives us psychological comfort and a sense of belonging and binds us more closely together as social groups.

In chapter 4 we move from an examination of "roots work" around the world to consider the ways memory and "memory work" are being revolutionized by new technologies and new ways of life. Our current fascination with the past is readily observable through the popularity of such things as historical films and novels, historical sites and monuments, or antiques and ancestry. And our often obsessive devotion to social media demonstrates an increased commitment to documenting (in effect, memorializing) our lives. The question is, of course, what is prompting these changes? What factors are fueling what some scholars have called a "memory boom"?[10] And how is this increased attention to memorialization reshaping the way we understand ourselves, our kinship networks, and our world?

Chapter 5 delves into one defining characteristic of our current genealogical era: the increasing use of DNA evidence. Of particular interest are DNA testing services that promise to reveal our deep genetic heritage—reaching back thousands or even tens of thousands of years—and link us to countless "cousins" across the globe for as little as $99. But do they deliver on these claims? And how will the increasing reliance on biological evidence potentially alter our ideas of self and family? In this chapter, we examine both the promises and the perils of genetic genealogy.

Chapter 6 examines both the production and the reception of televised roots quests. First we consider how roots TV shows such as *Who Do You Think You Are?* are structured to maximize suspense and emotional impact. Then we dig a bit deeper into certain underlying messages in the shows— about the value of multiculturalism, the American Dream, religious faith, and progress, among others. Next we look at the complicated relationship genealogists themselves have with these shows, an ambivalent relationship that vacillates between fascination and frustration. And, finally, we consider the ways the mass-mediatization and virtualization of social life may be changing the ways we perceive ourselves and our family connections.

Chapter 7 probes the spiritual dimension of American roots quests in the twenty-first century and, in particular, the impact of secularization on American genealogy. Religious affiliation has been changing rapidly over the past decade in the United States. The fastest growing religious category in the United States is "religiously unaffiliated" (the so-called Nones). One-fifth of all adults now identify as "unaffiliated," a dramatic increase over the past decade. At the same time, the global membership of the Church of Jesus Christ of Latter-day Saints (LDS)—a leader in the current genealogy boom—has continued to increase modestly.[11] It would appear that even as more people are stepping away from organized religion, there remains a desire to belong to something larger than any one individual, something enduring and transcendent. I argue that we meet this need, in part, through our roots quests.

In chapter 8, I examine our changing experiences of time, space, and homelands. Americans are traveling more than ever, and our virtual access to distant locations has increased exponentially, broadening the reach of our senses, broadening our range of experiences, and potentially broadening our social (and kinship) networks. At the same time, our hypermobility flattens out differences that were once preserved by geographical barriers. Many of the cultural markers that once gave us a sense of belonging (things such as distinctive clothing, cuisine, architecture, language, and music) are now either disappearing or becoming global communal property.[12] I argue that as everyone and every place starts to look the same, Americans have sought out new sources of distinction and uniqueness, in part through their roots work. Today, for instance, tourists can seek ancestral encounters on tours of the slave forts of western Africa or the concentration camps of the Third Reich, or at "homecoming" events in Ireland, the Scottish Highlands, or countless other locations.[13] In this chapter, I consider the experiences of roots tourists—both what they seek and what they find in roots tourism—as well as the impact of roots tourism on "homeland" destinations.

The concluding chapter considers the ways contemporary genealogy helps to shape our own identities. All genealogists face decisions about which lines of research to pursue and which to ignore (at least for the time being), about which forebears to examine more carefully and which to leave in the shadows of our family trees. In making such choices, genealogists are making choices about how to construct our own histories, our own narratives, our own projections of self. I consider not only the details that are included in family history narratives but also the details that are ignored or downplayed by genealogists as we construct our family histories. I also examine the ways the rapid commercialization of genealogy is reshaping personal and collective identities. In a sense, online genealogy subscriptions, roots tourism providers, and countless other genealogical products and services allow us to selectively "purchase" our family histories, and thus our identities. And not everyone has an equal capacity to pay. This has implications for the kinds of stories that get told and for the quality and the extent of genealogical information bequeathed to future generations.

EVIDENCE AND APPROACH

Over the past five years, I have immersed myself in genealogy. I have interviewed more than seventy amateur and professional genealogists from across the nation, asking them about their motivations, their joys and frustrations, and their perceptions of the importance of roots research. I have been an active participant–observer at local, regional, and national genealogical conferences, on two roots tourism trips (including one international trip), and at genealogical research centers across the Midwest, in Salt Lake City, and in Ireland. I have analyzed more than eighty hours of American roots television programming, and ten years of genealogical magazine content. And I have amassed a sizable collection of genealogical promotional materials, including advertisements for everything from DNA testing kits to specialist hardware and software, from roots tourism packages, research services, and training and accreditation programs to website subscriptions and I SEEK DEAD PEOPLE T-shirts. It is to this eclectic body of evidence that I turn as I attempt to understand American roots quests today.

As a social scientist with a background in sociology and anthropology, I use the tools of my trade—theories, concepts, and analytical methods from these disciplines—to help reveal patterns that might otherwise escape everyday notice. That said, I am a firm believer that such tools should be used to bring clarity to arguments and evidence, and not simply to demonstrate the erudition of the author. After all, how valuable is even the most original argument or the most striking piece of evidence if only the initiated few can understand and make use of it? For this reason, the main body of the book provides social scientific insights relatively unencumbered by professional jargon. My esteemed colleagues in the academy will find the relevant scholarly sources and debates covered in the notes to each chapter.

My goal in this volume is not only to shed light on the desires and preoccupations of American genealogists today, but also to examine how our twenty-first-century genealogy boom fits into both the broader sweep of history and the tremendous diversity of related cultural practices around the globe. The material I present will challenge genealogists and non-genealogists, academics and students of history and culture, and the general reader to think about ancestry and identity in new ways.

In addition, there are three quite specific benefits to closely examining our own genealogical practices. First, while the desire to dig into family roots is motivated by a whole range of personal factors (perhaps the death of a loved one, the anniversary of a momentous event like the Civil War, or simply the realities of aging and coming to terms with our own mortality), to understand the current genealogy "boom," we must look beyond such personal motivations to broader social factors. If we are to understand why we do what we do—in this case, why we, like millions of others, choose to spend our time and our treasure in pursuit of the dead—we must look at the cultural, technological, and economic forces that help to shape our desires and guide our actions. As genealogists often observe, we can only really know ourselves when we come to understand our place in history. Not only does this entail understanding the lives of those who came before us, but also understanding the ways the unique character of the current era is shaping our choices, our values, and our ideas today.

This is crucial because, in a very real sense, genealogy does not simply trace and preserve family memories and family ties; it also actively *constructs* kinship and memory. As one scholar has observed, "Genealogists are in the business of constructing symbolic ancestors out of the evidence available to them."[14] This is not to say that we invent stories and characters out of pure imagination. Instead, we take the often incomplete, fragmented, skewed, and contradictory evidence of our ancestors' lives and attempt to weave it into cohesive stories that help to bring meaning to our own lives. So understanding the forces that shape our thinking in the here and now can help guide our interpretations of the genealogical evidence.

Next, like most realms of human activity, genealogy reflects, reinforces, and occasionally even challenges existing power relations. In particular, it both mirrors and sustains certain social imbalances that we would do well to put behind us, namely inequalities based on gender, race, ethnicity, and class. Understanding how genealogy is implicated in such ongoing inequalities is part of the larger project of building a more just society. Let me clarify that I will not be arguing that American genealogists today are sexists or racists or snobs. Indeed, my data suggests that attitudes and social values in the genealogical community are quite varied. But, as we will see in chapter 2, genealogy by its very nature is always gazing backwards. It is firmly rooted in traditions, techniques, and perspectives established in less egalitarian times. Thus, even genealogists of the most egalitarian mind-set may unintentionally perpetuate some of the very injustices that offend us, by giving greater voice to the historically advantaged few while glossing over unsung others—especially women, people of color, and the poor.

This has consequences for us as a society, and for each segment of our society. The more we focus on the lives of men, on the white Christian majority, on the well-heeled, and the more we are told that they are the ones who forged the nation out of their trials and tears, the more likely we are to imagine these groups as the natural proprietors of the nation. Such imaginings stifle positive social change by making it more difficult for us to envision women, racial or ethnic minorities, or other less powerful groups in positions of authority and leadership. And, in extreme cases, notions of ancestry can be used in quite insidious ways, for instance, to legitimate the mass incarceration of Japanese Americans during World War II, to disenfranchise people of black African and "mixed" ancestry under apartheid, and even to justify genocide during the Holocaust. On a more hopeful note, however, I will also examine evidence of growing inclusivity and egalitarianism in American genealogy today.

Finally, while millions of Americans are engaged in family history research today, there has been relatively little discussion of the broader social impact of this activity. But researchers out of Emory University's Center for Myth and Ritual in American Life (MARIAL) recently found that children with greater knowledge of their own family history had higher self-esteem, lower levels of anxiety, and greater confidence in their own ability to overcome adversity.[15] The authors stress that it is not the specific knowledge itself but rather the process of transmitting intergenerational knowledge that allows children to develop a more resilient sense of self. The study bears out a frequent claim by genealogists—that genealogy gives people a firmer sense of who they are. But if self-knowledge is one of the primary goals of contemporary genealogy, then genealogists have a duty to put our own motivations and practices under the microscope to more deeply understand the nature of our roots quests.

AMERICAN GENIES

Among the many genealogical novelty products available in the burgeoning marketplace today are bumper stickers, mugs, tote bags, and T-shirts with pithy slogans like "I Used to Have a Life. Then I Started Doing Genealogy." One prominent genealogical retailer even sells a tongue-in-cheek "Genealogist's Prayer," which begins,

> Genealogy is my pastime; I shall not stray.
> It maketh me to lie down and examine half-buried tombstones;
> It restoreth my ancestral knowledge;
> It leadeth me into the paths of census records and ship passenger lists.[16]

Who are these genealogists—or "genies"—who dig with such dedication into the roots of their family trees? There is a widespread perception that genealogy is primarily the pastime of elderly women—the clichéd maiden aunt—but solid demographic data on the American genealogical community is hard to come by. One systematic study from 2001 found that 72 percent of genealogists in a national sample were indeed women, but the mean age of genealogists was just fifty-four years—more middle-aged than elderly, by common definitions. Furthermore, the study found the median income of genealogists in the sample was between $40,000 and $60,000 (on par with the national average in 2001).[17] The study did not collect data on race or ethnicity.

My own numbers are broadly consistent with these previous findings. Based on observational data on 4,611 visible participants at six large regional or national genealogical conferences and one local conference, the majority of participants (77 percent) were women. In fact, the skewed gender ratio at one conference prompted organizers to commandeer a men's bathroom and turn it into a ladies' room, which one woman gleefully proclaimed "Potty parity!" In a broad measure of ethnicity, participants were also classified as either phenotypically white or phenotypically nonwhite (most of African, Asian, nonwhite Hispanic, or indigenous descent).[18] The vast majority of participants (98 percent) were phenotypically white.[19] Furthermore, the average age of genealogists who completed a questionnaire about their family history activities was sixty years old.[20] And, while income data was not available, questionnaire respondents reported spending an average of $1,500 per year on genealogy, and traveling throughout the United States and to a variety of overseas "homeland" destinations for genealogical purposes, all indicators of relative economic security.[21]

These data suggest that American genealogists are more likely to be female, white, and older with sufficient disposable income to pursue what can be a rather costly pastime. However, the demographic picture may be more complex than this. First, data indicate that the American genealogical community is markedly segmented along racial and ethnic lines. At one recent national conference,[22] for example, only 2 percent of the roughly two thousand observable participants were people of color, and yet sessions on Civil War "Colored Troops" and abolitionist societies attracted audiences that were between 61 percent and 73 percent African American. In a session on Irish genealogy, by contrast, not a single person of color could be seen. Specialist genealogical societies, resources, conferences, and services cater to racial, ethnic, and religious minorities within the United States. Such segmentation is rooted in both practical and historical realities. In practical terms, different and quite specialized skills are required for effective genealogical research on different ethnic groups, making some segmentation in the research community inevitable. In historical terms, as we shall see in chapter 2, American genealogy was long fixated on elite pedigrees and racial purity, to the extent that racial and ethnic minorities were effectively barred entry to some of the nation's most prominent genealogical and lineage societies (a legacy that still mars the reputation of groups such as the Daughters of the American Revolution, which notoriously prevented African American soprano Marian Anderson from performing in their concert hall in 1939).[23] Surveys of specialist genealogical communities would no doubt yield starkly different demographic results.

Second, gender dynamics within the genealogical community are complicated by historical, cultural, and institutional factors. As noted above, the data suggest that women account for roughly three-quarters of American genealogists. As other scholars have noted, women have long served as the key managers of kinship knowledge and kinship networks in industrialized societies such as the United States. In a classic study of gendered labor within American households, for instance, one scholar found that women bear a much greater responsibility for "kin work," the construction and maintenance of extended family ties through labor such as hosting family dinners, sending holiday cards, buying presents, and coordinating visits.[24] Indeed, kin work has become such specialized "women's work" that when wives are absent (due to divorce or death, for example), such tasks typically go undone—no more holiday meals, no more cards or presents or telephone calls to elderly relatives. And thus kinship networks often simply languish. Likewise, we can think of genealogy as one kind of kin work, dedicated as it is to uniting extended family members. It is possible that more women than men engage in genealogy because it is seen as a natural extension of their other domestic, nurturing, and kinship roles. Additionally, in a world where women still routinely earn much less than men and face barriers to promotion and hiring, kin work is one realm where women are the acknowledged specialists.[25]

Indeed, a survey of registered certified professional genealogists at two of the leading certification bodies in the United States reveals that roughly three-quarters of genealogical professionals today are women.[26] Yet in my sample of genealogy conferences, women made up just over half (55 percent) of all conference speakers, and, with one exception, all opening keynote speakers were men, a significant underrepresentation of women. To explain this disparity, it is useful to look at another realm of female labor and culturally acknowledged female expertise—cooking. According to the US Bureau of Labor Statistics, women spend more than twice as much time as men cooking in the home, and women make up the bulk of the workforce in the US food service industry, and yet a study by Bloomberg Business found that women account for just 6 percent of head chefs in the nation's most prominent restaurant groups.[27]

Such disparities reveal the underlying patriarchal structure of American society today. Yes, women are widely considered the "natural" experts in the time-consuming, everyday task of home cooking, but when cooking is elevated to a high-status profession, the "natural" experts are seen to be men. Because the United States, like all other Western industrialized nations, has a long history of regarding men as natural leaders and authority figures, men in female-dominated occupations are often more quickly elevated to positions of leadership and authority. This is what social scientists call the "glass escalator" effect.[28] So it is not surprising that genealogy conference organizers are more likely to choose men as their headline speakers, nor that men are overrepresented in the slate of experts leading conference sessions.

American genealogy is also gendered in another way that practitioners readily acknowledge: in its sometimes disproportionate emphasis on paternal lines. In many ways, for instance, the Bible is the model on which Western European genealogy developed.[29] In its lengthy passages of "Irad begat Mehujael; and Mehujael begat Methusael; and Methusael begat Lamech . . . ," women are conspicuously absent. The only lineage that matters is the father's lineage. To some extent, modern American genealogy demonstrates a similar tendency in its emphasis on surname groups, traditionally passed through the father. In fact, such priority is given to the paternal line that standardized family group sheets are organized with fathers always listed above mothers. As one conference presenter said, "Sorry, ladies. I know it's not fair," but we must follow standard documentary practice. Again, there are both practical and historical reasons for this institutionalized male dominance. In practical terms, because historically women have had fewer rights than men and fewer public roles, typically far fewer records document their lives. This is compounded by the Western European tradition of women adopting their husbands' surnames, which can make it difficult to track women back in time. So American genealogists may have little choice but to focus (at least in the early phases of their research) on the better documented lives of their male forebears. The irony, of course, is that while women are spending considerably more time than men tracing and preserving family history, it is often largely the history of *men* that we are documenting.

"WE'RE HOPELESSLY ADDICTED": THE NATURE OF AMERICAN ROOTS QUESTS

When I interviewed Beth and John, a Wisconsin couple in their seventies, about their motivations for devoting so much time and energy to tracing their ancestors, their first response was "We're hopelessly addicted!"[30] And I heard this sentiment repeated countless times by amateur and professional genealogists alike: "addicted," "obsessed," it's "never enough," it's like "crack." But what drives this "addiction"? Survey responses suggest that American genealogists today are motivated by a number of overlapping factors—principally mystery, identity, duty, and a sense of connection.

Mystery

> As a kid, I grew up reading Nancy Drew and Hardy Boys mystery novels. [Genealogy] is my own true mystery. (Anna, 56, California)

Many genealogists report that they started their roots quests after the death of an elder, the protracted illness of a parent, or the discovery of a box of family photos or documents, a "treasure trove of old letters" (Madeline, 69, Missouri), a "trunk of family pictures" (Bill, 71, Oklahoma). Such experiences often prompt us to recognize how little we know of our own family histories, and thus frequently drive us to start asking the questions that lead us to genealogy.

But by far the most common motivation genealogists give for maintaining and intensifying their activities is a love of the "mystery" or the "puzzle." "I feel like a detective trying to solve mysteries. It's exhilarating when I find something new," remarked Camille (59, of Missouri). Conference sessions build on this motivation with titles like "Unleash Your Inner Private Eye" or "Solving the Mystery of the Disappearing Ancestor." One prominent presenter began her session with an image of Sherlock Holmes, and ended by wishing the audience "Happy sleuthing!" Genealogists talk about the challenge of finding clues and piecing them together, about the thrill of "the chase" or "the hunt." It's like being on *CSI*, one conference speaker said: "You're trying to convict someone of being your ancestor."[31]

Similarly, practitioners liken genealogy to a "treasure hunt" and a never-ending jigsaw puzzle. It is so addictive, they say, because every piece you find creates at least two more pieces. Every answer creates more questions. And particularly for older genealogists, the mental and organizational challenges of genealogy are seen as ways of keeping their brains active while doing something "productive" rather than spending their retirement "rocking on the porch" or watching television (Angela, 78, Virginia).

We need to understand the appeal of mysteries and puzzles in a twenty-first-century context, where detective novels, television mystery series, and games like Sudoku are ubiquitous. While precursors of these phenomena have long existed, it was only in the twentieth century that they became mass sensations. Both crossword puzzles and detective novels, for instance, came to full flower in the 1920s and 1930s, with authors like Agatha Christie and Dorothy Sayers, and the first crossword collection by Simon & Schuster.[32] It is little wonder that, after the unprecedented mass violence and trauma of World War I and rapid technological and social changes at the turn of the century, we developed a taste for detective stories and puzzles with tidy solutions. One hundred years later, we are facing new challenges and new changes, and we still derive satisfaction from detective novels, brain games, and genealogical puzzles and mysteries.

Identity

> To know who you are, you have to know where you came from. (Jillian, 60, Indiana)

Another strong motivation for engaging in genealogy is the desire for deeper self-knowledge. Genealogists frequently recount striking similarities between their own lives—and character traits and interests—and those of their ancestors. Such similarities, many genealogists claim, help explain "why you do what you do" (Helen, 77, Illinois), "why you are the way you are" (Harold, 48, Illinois).[33]

This comes through perhaps most clearly in roots television programs, such as *Who Do You Think You Are?* and *Finding Your Roots*, where the choices and traits of ancestors are often used to help explain the choices and traits of the current generation. Political activism, civil disobedience, adventurousness, leadership, spiritual devotion, artistic talent, a passion for farming, for cooking, for architecture, for education—guests and hosts alike suggest that all of these traits, and more, have been passed down through the generations. In an episode of *Who Do You Think You Are?*, for instance, celebrity guest Brooke Shields experiences a moment of clarity when she discovers an ancestral connection to France.

> That is fascinating to me. There's this other side of my brain which is just so French, so comfortable in France. I even majored in French literature. So maybe that was it. Somewhere deep inside I knew that there was something in my makeup that came from France.[34]

Likewise, on *Finding Your Roots*, host Henry Louis Gates tells doyenne of domesticity Martha Stewart that her family tree

> is populated with butchers, gardeners, shoemakers, decorative ironworkers, seamstresses. . . . You are an extension of this concern with sewing and craftsmanship and gardening . . . on every branch of your family tree. It just kept repeating. . . . It makes you believe in genetic determinism.[35]

And on *The Generations Project*, a web series from BYU-TV, a guest identified as Vicki is thrilled and amazed to discover that her ancestors were German stonemasons. Without knowing that fact, she had designed her own home with "tons and tons and tons" of German limestone. "Can you believe it?" she asks the host. "I don't think it's a coincidence." Now, she says, she can understand her love of architecture, of design, and of stone.[36]

When we come to know our ancestors, genealogists argue, we come to know ourselves. As Deidre (58, from Texas) remarks, genealogy "somehow grounds me and helps me to understand myself better." But, more than this, many genealogists report learning important lessons from the ancestors—inspirational lessons about the importance of perseverance, loyalty, or faith, but also cautionary lessons about the kinds of destructive behaviors we should avoid. Or, as Serena (50, New York) puts it, genealogy gives us the opportunity "to learn from family mistakes and not repeat them."

One way identity surfaces here is in the stories genealogists tell about their forebears. As we shall see in chapter 2, historically American genealogy has strongly focused on establishing elite pedigrees. Only a small number of genealogists today, however, say that their research is motivated by the desire to gain membership to groups such as the Daughters of the American Revolution (DAR), Sons of the American Revolution (SAR), or the Mayflower Society.[37] Instead of making such elite identity claims, genealogists today are more likely to regale listeners with stories of outlaws and eccentrics in their family trees. As Abigail from Massachusetts told me, genealogists today don't care much about trying to find links to royalty, or to the rich and famous. What they want are colorful characters and memorable stories to add to their family narrative. To today's genealogists, she said, "A rogue is as good as a king."

We can understand genealogists' focus on identity in the context of broader social changes that are destabilizing traditional identities in the twenty-first century. As populations become more mobile, as families and communities become more fragmented, as our connections to land and to history become more tenuous, we look for new ways to define and distinguish ourselves.

Duty

> For me, walking through a cemetery is a most powerful experience. To some, it's a creepy place full of dead people. For me, it's walking amongst the last earthly fragments of someone who lies below whose story is begging to be told. (Glen, 44, Indiana)

Related to the perceived power of genealogy to illuminate and guide us, many genealogists are also motivated by a strong sense of duty to share what they learn with others. This primarily takes the form of leaving an accurate and detailed account of family history to their children and grandchildren, "to give those who come after [us] a sense of place in the family line" (Nancy, 79, Illinois). "We have a duty to our families, but also to everyone in the younger generation," one conference speaker exhorted his audience.

Perhaps the term most often used here is *legacy*. Everyone from a digital scrapbooker in Virginia to a volunteer at the Family History Library in Salt Lake City, to an archivist in Chicago, to retirees in Florida, Texas, and California talk about the desire to leave a legacy for their families—a resource to enlighten and provide them with a "blueprint" for their lives. In bequeathing this legacy to their descendants, however, genealogists are of course also ensuring that they themselves will be remembered. Genealogy "gives us a certain amount of immortality," observes Glen in Indiana. You cannot literally meet the ancestors, but you can get to know them by reading about their lives and times. "Wouldn't it be nice to know someone in the distant future can do the same about you and your life when you are long gone from this Earth?" So precious is hard-earned family history knowledge to genealogists that many express serious concerns about how to safeguard it after they are gone. Retired couple Beth and John of Wisconsin have written provisions in their will to ensure that their research will pass safely to future generations.

Many genealogists also express a sense of responsibility toward the ancestors, a mission to unearth long-buried details and bring the ancestors, in some sense, back to life. For some, the focus is on telling the stories of those who have been largely ignored or forgotten. Julia (39, of Maryland) says she turned to genealogy because there were so many "silences" in her family. Everyone worked so hard to keep family "scandals" hidden—an unwed mother, an alcoholic, an interracial affair—that they had lost touch with their ancestors. Julia hoped to bring some of those silenced voices back to her family history. As a conference speaker from the LDS organization FamilySearch put it, "We believe every person's history deserves to be told."

For others, giving voice to the ancestors is a way of expressing appreciation for them. Ramona (46, from New York) says that genealogy has given her a "deep appreciation for my ancestors and . . . immense gratitude for the sacrifices of the previous generations that have enabled me to have the life I enjoy today." Genealogists from across the nation report feeling a profound sense of gratitude for those who came before us, and many see their work as a way of giving back to the ancestors. "We know times were hard and [our ancestors] endured great sacrifices for us to be here today.

Maybe genealogy, documenting their journey, is our way of saying thank you" (Beth and John, Wisconsin).

For many genealogists, this sense of duty to the ancestors extends to a sense of duty to the larger genealogical community. Many report spending countless hours volunteering in local archives and historical societies, providing photographs, transcriptions, and even GPS coordinates for tombstones around the country, and transcribing and indexing cryptic handwritten records. Indeed, in a massive "indexathon" in 2012, some 163,000 volunteers indexed in excess of 132 million names from the 1940 US Census in only four months.[38] As one conference speaker put it: "When you get down to it, we're all related." So in serving the whole genealogical community, you are serving your own family.

We can understand this extraordinary commitment to the mission of excavating long-buried stories and breathing life into the bare names and dates found in official documents by considering the secular and rather anonymous nature of twenty-first-century industrial societies. In large-scale societies with their huge populations, impersonal interactions and complex divisions of labor are necessary for the smooth operations of everyday social, political, and economic life.[39] (Imagine how much extra time it would take if you had to cultivate close personal relationships with the grocery store clerk, the gas station attendant, the road maintenance crew, and so on.) Fleshing out the ancestors may be one way of pushing back against such an impersonal social structure. Moreover, as we shall see in chapter 7, as increasing numbers of Americans are stepping away from organized religion, they face disquieting questions about life after death. If the immortal soul is no longer a certainty, if we can no longer be confident that a wholesome life on this Earth will earn us a place in paradise, at least we can try to ensure—through genealogy—that our name and lifeworks will live on.

Connection

> It's the connection I crave, I think. (Deidre, 58, Texas)

> We all have a need to feel connected—to know where we come from—to know who we are. (Marlene, 66, Florida)

A further motivation expressed by many genealogists is the desire to strengthen existing social connections, and to form new ones. These connections may be to living relatives, to deceased ancestors, to other genealogists, or to the nation and to history more generally. While the image of the solitary genealogist toiling away in a library is a common one, in reality genealogy is often a social and communal pursuit. Husbands and wives, cousins, siblings, and friends routinely travel together to conferences, archives, cemeteries, and even overseas "homeland" destinations in pursuit of their ancestors. Genealogy "brings families closer together," they say.[40]

Belinda (61, Indiana) had an experience that many in the genealogical community share. When her elderly father became ill, she sat for hours with him listening to family stories. It was a new way for them to connect, and it strengthened their bond. After her father passed away, she began intensive research based on the details he had given her. Other genealogists organize family reunions and family trips, both as opportunities to share what they have learned and to gather additional information (sometimes including DNA samples) from family members. Holly (54, Texas) takes every opportunity she can to share her research with family members. "It makes me the center of attention at family gatherings, which I really enjoy." And she adds that because she is not good at making small talk and does not have much in common with her relatives, genealogy "gives me something to help me fit in."

Some are also motivated by the desire to find unknown living relatives, often simply called "cousins," particularly those still residing in ancestral homelands. Barbara (57, from West Virginia) recounts an emotional trip she took to Wales to visit her father's ancestral stomping grounds. There she was able to visit the family farm and meet distant cousins who previously had no knowledge of her branch on their family tree. The trip gave her such a sense of belonging that she is currently in the process of planning a similar trip to Scotland to find her mother's family. Genealogical service companies capitalize on this desire to find far-flung relations. DNA testing companies, in particular, promise to match clients with "cousins" around the globe. One conference vendor pledged an average of 2 third cousins, 50 fourth cousins, and 5,500 "distant" cousins—although he noted that such distant matches had a 50 percent error rate. There is some awareness within the genealogical community, however, of a qualitative distinction between such genetic kinship and more meaningful social kinship. One conference participant told her friend about a recent gathering. "I was getting together with my DNA cousins," she said, "as opposed to my *real* cousins."

In addition to strengthening connections with living relatives, some genealogists (although admittedly a smaller number) also talk about feeling spiritually connected with deceased ancestors. Judy from Maryland told me that she felt her deceased father's spirit guiding her to crucial family records. One conference speaker told the audience that she sensed her great-grandmother calling to her to reunite their fractured family. And Celia in California said she knows that her "family on the other side" wants her to find them, and that is what keeps her going.

This spiritual connection is also a strong theme in roots television, particularly on *The Generations Project*, produced by the LDS-affiliated BYU-TV. One featured guest, Maile, a native Hawaiian, says she feels a close and personal link to her ancestors. The ancestors "help us, they guide us, they give us the knowledge they had." They are "waiting up there. They just don't want us to forget them." Another guest, Anglo-American Emily, gets strong "impressions"—images, emotions, and sensations—from her ancestors. She follows her genealogical trail through a long line of spiritual women, and finally focuses on a male ancestor who died amid scandal. Emily receives such powerful messages from him that she arranges to exhume and relocate his remains.

While such otherworldly experiences appear quite rare (or perhaps people are simply reluctant to talk about them), most genealogists say they are motivated by a desire to know "what part my family played in history" (Serena, 50, New York). Many report investigating not only their own lineages but also historical places and settings, and everything from the hats and hairstyles to the medical treatments and harvesting techniques of their ancestors' times. It is this broader knowledge, they say, which helps us to better understand our forebears' experiences and decisions. And it is this broader understanding that makes history more personal and more alive for us. "Genealogy is history come home," observes Harold (48, Illinois).

Roots television programs build on this desire to place individual families in the context of significant historical events. On one episode of *Who Do You Think You Are?*, actress Sarah Jessica Parker recalls feeling as a child that her family was "common," insignificant, with no real connection to the nation's history. In the course of the episode, she finds her roots in Colonial New England, the Salem witch trials, the Civil War, and the California Gold Rush. She is overcome with emotions, and says that before her genealogical journey,

> I believed in America. I believed in the things I love about being American. But I never really felt that I was really American. . . . What I've learned is I have real stock in this country, and real roots, and I have belonging. . . . You know, I'm an American. I'm actually an American.[41]

Clearly, twenty-first-century genealogy helps us feel more connected—to our family members (both living and dead), to our communities, and to our nations. As the world becomes more globalized, more anonymous, and more secular, and our historical awareness is undercut by rapid and shallow flows of information, such connections take on increasing importance. We explore these dynamics in greater depth in later chapters.

UNDERSTANDING ROOTS QUESTS

As we delve into roots quests—both in America and around the world—certain questions will guide our inquiry.

Why are so many Americans interested in genealogy? And how can we explain its dramatically increased popularity? Specifically, what do Americans seek through genealogy? And what is it about this moment in time that is driving the American quest for roots?

How has American genealogy changed over time, and what factors have shaped and reshaped it? Specifically, what are the key concerns and methods of American genealogy today, and how can we explain those priorities and procedures?

Why do people in cultures worldwide engage in "roots work," what forms does it take, and, despite surface appearances, is it actually all that different from twenty-first-century American "roots work"? Perhaps more importantly, why do humans have such a powerful drive to trace our origins and maintain links with our kin, both living and dead?

And how do Americans today and people in cultures around the world "construct" their ancestors and their kin? And how do such constructions both reflect and reinforce social norms, values, and hierarchies of power?

As we answer these questions and more we will gain insights not only into roots quests but also into the nature of American society in an age of rootlessness.

2

A GENEALOGY OF
AMERICAN GENEALOGY

As we saw in chapter 1, a key assertion of American genealogists today is that we can only truly know who we are when we understand where we came from.[1] By extension, we can only fully understand the nature of American genealogy today by tracing the history of genealogy, to see how ideas, practices, and priorities have developed and changed over time.[2] This chapter will examine American genealogy from Colonial times through to the present. As we shall see, our current genealogy "boom" is not the first of its kind in the United States. The popularity of genealogy has waxed and waned considerably over time in response to political, cultural, economic, and scientific changes. Figure 2.1 provides a brief overview of the genealogical "eras" and charts the changes to American genealogy. Each period is examined in greater detail below.[3]

OLD WORLD AND AMERICAN
ARISTOCRATIC GENEALOGY

Eighth-Century Europe to Colonial-Era America

- Pedigree
- Hereditary and colonial rule
- Inheritance and property claims
- Political and economic alliances
- Blood-borne traits

We can trace early American genealogical practice back to what historian François Weil calls "Old World" genealogy.[4] As far back as the eighth and ninth centuries, noble Anglo-Saxon families were recording sometimes

21

Figure 2.1. American Genealogical Eras

	Old World Aristocratic Genealogy	American Aristocratic Genealogy	Democratic Genealogy	Eugenic, Nationalistic, and Aspirational Genealogy	Multicultural, Self-Revelatory Genealogy	Quantum Genealogy
Genealogical Eras	8th c. onward	Colonial America 17th–18th c.	Post-Revolutionary War Late 18th–early 19th c.	Post-Civil War to Civil Rights Era 1860s–1960s (Eugenics dropped after WWII)	1970s onward	1990s–present
Primary Focus	Pedigree Hereditary rule, property rights Inheritance, succession Alliances through marriage	Pedigree Colonial rule Social status Land claims	Democratic values Strengthening links to kin and country Substantiating land and inheritance claims	Racial distinctions (white superiority) Hereditary privilege, elite status based on links to significant people and events in American history Blood-borne traits	Pride in racial/ethnic identities Personal fulfillment, individual identity Affirmation of multiculturalism	Individual identity narratives Scientific/technological tools, methods, data Global interconnections
Contributing Factors	Minimal state recordkeeping allowed inventive pedigrees Belief that nobility was divinely ordained	Distance from Old World allowed inventive pedigrees Belief in blood-borne traits	Spread of literacy and printed texts Westward expansion Bounty land claims	Industrialization, urbanization, economic inequalities Rapid technological, scientific changes Mass immigration	Self-empowerment movements Embrace of multiculturalism Haley's *Roots* Postmodern turn	Digital and genetic technologies Globalization Mass media and virtual realities Secularism and relativism

rather imaginative pedigrees that were used to legitimate their rule and land claims, ensure succession and inheritance, and forge alliances through marriage and kinship ties.[5] By the fifteenth and sixteenth centuries, such pedigrees had become even more important to the nobility, who felt their position threatened by the growing number of nouveau riche families. Genealogical pedigrees became a way for nobles to distinguish themselves as the natural and rightful rulers of their nations at a time when royal birth was widely believed to be divinely ordained. Indeed, these noble pedigrees took on such importance that by the late sixteenth and early seventeenth centuries, the aristocracy in nations including England, France, and Spain had instituted "genealogical bureaucracies," official bodies charged with keeping aristocratic genealogical records.[6] For the most part, genealogy remained the pursuit of wealthy elites with the time and resources to devote to formalizing their lineages, and with concrete motivations for doing so.

Likewise, in Colonial America, genealogy was primarily an elite pursuit. Ruling Colonial families used illustrious pedigrees to assert their right to rule. Although the notion of divinely sanctioned rule was losing ground in the less tradition-bound colonies, a belief in blood-borne traits (such as an innate nobility or depravity of character) was still alive and well, and useful for assertions of "natural" superiority. And since Colonial elites were far from the European recordkeeping bodies, their pedigrees could be quite inventive. As the colonies grew wealthier, elite pedigrees took on even greater importance, and status-conscious families increasingly took to displaying family crests and coats of arms, the use of which was unregulated in the colonies (unlike in the Old World), and therefore could be purchased by families with the means to do so.[7]

AMERICAN DEMOCRATIC GENEALOGY

Post–Revolutionary War Era

- Democratic values
- Links to kin and country
- Land and inheritance claims

In the wake of the American Revolution—a war against the hereditary English monarchy—genealogical pedigrees fell from favor in America. They were seen to be elitist, pretentious, and decidedly undemocratic, which ran contrary to one of the republic's founding principles, that "all men were created equal." At the same time, two important developments were helping to popularize basic genealogical recordkeeping among ordinary Americans—westward expansion and the rise of literacy and the printed word. As increasing numbers of people pushed into the western frontier, families were becoming more fragmented. Because older generations typically stayed behind while younger generations moved west, opportunities for passing down family history through face-to-face storytelling grew more limited. In danger of losing this family lore, Americans increasingly turned to recording at least births, deaths, and marriages in a family Bible.[8] Of course even this rudimentary genealogical recordkeeping was contingent on two things: the ability to write (or access to someone who could write), and the possession of a family Bible or other record book. And by the early nineteenth century, both literacy and printed texts were on the increase.[9] By the early 1800s, many Bibles came with a preprinted page for recording genealogical information.[10]

It should also be noted that many families had practical and legal reasons for maintaining at least basic genealogical records. Such records could help to solidify inheritance and land rights claims. In particular, at least a portion of those moving west were drawn by bounty-land warrants—land granted by federal and state authorities to Revolutionary War veterans and their survivors.[11] Widows applying for bounty land often submitted whatever marriage records they could, including genealogy pages torn from family Bibles.

So it was that in the post–Revolutionary War era, American genealogy was democratized. That is, it came to be practiced by a broader segment of the population, rather than simply by elites; and it came to be focused less on aristocratic pedigrees and more on the family histories of ordinary Americans. Indeed, early in the nineteenth century, genealogy became one way to demonstrate one's connection and commitment to the fledgling nation. And, by the 1840s, genealogy was enjoying a comeback. The first genealogical societies were founded and the first genealogical periodicals and how-to manuals were published.[12] Amid the rapid social and technological changes of the early nineteenth century, genealogy helped to keep Americans connected to kin and country.[13]

EUGENIC, NATIONALISTIC, AND ASPIRATIONAL GENEALOGY

Post–Civil War Era to Civil Rights Era

- Racial distinctions
- Elite status
- Hereditary privilege
- Blood-borne traits

Perhaps the first genealogy "boom" in American history arrived in the wake of the Civil War, a conflict in which more than six hundred thousand soldiers died.[14] Certainly, after a conflict that divided families and sometimes literally pitted brother against brother on the battlefield, many Americans looked to genealogy as a way to reconcile families and communities fractured and traumatized by war, and a way to honor the memory of those who had perished.[15] Additionally, a whole host of social, economic, demographic, and technological changes in the decades after the Civil War contributed to the popularity of genealogy.

Consider, for instance, that the post–Civil War period witnessed dramatic economic changes and upheavals. As the South struggled to rebuild its war-torn infrastructure and cope with the demands of Reconstruction, the nation as a whole saw the gap between rich and poor increase exponentially.[16] In fact, in the last three decades of the nineteenth century (the Gilded Age), massive corporate trusts so dominated the US economy that almost three-quarters of the wealth of the nation was concentrated in the hands of just 10 percent of the population, most notably the so-called robber barons, with names like Rockefeller and Vanderbilt.[17] The chasm between rich and poor was further deepened by the banking crisis of 1873, when lenders found themselves overextended by speculative postwar loans. When the "credit bubble" burst, banks began to fail and the stock market panicked, closing down entirely for ten days, setting in motion a chain reaction that led both the United States and much of Europe into an economic depression that lasted six long years. During those years, interest rates rose, real estate values dropped, factories laid off workers, businesses failed, and wages fell.[18] So ordinary Americans faced economic hardships, economic uncertainty, and increasing economic inequalities in the post–Civil War era.

At the same time, they were witnessing extraordinary scientific and technological changes. With the rapid development of railroad infrastructure (some 33,000 miles of new track were laid between 1868 and 1873 alone),[19] distances seemed to collapse. A journey that once took months could now be completed in days, thanks to the transcontinental rail network. Likewise, with improvements to telegraphic technology and the spread of electricity and telephones in the closing decades of the nineteenth century, both communications and the rhythms of everyday life were forever changed. Meanwhile, more nuanced understandings of disease mechanisms and improvements to water and sanitation systems began to prolong our lives, even as evolutionary science was challenging traditional notions about the relationship between humankind and the rest of the animal kingdom.

Amid such dramatic economic, scientific, and technological changes, the United States was also experiencing monumental demographic changes. Industrialization increased rapidly in the North in the decades after the Civil War, drawing populations away from rural agricultural areas into urban manufacturing centers. Contributing to this massive urbanization were millions of African Americans who migrated from the South to the North, Midwest, and West after the Civil War.[20] At the same time, great waves of immigrants arrived in the United States, particularly from Ireland, and Eastern and Southern Europe—almost ten million people between 1880 and 1900 alone.[21]

There is little doubt that such significant changes contributed both to the rising popularity of genealogy and to its shift in focus. Amid an influx of immigrants, genealogy became a way to distinguish oneself as authentically American; it also provided a sense of stability and permanence during the economic uncertainties of the 1870s. And while most Americans could not hope to achieve the levels of wealth enjoyed by the robber barons of the Gilded Age, genealogy could potentially provide a source of distinction and family pride, particularly if one could brag of family connections to the *Mayflower*, the founding fathers, or war heroes. In an increasingly mobile, urbanized, technologically complex society, genealogy connected people to a seemingly simpler past. For African Americans, genealogy offered the possibility of discovering a family history before the trauma of slavery (although African Americans would not come to genealogy in significant numbers until the 1970s). And for whites in an increasingly diverse society, genealogy offered a way to prove their racial purity and assert their racial superiority. It is perhaps not surprising, therefore, that genealogy in the late-nineteenth and early-twentieth centuries became increasingly focused on racial identity, on connections to important American people, places, and events, and on claims of exclusivity.

This period witnessed a proliferation of voluntary associations, such as fraternal organizations and benevolent societies.[22] No doubt as people moved from rural to urban areas, they sought substitutes for the kin and community groups they had left behind. Notable among these were exclusive hereditary societies, such as the Sons of the American Revolution (SAR, founded in 1889) and the Daughters of the American Revolution (DAR, founded in 1890) for those descended from a Revolutionary patriot, and the Mayflower Society (founded in 1897) for descendants of those who arrived on the *Mayflower*. Not only did admission to such societies affirm one's status as a "true American"—in contrast to Johnny-come-lately immigrants or increasingly mobile African Americans—but members were also charged with defending the values and the integrity of the homeland.[23] In particular, many of these groups voiced concern over national "degeneration"—the perceived decline of traditional morality and national vigor believed to result from race-mixing and contact with "lower orders" of immigrants.[24]

In their concern over racial "contamination," these groups were not alone. While such fears may strike readers today as the fevered imaginings of fringe racists, at the turn of the twentieth century, such views were mainstream. Rapid urbanization, an influx of poor immigrants, and the concentration of the nation's wealth in the hands of the few had created a surfeit of social problems—crime, disease, grinding poverty, and appalling living and working conditions. And amid rapid scientific and technological changes, Americans were eager to find scientific solutions to these troubling developments. One such proposed solution was eugenics, a field dedicated to improving humanity through selective breeding.[25]

Eugenics was premised on the notion that undesirable traits such as criminality, immorality, and "feeblemindedness" (as well as desirable traits such as intelligence and virtuousness) were carried in the blood. To strengthen and improve one's bloodline, it was therefore vital to carefully investigate potential mates and select only those with superior traits. By extension, to improve the "racial stock" of the nation, it was vital to avoid race-mixing, as the "inferior" races were more likely to carry pernicious traits in their blood. Moreover, some eugenicists argued, it was advisable to prevent certain "unfit" populations from reproducing and passing on their deleterious traits. Although such assumptions may appear extreme from a twenty-first-century vantage point, at the turn of the twentieth century, they were so uncontroversial that eugenics how-to articles were carried in such mainstream publications as *Good Housekeeping* and the *Saturday Evening Post*.[26] And by the early 1900s, several US states had passed laws allowing the forced sterilization of certain criminals and those deemed insane or "feebleminded." Many more states had outlawed mixed-race marriage, and even US immigration policy was being informed by notions of desirable and undesirable "racial stock."[27]

The popularity and perceived benefits of eugenics were clearly reflected in American genealogy at the turn of the twentieth century. At the first International Congress of Genealogy, convened in conjunction with the 1915 Panama-Pacific International Exposition in San Francisco, a number of prominent speakers endorsed the principles of eugenics, and enjoined genealogists to use their family research not for self-aggrandizement but for the betterment of the nation as a whole. Genealogists were encouraged to submit their family histories to eugenics organizations for the purposes of furthering scientific understanding of heredity, and, ultimately to help inform legislation designed to strengthen the national stock.[28] Such aims complimented the exclusionary, status-oriented focus of American genealogy in the first decades of the twentieth century.

Eugenics began to lose favor in the 1930s. First, the Great Depression saw families of all backgrounds—even those of supposedly superior racial stock—fall into hardship. Such dramatic reversals of fortune challenged the notion that one's success or failure in life was largely determined by "blood," or genetic inheritance.[29] And second, German Nazis took eugenicist principles to genocidal extremes. They began by forcibly sterilizing those deemed "unfit" to reproduce, then instituted "euthanasia" programs for institutionalized "undesirables," and finally adopted mass extermination programs aimed at purifying the Aryan racial stock and strengthening the nation. After the horrors of the Holocaust became known, eugenics was no longer respectable, and it largely disappeared from American genealogical discussions. Although eugenics and more explicitly racialist language fell out of fashion after World War II, amid the conservativism and affluence of postwar America, hereditary-patriotic organizations such as the SAR and DAR continued to thrive, and to provide Americans with the motivation to engage in genealogical research.

MULTICULTURAL, SELF-REVELATORY GENEALOGY

1970s Onward

- Racial and ethnic pride
- Individual identity and fulfillment
- Multiculturalism

As we have seen, during the one hundred years between the 1860s to the 1960s, America witnessed overwhelming social, technological, and demographic changes. Consider, for instance, the enormity of the transition from horse-drawn carriage to train to automobile to plane to lunar landing craft in this one compressed period. Consider the transformative impact of massive human migrations and two devastating world wars. The conservative, almost defensive character of American genealogy during this period may well reflect nostalgia for simpler times, and a longing for firmer, more familiar ground in an age of uncertainty and upheaval.

The late civil rights era, which overlapped with the women's movement and a host of antiestablishment and self-empowerment movements, ushered in a new genealogical era, one focused on self-discovery and the celebration of diversity. Alex Haley's book *Roots* (1976) and the blockbuster television miniseries based on the book (1977) inspired a boom in what we might call multicultural and self-revelatory genealogy. African Americans, eager to embark on their own roots quests, made inroads into genealogical domains previously dominated by whites more interested in maintaining racial boundaries than in exploring the racial and ethnic complexities of American family trees. And Americans of all backgrounds embraced Haley's message—that by tracing family origins, we can find meaning and a deeper sense of belonging in an increasingly complex world.

One historian at the time observed that while Americans had long cherished desires to know where they had come from, Haley's *Roots* inspired many to act on that desire for the first time.[30] For African Americans, in particular, whose formal genealogical records often began only with Emancipation in 1865, links to ancestral homelands were often thought to be irretrievably lost. But Haley gave people of African descent hope that they too could find their deep ancestral origins, as he apparently did in the course of his book.[31] So Haley's book helped prompt would-be genealogists to action. But a whole host of social changes would transform American genealogy from its previous focus on exclusive status and hereditary privilege to a new concern with self-knowledge and the complexities of heritage.

First, it should be noted that Haley's book came out in the midst of the nation's bicentennial celebrations, so Americans were already in a retrospective mood. But this was also a decade that had witnessed the full flowering of the black pride and black power movements, the women's rights movement, and the gay rights movement. And these movements, aimed at empowerment, social recognition, and equal treatment for less-powerful groups, had grown out of the tumultuous changes of the 1960s, with the civil rights movement, and the antiwar, counterculture, and hippie movements. Although each of these movements in the 1960s and 1970s had distinctive aims and modes of action, their net effect was, first, to challenge the long-standing dominance of whites, of men, of heterosexuality, and of established social norms and institutions, and, second, to affirm the value of diversity in all its forms.

Roots also came out at a time when historians, social scientists, and other scholars were rethinking their approach to knowledge itself. As more women and students of color entered graduate programs in the 1960s and 1970s, scholars began asking new questions that challenged long-held theories about history and society.[32] In particular, they began asking why women and minority groups had been largely ignored or marginalized in academic scholarship. Such questions sparked an intellectual revolution. Historical research shifted away from a more traditional focus on rulers, military generals, and captains of industry, to an examination of the experiences of "ordinary" people—history from the bottom up.

At the same time, there was a growing recognition among scholars that our understandings of the world are profoundly shaped by the ways stories and theories and "facts" have been presented to us by those with the most powerful and authoritative voices—politicians, intellectuals, and the mass media, among others. In other words, scholars came to see human experiences, perceptions, and thoughts (including ideas about morality, gender, sexuality, and race) as socially constructed in complex ways.[33] This intellectual shift is often called the "postmodern turn," because it represented a turn away from the "modern" perspective on the world (with its seemingly objective facts and well-established rules and orders) toward more fluid, diverse, and relativistic perspectives.[34]

These shifts in the intellectual and social climate of the 1970s were reflected in American genealogy. Fewer genealogists were overtly focused on finding illustrious forebears—princes and patriots—and more professed an interest in better understanding the lives of the ordinary people in their family trees. Fewer genealogists focused simply on family pedigree charts, and more began to focus on piecing together ancestral stories that would help them make sense of their own lives. Fewer genealogists were overtly focused on establishing their racial purity and superiority, and more sought out the ethnic diversity that was thought to make their family trees more "colorful." Indeed, as America was increasingly defined as a multicultural nation, having a diverse cast of ancestors became a new way of proving one's essential Americanness. Even hereditary organizations with a history of racial exclusion began courting greater diversity. The DAR, for instance, admitted its first African American member in 1977.[35] And a burgeoning market developed for specialist genealogical how-to books and organizations designed to help Americans trace their African American, Hispanic, Native American, Jewish, and other ethnic minority ancestors.[36]

Perhaps the primary focus of this new era of genealogy was self-discovery. Consistent with one of the core messages of Alex Haley's *Roots*, American genealogy came to emphasize the notion that we can only truly understand ourselves and find fulfillment when we understand our origins. As Haley put it,

> In all of us there is a hunger, marrow-deep, to know our heritage—to know who we are and where we have come from. Without this en-

riching knowledge, there is a hollow yearning. No matter what our attainments in life, there is still a vacuum, an emptiness, and the most disquieting loneliness.[37]

This focus on self-discovery was consistent with the value orientation of the so-called Me Generation, those people who came of age in the 1960s and 1970s amid a countercultural push for self-realization. Given that the majority of genealogists today are drawn from this generation, it is not surprising that this emphasis on self-knowledge persists into the current era of American genealogy.

QUANTUM GENEALOGY

1990s to Present

- Digital and genetic technologies
- Globalization
- Mass media and virtual realities
- Secularization and relativism

While the current genealogical era retains a focus on self-discovery, on "ordinary" people and on "colorful" diversity, it also reflects certain twenty-first-century social and technological developments. American genealogy today is characterized by a preoccupation with scientific and technological methods, an emphasis on global kinship connections, highly mass-mediated and commercialized genealogical narratives, and a certain fascination with the spiritual dimension of family history research. We will examine each of these trends in greater detail in subsequent chapters, but let us briefly consider how each of these developments has reshaped twenty-first-century American genealogy.

SCIENCE AND TECHNOLOGY

Genealogy has long suffered from comparisons with academic history. Genealogists have been considered by many academic historians and archivists as status-driven and rather slapdash ancestor hunters with little concern for broader historical issues or for sound research methods.[38] Despite this negative image, and likely *because* of this negative image, twenty-first-century American genealogists demonstrate a strong commitment to rigorous scientific methods and to detailed understandings of the historical contexts that shaped their ancestors' lives. One recent promotional pamphlet for a national genealogical society, for example, set out the organization's key mission: "To advance genealogical research . . . [and] to secure recognition of genealogy as a serious subject of research in historical and social fields."[39] The pamphlet boasted of a membership including "distinguished academics" who employ "proper documentary evidence" and come to "sound conclusions." Likewise, genealogy conference presenters employ scientific jargon, such as "double-blind" indexing, data "extraction," and "probability tools" to discuss their research. And both amateur and professional genealogists alike frequently stress the importance of the Genealogical Proof Standard, which requires exhaustive searches, the corroboration of evidence, tests of validity, painstaking documentation and citation, and well-supported conclusions.[40]

The current preoccupation with scientific and technological methods has also grown out of advances in computing technologies and genetic science in recent decades. Consider the impact of the so-called digital revolution on American genealogy. Over the past twenty years, in particular, dramatic increases in computing speed, digital imaging, and data storage capacity, along with improvements to global networking infrastructures, have facilitated the exponential growth of digital data.[41] Every *second* of 2016, for instance, we collectively sent 2.6 million e-mails, posted more than 7,000 tweets, did almost 63,000 Google searches, and viewed 71,000 YouTube videos.[42] Ancestry.com alone hosts more than 20 billion digital records on its site, adds 2 million new records each day, and processes more than 75 million searches on its site daily.[43] The company is constantly acquiring access to more archives both in the United States and around the globe, which it claims to integrate into easily accessible genealogical information with the use of "Big Data analytics, artificial intelligence, and state-of-the-art search solutions."[44] By far the most prevalent answer I get when I ask genealogists why they think family history has become so popular is that the mass digitization of historical records has made once time-consuming and expensive archival research as easy as clicking a mouse.

At the same time, developments in the field of genetics have now made DNA analysis increasingly affordable and easy, which has led to the rise of "genetic genealogy."[45] For as little as $99, DNA testing firms promise to reveal your ethnic composition and show you "the places and cultures that make you who you are."[46] Such services pledge to uncover hidden and "surprising ethnicities," reveal distant relatives and "ancestors you never knew you had," and provide you with "new details [to add] to your family story."[47] Some services offer to provide you with a precise ethnic breakdown, measured to one-tenth of 1 percent (20.5 percent East Asian, 38.6 percent Sub-Saharan African, 24.7 percent European, for example).[48] Some offer to take your family history back as much as 340,000 years,[49] a remarkable claim, given that most current science dates the emergence of modern humans (*Homo sapiens sapiens*) to between 150,000 and 170,000 years ago.[50]

Genealogists are told that genetics have the power to unlock family secrets that would be difficult or impossible to access in any other way. (Prehistoric humans did not, so far as we know, carve pedigree charts on cave walls!) We are also told that genetic information can transform our identities. Ancestry.com has promoted its DNA services with a national television advertisement in which an American man talks about growing up with such a strong German ethnic identity that he wore lederhosen and danced in a German dance group.[51] But his DNA test revealed that his family was "not German at all," but primarily Scottish and Irish. He jokes that he has since traded his lederhosen for a kilt.

Several things stand out here. The first is the power of DNA data to override information from other family history sources, and to fundamentally transform personal identity. The man in the ad clearly experiences this transformation as a novel and pleasant surprise, which he easily accommodates by simply changing his ethnic costume. A second and related point is the apparent superficiality of ethnic identities—reduced here to styles of dress and dance. It should also be noted that this man's transformation from German to Scottish/Irish is relatively easy and without social cost because he is phenotypically white. Because he belongs to America's dominant ("unmarked") ethnic group, he has the luxury of adopting multiple "symbolic" or "optional" ethnicities.[52] He could emphasize his Irish heritage on St. Patrick's Day, the German heritage of his childhood during Oktoberfest, and his English Puritan heritage on Thanksgiving, and no one would likely challenge the authenticity of his claims. However, if a phenotypically African American or Asian American man claimed Irish or German or English heritage as his primary ethnicity, he would likely face challenges ranging from questions like "No, but what are you, *really*?" to more hostile repudiations.[53] As a visibly African American student once told me, her Scottish grandmother had given her a KISS ME, I'M SCOTTISH T-shirt, but she felt she could not wear it because she would attract too much negative attention. Clearly, visible minorities in the United States cannot shift between "optional" ethnicities as easily as whites can.

Another point that stands out here is in the ad's claim that, contrary to the man's family traditions, DNA evidence shows that they are "not German at all." The implied certainty and objectivity of genetic data actually obscures the complexities of DNA results. For instance, certain tests (those for Y-DNA) only trace results through the direct paternal line, and some (mitochondrial DNA—mtDNA—tests) only trace the direct maternal line. So taking either of these DNA tests will yield results that ignore one-half of my genetic material. Even autosomal DNA tests that chart genetic markers on both sides of the family will not necessarily capture my full ethnic heritage. Because we each receive half of our genetic material from our mother and half from our father, we likely do not carry a full complement of our family's ethnic heritage in our DNA. (For instance, if my mother carried a trace of Native American heritage in her DNA, but I didn't happen to inherit it, my DNA tests will not indicate any Native American ancestry. In effect, my Native American ancestors are simply rubbed out of my record. But does this mean that I can no longer claim Native American ancestry?) Indeed, even full siblings may turn out to have quite different ethnic composition results when they take these tests, because each sibling gets a slightly different mixture of genetic material from the same mother and father. So while DNA testing firms may promise to transform and deepen our understandings of our ethnic origins, test results inevitably provide us with an incomplete picture of our family's full ethnic heritage.

The increasing popularity of genetic genealogy also raises concerns for some genealogists and scholars, as well as for the DNA testing firms themselves. While genealogists at conferences across the nation voice enthusiasm for the potential of this technology to push family histories further back in time and to provide more "objective" proof to substantiate (or challenge) family lore, they also express misgivings about how their DNA evidence might be used for other purposes—for instance, by insurance companies, by government agencies, or by commercial entities who might try to wring profits from their genetic material. At the same time, social scientists and historians are also raising concerns about disquieting similarities between the current genetic genealogy boom and biologically based, racialist notions of heritage that were dominant in the heyday of American eugenics.[54] And DNA testing firms themselves appear to be conscious of the potential for their results to reduce complex individual identities and experiences to seemingly discrete biological components. Typical results that define an individual as 21 percent Northern European, 16 percent West African, and so on (often displayed in a pie chart) can seem uncomfortably similar to the racialist calculations that were once used to classify people into categories such as "mulatto," "quadroon," or "octoroon" (those with one-half, one-quarter, or one-eighth African ancestry, respectively). Perhaps to distance themselves from such associations, DNA testing firms often stress the potential of genetic technology to link people to a diverse, interconnected global family. Indeed, world maps and globes are prominent design motifs for many genetic genealogy firms.

GLOBAL CONNECTIONS

With the global reach of genealogy websites and the global scope of genetic testing, it is perhaps not surprising that American genealogy is increasingly focused on forging global kinship connections. Both DNA testing firms and genealogy websites promise to link customers with "cousins" around the world, and invite customers to become part of a global kinship "community." One company, Geni.com, even aims to create a World Family Tree encompassing everyone on Earth. As of this writing, the massive tree project includes more than 126 million "cousins" worldwide and is being promoted by best-selling author A. J. Jacobs in newspaper and magazine articles, TED talks, and live events such as the world's "Biggest Family Reunion" in New York City in 2015. Jacobs talks about the potential of this globalized genealogy to lead to scientific breakthroughs, a deeper appreciation of history, and "a kinder world" in which we all treat each other better because we recognize that we are part of the same family.[55]

The global reach of genealogy is also celebrated in popular roots television shows, like *Who Do You Think You Are?* and *Finding Your Roots.* Just as each guest's genealogical quest is a journey of self-discovery, each quest also involves literal journeys across the United States or across the world to trace their family origins. When actor Martin Sheen travels to Spain and Ireland, when football star Emmitt Smith goes to Benin, when actresses Susan Sarandon and Gwyneth Paltrow travel to Tuscany and Barbados, respectively, the audience is treated not only to the unfolding of historical mysteries but to contemporary travelogues, complete with picturesque landscapes, friendly locals, and moving scenes in which celebrities "walk in the footsteps" of their ancestors.

Roots tourism companies build on the popularity of such shows by promoting family history tours as an opportunity for visitors to research their family trees, experience the natural beauty, culture, and hospitality of their ancestral homeland, and "stand in their ancestors' shoes."[56] Some tour providers offer the tantalizing possibility of meeting "long-lost cousins," thus expanding one's global kinship network.[57] And some offer add-on packages including professionally produced family heritage books, containing a family tree, a personalized family history narrative "designed to make interesting reading," copies of relevant historical documents, and photographs.[58] One roots tourist I interviewed even had her own overseas genealogical journey professionally filmed and edited into a *Who Do You Think You Are?*–style story of discovery. It was "the trip of a lifetime," she said, with visits to an ancestral home and the opportunity to create links with "distant cousins" on the other side of the world.[59]

MASS MEDIA AND COMMERCIALIZATION

The influence of roots television shows and advertisements on the practices, priorities, and perceptions of American genealogists today demonstrates another key characteristic of the current genealogical era—the important role of the mass media and commercial interests. And, arguably, no company has done more to commercialize and mass-mediate twenty-first-century genealogy than Ancestry.com.

The company has embarked, for instance, on national ad campaigns that promote both its services and the existential value of family history research. As amateur and professional genealogists alike frequently note, the ads make genealogy look so deceptively easy that it draws many new recruits to the activity. One recent television ad is typical of Ancestry's approach. We see a contemporary woman sitting down at her computer as a voiceover says, "I typed my name, and Ancestry opened the door to my past. Before my eyes, my family story was revealed. And the further I traveled back, the more I discovered." We see footage of a nineteenth-century suffragette, an eighteenth-century elopement, and a seventeenth-century foundling.[60] So, in three quick steps, we see a twenty-first-century woman reach back almost four hundred years into her family history, a journey that would, in all likelihood, take many years of hard work for a seasoned genealogist. The fictionalized footage of past events here is filmed in vivid color, with close-ups of the "ancestors" at dramatic moments in their lives. No blurry black-and-white photographs or dusty courthouse records here. Rather, the message is that family history research is exciting, engaging, and simple; it will unfold on our computers like personalized historical dramas.

Perhaps even more importantly, the highly successful television show *Who Do You Think You Are?* is actually sponsored by Ancestry.com, and the company's products are quite conspicuously integrated into each episode. Genealogists today sometimes joke about playing a drinking game while watching the television show. Every time someone on the show mentions Ancestry.com, players must take a drink, and by the end of the episode they are usually rather tipsy. Whether or not genealogists actually play such a game, the fact that they joke about it reveals the degree to which Ancestry .com promotes itself through the series. At crucial points in each episode, guests turn to Ancestry.com to push further back into their family's past. And genealogical professionals in the episodes are often shown using the site as well, reinforcing the notion that a subscription to the service will grant new and privileged access to one's family history, and, by extension, fresh insight into one's identity. The show illustrates the degree to which genealogy today is commercialized. In effect, purchasing genealogical products (an Ancestry.com subscription, a genealogical tour, a professionally produced family history book or video) is promoted as a way of purchasing a more colorful and more complex self.

THE SPIRITUAL DIMENSION OF GENEALOGY

As mentioned in chapter 1, religious affiliation in the United States has been changing rapidly in recent decades. One-fifth of all adults (some forty-six million Americans) and one-third of all adults under thirty now identify as religiously unaffiliated, making this the fastest-growing population in the American spiritual landscape.[61] Despite the growing disenchantment with organized religions, the desire to be part of something transcendent, authentic, and deeply meaningful clearly remains. And that desire is evident in twenty-first-century American genealogy.

I have already briefly discussed the prominence of spiritual or supernatural themes in roots television programs, a topic we will explore in greater detail in chapters 6 and 7. Such programs frequently emphasize uncanny similarities between the ancestors and featured guests, and highlight seemingly mysterious patterns in a family's history. Guests themselves often view such discoveries as a way to explain or justify their own choices. Some feel that the spirits of the ancestors have been subtly guiding them toward certain professions, hobbies, fields of study, political engagement, or other courses of action.

The spiritual dimension of family history research today cannot be discussed without reference to the genealogical mission of the Church of Jesus Christ of Latter-day Saints (LDS), the Mormon Church. The LDS organization FamilySearch rivals—and, in some ways, surpasses—Ancestry.com in the extent of its family document holdings. And unlike Ancestry.com, where an annual subscription can cost almost $400, access to FamilySearch.org is free. Likewise, the LDS church offers free access to its Family History Library in

Salt Lake City, which boasts "over 2.4 million rolls of microfilmed genealogical records; 727,000 microfiche; 356,000 books, serials, and other formats; over 4,500 periodicals and 3,725 electronic resources," giving it the largest collection of family history documents in the world.[62] In addition, the LDS church maintains more than 4,700 Family History Centers around the world, where people of all backgrounds can access the genealogical holdings of the Church and get help with family history research at no charge.[63]

This commitment to facilitating family history research around the world is grounded in the LDS religious mission to posthumously baptize forebears into the Mormon Church, both to ensure their salvation and to unite complete families in the afterlife. In order for such baptisms to take place, however, proper genealogical documentation is necessary. Thus, collecting, safeguarding, and granting access to family records around the world, and learning and teaching genealogical research techniques, have been key missions of the Church for at least one hundred years. As LDS genealogist Nephi Anderson put it in 1911,

> Every well-informed, consistent Latter-day Saint should believe in genealogy as much as he believes in faith, repentance, and baptism for the remission of sins; and this belief should be manifested in works, the same as belief in baptism, tithing, or any other gospel principle is shown to be genuine by its fulfillment in actual practice.[64]

While researching one's own family history is an important obligation for Mormons themselves, they are also exhorted to help others research their family trees. For, ultimately, we are all connected in a "grand family," and God has given Mormons the responsibility of reuniting that family.

While Mormons constitute only about 2 percent of the US population today, FamilySearch and other LDS-supported genealogical efforts (such as the *Generations Project* produced by BYU-TV), with their impressive resources and reach, have left a distinctive moral and spiritual imprint on twenty-first-century American genealogy.

WHY "QUANTUM" GENEALOGY?

Finally, I have used the term *quantum genealogy* to characterize the current American genealogical era, a label that requires some explanation. The term *quantum*, in its associations with theoretical physics, captures an important aspect of American genealogy today—its preoccupation with scientific and high-tech tools and methods. Specifically, the term evokes attempts within theoretical physics to reconcile and integrate the insights of quantum mechanics and general relativity into a so-called Theory of Everything. Just as physicists seek to uncover the underlying and unseen forces that govern all physical interactions in the universe, today's quantum genealogy seeks to uncover deep and hidden kinship networks that, if taken far enough, would link all of humanity in a single unified family tree. Additionally, the term *quantum* can indicate a discrete amount. This was the sense in which the term was used in "blood quantum" calculations once used to quantify degrees of Native American descent—"full-blood," "half-blood," and so on. In this sense, the term captures an increased emphasis on genetic kinship and DNA evidence in American genealogy. Not perhaps since eugenics fell out of favor in the United States has there been such a concerted effort to quantify ethnic admixtures.

As with all past genealogical eras, American quantum genealogy reflects the social, political, economic, and technological developments of our particular time and place. Likewise, genealogical practices around the world reflect and help to sustain the values, beliefs, worldviews, and power relations of the cultures that engage in them. In the next chapter, we will examine "roots work" in cultures around the world. Even as we survey the tremendous diversity of practices, we will find a common core of motivations and human needs that drive people worldwide to seek out their ancestors.

3

ROOTS WORK

Genealogy across Cultures

Death is a fact of life, and all cultures have developed their own ways of coping with it. There are, for instance, culturally specific rules about handling human remains, about proper funerary and memorial rituals, about how to treat the bereaved, about how the bereaved themselves should behave, and about the disposal or distribution of the property of the deceased. Underlying these rules are notions of kinship rights and obligations, and conceptions of what happens to us after death—specifically, whether we simply cease to exist or some part of us lives on in spirit form. Taken together, all of these rules, beliefs, and practices constitute each culture's "death system."[1]

In the contemporary United States our death system arguably reflects the high value we place on efficiency, rationality, consumerism, and individualism. We routinely employ a whole range of paid professionals, from end-of-life health-care workers, to morticians, funeral directors, and estate attorneys to help us efficiently navigate the deaths of our loved ones. Human bodies are discreetly removed from the place of demise to state-regulated processing facilities where they are often carefully preserved, dressed, coiffed, and painted for display in luxurious coffins. Funerals and obituaries celebrate the accomplishments and distinctive traits of the deceased, and their remains are customarily interred in well-ordered burial grounds where numbered plots are purchased and headstones with the individual's name and epitaph are erected. After a short period of mourning, the bereaved are expected to return to life as usual, and divest themselves of all but the most sentimental or valuable property of their loved ones. And if the bereaved suffer with prolonged grief they may be given psychological counseling or medication designed to help them let go of the deceased and move on with their lives. "Excessive" grief is seen as both irrational and unhealthy.[2] While the bereaved may quietly mark birthdays, anniversaries, or other significant dates associated with the deceased, conversing with the dead, seeing the dead, or offering sustenance or gifts to the dead are generally regarded as pathological behaviors in the American death system.

In a large number of societies around the world, however, the spirits and often the remains of the dead are kept close at hand, the living regularly address the dead and offer them food, drink, and gifts, and the dead are believed to communicate with the living and even reward or punish them. Such beliefs and practices are particularly widespread in Sub-Saharan Africa, East Asia, Polynesia, Melanesia and the Pacific Islands, and in some parts of the New World, such as the Caribbean. While there is great diversity in systems of ancestor veneration (or "ancestor worship")[3] worldwide, these systems are always premised on the notion that the dead live on in some kind of spirit form after biological death, that they continue to be involved in the affairs of the living, and that they have at least some power to influence events in the physical world.[4]

While communing regularly with the dead may at first glance appear quite at odds with rational American deathways, I will argue in this chapter that practices as diverse as African and East Asian ancestor veneration, Micronesian spirit possession, and contemporary American genealogy are all forms of "roots work"—ways of cultivating and managing our links to those who have gone before us. Arguably, whether roots work takes the form of animal sacrifices, dances of the dead, or the collection of census records, I argue that it affects us in three important and interconnected ways. Roots work has *psychological effects*—it comforts the living. It has *identity effects*—it helps to define membership in social groups, such as families or ethnic groups. And it has *social order effects*—it helps to reinforce shared norms, values, and social ranks (see figure 3.1).

THE PSYCHOLOGICAL EFFECTS OF ROOTS WORK

Roots work: Activities aimed at elaborating and maintaining links with the ancestors. Examples include, but are not limited to, funerary practices; rituals of veneration, supplication, and appeasement; spirit possession; divination; lineage recitation; and the collection, preservation, and ordering of genealogical records.

Roots work involves everything from constructing carefully documented family trees to hosting elaborate feasts for the dead. As diverse as these practices are, they are all aimed at defining and maintaining links with the

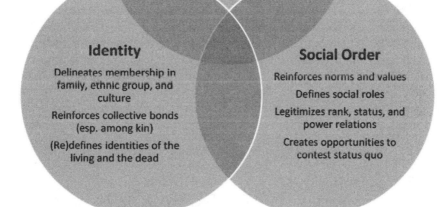

Figure 3.1. Social Effects of Roots Work

ancestors, and they all provide psychological comfort to the living. For those who believe that the deceased live on in spirit form, honoring the dead through ritual or documentary practices can help to ease the grief of losing a loved one. After all, there is consolation in the belief that our loved ones are not really gone, but rather continue to reside in heaven (for Christians), on an island of the dead (for Trobriand Islanders), or even beneath the floorboards of our homes (for many West Africans). In all cultures, mourning involves a complex balancing act between remembering and forgetting, between holding on to the dead and letting them go.[5] Roots work, in its many forms, helps us order our memories of the dead and manage our emotions.

Consider, for instance, the Kasena of northeastern Ghana. Among the Kasena, treatment of the newly deceased broadly mirrors the treatment of newborn babies.[6] It is women, for instance, who oversee childbirth, and women who attend to the dying in their final moments of life. And, as is the case with newborn infants, the newly dead are carefully washed with herb-infused water, regularly massaged, and never left alone. Once the body is thus carefully prepared, it is placed in a womb-shaped burial chamber and arranged naked in a fetal position with its head toward the opening of the grave. Essentially the deceased is returned to the womb of Mother Earth in order to be reborn into the realm of the ancestors. Kasena deathways are clearly "pregnant with life," bearing countless reminders of the cycle of birth, death, and rebirth into the spirit world.[7] Through such positive associations with childbirth, death is framed as a natural step in the life cycle, not a loss as much as a transition to a new state of existence. Such roots work "overcomes death's destructiveness."[8] In other words, in the face of death, this roots work comforts the bereaved with an affirmation of life and the promise of life after death.

Christian death rituals in the contemporary United States likewise often stress a return to the earth ("ashes to ashes, dust to dust") and the promise of life after death.[9] Members of some Christian denominations regularly pray for the peaceful repose of the dead in the afterlife, for instance, on All Saints' Day and All Souls' Day. In addition, American genealogists often report that the death of a loved one prompted them to begin their family history research in earnest. For some, the personal loss made them realize how little they knew about their own family history. For some, the death made them more aware of their own mortality, and more concerned about leaving a record of their own lives for generations to come. Still others report feeling a sense of duty to the deceased to honor and preserve their memories. Whether we participate in religious rituals for the dead or undertake archival research to document the lives of our forebears, we are keeping them alive in our minds and organizing and editing our memories of them. We are allowing ourselves both to remember certain things and to forget others, both to hold on to and to let go of the dead. This provides solace in our grief.

In addition to roots work providing consolation to the bereaved in cultures around the world, it also provides comfort by supplying explanations for hardships or turns of fortune. In cultures with ancestor veneration, ancestral spirits are believed to be able to intervene in the affairs of the living. In some cultures, ancestral spirits are thought to guide and protect living kin from a distance, and they are perceived as rather aloof and benign with fairly limited powers. In other cultures, however, ancestral spirits are believed to be more active participants in human affairs; they are powerful, easily offended, and potentially dangerous. They reward proper behavior with bounty and punish improper behavior with calamity—illness, accident, crop failures, and more. However, in such systems, one always has the option of appealing to the ancestral spirits for help, for cures, for answers, for relief. If only the will of the ancestors can be determined and the appropriate actions taken, assistance will be forthcoming. Such beliefs provide a measure of psychological comfort—first, by offering explanations for calamities or extraordinary good luck, and, second, by giving the living a sense of hope and control. Yes, circumstances may be dire, but if we please the ancestors, they will come to our aid.

Let us consider the psychological effects of such beliefs in a cross section of African cultures. Among the Igbo, Tuareg, and Ohafia peoples of Nigeria; the Akan peoples of Ghana and the Ivory Coast (including the Asante/Ashanti); the Tallensi, Sisala, and Ewe peoples of Ghana; the Yoruba of Benin; the Lugbara of Uganda and the Democratic Republic of the Congo; the Chagga of Tanzania; and the Mozambican refugees and Xhosa-speakers in South Africa, various forms of ancestor veneration are practiced (see figure 3.2).[10] While beliefs and practices vary a great deal from culture

Figure 3.2.   Select African Societies with Ancestor Veneration

to culture, in all of these societies, people look to ancestral spirits to explain family misfortunes and social calamities such as food shortages and natural disasters, and they take pains to please the ancestors through offerings such as drinks poured on the earth (libations), food dropped through the floorboards, animal sacrifices, drumming, dancing, processions, praise, and prayer. When misfortune strikes, efforts are made to determine what has displeased the ancestors (leading them to actively punish or withdraw protection from their descendants). And diviners and healers are consulted and dreams analyzed to identify the will of the ancestors and the cure for the struggle at hand.

As scholars of Africa point out, these ancestral spirits typically are not regarded as all-powerful gods. Rather, they are more like guardian angels or Catholic saints, who protect and aid the living and intercede between the living and higher deities.[11] Nonetheless, communing with the ancestors can provide the living a glimmer of hope amid despair, and a familiar touchstone amid unsettling social changes. Researchers note, for instance, that for Mozambican refugees fleeing war and living in poverty in South Africa, engaging in rituals of ancestor veneration gave them hope of overcoming adversity, and allowed them to create a sense of home even in the midst of their displacement.[12] Likewise, for the Chagga of Tanzania, ancestral beliefs provided explanations for the AIDS epidemic that swept the region and gave solace as the death toll rose.[13]

Among the Igbo in southeastern Nigeria, there is another form of solace. A limited number of families are given the opportunity to commune one last time with deceased loved ones. Communities stage masquerade festivals in which select ancestors are believed to return to their families by temporarily incarnating in dancers who wear sacred *Odo* (ancestral spirit) masks. While it is an honor and a blessing to have your loved one incarnated in the masquerade, it often reignites intense grief in family members. Nonetheless, these rituals give the living a chance to voice their emotions, receive support and consolation from the assembled community, and strengthen perceived ties to the spirit realm.[14]

Similarly, for many Akan peoples of Ghana (including the Asante/ Ashanti), crucial roots work is accomplished at elaborate funerals. Family members of the deceased will spend as much money as they can assemble, and potentially go into debt, to stage an impressive funeral with amplified music, dancing, refreshments, electric lighting, video recording, specially commissioned funeral clothes for mourners, and expensive clothing, jewelry, and an ornate golden bed for the deceased.[15] Indeed, the social pressure to hold a "good" funeral is so strong that many families will spend more money on the gathering than they spend on end-of-life care for the deceased.[16] Scholars point out, however, that a key aim of these lavish funerals is to successfully initiate the transformation of the deceased into a revered ancestral spirit. Not everyone who dies will be revered as an ancestor—typically only those who lived good lives and left descendants. So staging a successful funeral with conspicuous displays of prosperity and a large contingent of mourners (who are drawn, in part, by the promised festivities), is a way to show the community at large that the deceased is worthy of veneration as an ancestor. The funeral helps to shape mourners' recollections of the deceased and build the reputation of the deceased so he will be revered as an ancestral spirit.[17] Such roots work provides family members with the comforting knowledge that, although they could not prevent the death of their loved one, they did all they could do to ensure that he would live on through ancestor veneration.

Researchers find similar forms of psychological consolation arising from ancestor veneration practices in East Asia, Melanesia, Micronesia, and the New World, cases which will be discussed below.[18] In the contemporary United States, ancestors are not typically given offerings, petitioned, consulted, or believed to directly commune with the living. So ancestor veneration is not a feature of the dominant US death system. Nonetheless, the roots work Americans undertake through memorial and genealogical practices serves the same psychological functions. Memorializing the dead, and documenting their lives through vital records, photographs, and other evidence, is a way of ensuring a kind of immortality for the ancestors. Indeed, genealogists often speak of keeping a forebear's memory "alive" through such practices. Likewise, genealogists not only document the lives of their ancestors; they also document their own lives, engaging in a kind of "self-immortalization,"[19] ensuring that they will "live on" in documentary form. While most Americans would not assume that ancestral spirits are responsible for calamities or windfalls, it is not uncommon for genealogists to explain current circumstances with reference to the ancestors. Such explanations are especially prominent on roots television. When a young woman on one American roots program discovers that her ancestor was a cobbler, she decides that this explains her love of shoes. When another woman finds that her ancestor suffered through food shortages, she decides that this explains her own overeating and her struggles with obesity. And when a man finds prominent farmers among his ancestors, he feels that this explains his own commitment to eating locally grown food.[20]

While roots work clearly takes very different forms around the world, in most, if not all, cultures it has important psychological effects. It consoles and comforts the living by affirming some form of immortality for our loved ones and for ourselves; it provides hope and a sense of control over our own lives; and it helps to explain otherwise seemingly inexplicable circumstances.

THE IDENTITY EFFECTS OF ROOTS WORK

In addition to having important psychological effects, roots work—whether in the form of sacred rituals of ancestor veneration or the documentary rituals of genealogical research—also serves to define and strengthen individual and group identities. When Japanese, Chinese, and Taiwanese families place daily offerings on their ancestral altars, when a Chuuk islander is possessed by an ancestral spirit who chastises his or her descendants for family discord, when Cubans, Haitians, Puerto Ricans, and Brazilians consult the ancestors through divination rituals, and when contemporary American genealogists proudly display family trees reaching back to Colonial settlers, they are all asserting a sense of belonging. Belonging to a particular family, to a lineage, to an ethnic group, and belonging to the flow of history more generally. This desire to belong to social groups is universal. Humans, like other higher primates, are social animals. Indeed, some researchers suggest that this highly developed sociality evolved in humans and other primates because it helped us to survive.[21] Belonging to social groups affords protection when faced with threats; it provides food in times of shortage; and it offers assistance with crucial tasks like raising offspring. Drawing on select examples from the Asia-Pacific region and the Americas, let us consider the ways roots work serves to define identities (see figure 3.3).

We begin in China, with its rich history of ancestor veneration. Traditionally, Chinese families were patrilineal (ancestry was traced only through the father's line) and patrilocal (brides moved into the husband's household and lived together with his parents, his brothers, and all of their wives and children). In addition, daughters were considered only temporary members of their father's lineage. When a woman married, she became a member of her husband's lineage, so her husband's ancestors became her own ancestors.[22] This system of organizing families and defining kinship links was arguably beneficial to Chinese families in several ways. It ensured the smooth transmission of wealth (from fathers to sons). It provided large extended families to care for the elderly and the young. And it reinforced bonds of loyalty and mutual aid along kinship lines.

These family arrangements were reflected and reinforced by the teachings of Confucius (551–479 BCE), whose moral philosophy stressed what

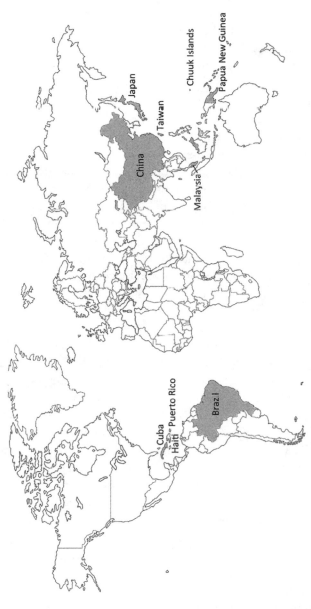

Figure 3.3. Select Asia-Pacific and New World Societies with Ancestor Veneration

he saw as natural authority relations—namely, father over son, husband over wife, and master over subject.[23] A key component of this moral system was filial piety: the duty of children to respect, obey, and give unquestioned loyalty to their parents—particularly to their father. In return, parents had a duty of care for their children, and were expected to rally their resources and connections to arrange advantageous marriages and livelihoods for their children. In all matters, the individual was expected to disregard his or her own interests and desires, and place the needs and reputation of the family and the will of parents and ancestors above all else.

In such a system, family membership defined individual identity. You were, in effect, an extension of your family, and your opportunities, roles, and social status were largely determined by your family's standing. Crucially, your individual actions could enhance or damage your family's reputation. So every day, in countless ways, you were reminded to serve the family well and safeguard its honor. One way this priority on family membership and family duty was reinforced was through rituals of ancestor veneration. Although specific practices varied from region to region and changed over time, they generally at least involved offering daily food, drink, incense, and prayers at an ancestral altar in the family home, and completing seasonal rites such as cleaning the family gravesite and making special offerings during the Lunar New Year and Tomb-Sweeping Day.[24]

Family membership and lineage continuity was so crucial, in fact, that when a man died without leaving any descendants, his family might arrange for him to posthumously adopt a living son who would then venerate his adopted father's spirit with the appropriate rituals. Likewise, if a woman died without marrying, it meant that she died without being situated in a permanent lineage—for her father's lineage was only temporary. Families often feared that such a spirit would become an angry "orphan ghost,"[25] which would wander around looking for a permanent home and potentially bring serious misfortunes to her household. These families might arrange "ghost marriages" for their deceased daughters, so they would be permanently adopted into a husband's lineage. This was thought to placate the woman's spirit and thus protect the family from her anger. Similarly, in Taiwan, widows were strongly discouraged from remarrying, out of concern that the ancestors would be angry to have women's family loyalties (and their immortal souls) divided between two families—that of their first husbands and that of their second husbands.[26] Permanent and unambiguous membership in a family was believed to be the will of the ancestors.

The basic principles of Chinese ancestor veneration were quite similar to those of African ancestor veneration, discussed above. Namely, if the living appropriately honored the ancestors, the spirits would reward them. If the living failed to adequately revere the ancestors, the spirits might punish them with illness, accident, or other bad luck. The ancestors were generally not regarded as all-powerful gods, but as spirit entities who could protect and bring good luck to the living and intercede with higher deities on behalf of the living, or bring calamity on descendants who failed in their duties to the ancestors.

Interestingly, scholars have noted that some Chinese today (and ethnic-Chinese in societies such as Malaysia and Taiwan) continue to observe ancestor veneration rituals without necessarily believing in the supernatural effects of the rites.[27] They continue the observances because they wish to show respect to their ancestors, because they want to preserve what they see as a distinctive Chinese cultural tradition, and because they fear that others will criticize them if they do not engage in the expected rituals. The fact that some Chinese continue to venerate ancestors even though they no longer believe in the power of ancestral spirits suggests that ancestor veneration is as much about identity (individual identity, family identity, and Chinese cultural identity) as it is about beliefs in the divine.[28]

The Communist state seems to have understood this. During China's Cultural Revolution the Communist state effectively barred ancestor worship, considering it superstitious and bourgeois.[29] Excessive concern about one's own family (one's individual and family identity) was seen to conflict with communitarian national values. Ironically, the state is now encouraging ancestor veneration again, hoping to draw wealthy ethnic-Chinese expatriates back to rural villages with the promise of reconnecting with their ancestry.[30] The ultimate goal of the state is to convince these ex-pats to invest in rural schools, roads, and other economic development projects. In effect, the Chinese state is using ancestral spirits (and the lure of family identity) as bait to attract foreign investment.

Over the millennia, Chinese cultural and religious values and associated practices have spread widely throughout Asia. Japan, for instance, adopted Buddhist beliefs and Confucian values from China. So, not surprisingly, the Japanese also have a long tradition of ancestor veneration. Indeed, even before the arrival of Buddhism (in the sixth century CE), the Japanese had their own system of ancestor veneration, rooted in the indigenous religion of Japan, Shinto. Within Shinto, an animistic religion with a host of deities and nature spirits (collectively known as *kami*), deceased kin could eventually become *kami*, spirits who guided and protected their households and their home villages. So when Buddhism and Confucianism arrived in Japan, Chinese rituals of ancestor veneration were easily incorporated into existing Japanese beliefs and practices.[31] In Japan today, families customarily maintain both a Shinto "spirit shelf" (a *kamidana*) and a Buddhist ancestral altar (a *butsudan*) in their homes, on which they make regular offerings of food, drink, flowers, and incense.[32]

Daily, seasonal, and other periodic rituals of remembrance in Japan reinforce the message that one's identity is firmly rooted in one's family, and furthermore, that one cannot achieve well-being through individual actions, but only through connection with others.[33] The living are enmeshed in a web of mutual obligations, and it is these social bonds that make us fully human. Likewise, the living and the dead are bound by mutual obligations. The living venerate the dead, allowing them to progress to higher levels of ancestorhood. And, in exchange, the dead provide protection and allow for the flow of good luck to their descendants.[34] Similar to recent developments in China, many young people in Japan today do not really understand the meaning or beliefs behind rituals of ancestor veneration.[35] (This reality was portrayed to humorous effect in Jūzō Itami's 1984 film *Osōshiki,* or *The Funeral.*) Younger generations often observe the rituals out of a sense of family duty, filial piety, and cultural tradition.[36] Nonetheless, in the process of coming together to venerate the ancestors, family members strengthen their communal bonds and their communal identity, their sense of belonging to a long, unbroken chain of ancestors that will continue in perpetuity.[37] The individual is just one small link in this chain, and his or her identity is virtually inseparable from the whole. Indeed, even the tombs that hold family members' cremains are not customarily inscribed with individual names. Rather, family members are laid to rest under one family name.

The Japanese state has long recognized the power of ancestor veneration to promote social solidarity and cultural/national identity. During the feudal era, the ruling elite monitored the population to ensure that they were performing proper rituals of ancestor veneration.[38] Such rituals were seen as proof that families were devout Buddhists, not upstart Christian converts whom the rulers saw as threats. Later, when Japan began to modernize in the nineteenth century, the Meiji state mandated that families keep accurate genealogical records and conduct appropriate rituals to venerate the ancestors, chief among them the emperor, who was portrayed as the father of the nation.[39] In these ways, the state used the power of roots work to solidify Japanese cultural and national identities.

In addition to helping define and solidify the identities of the living, Japanese ancestor veneration serves to transform the identity of the deceased. Through countless rituals that span decades, memories of the dead are edited down until all that remains is a rather generic image of benevolent ancestral spirits. Likewise, further afield in Melanesia, several Papua New Guinean peoples engage in roots work designed to transform the identities of both the living and the dead. Sabarl Islanders, for instance, undertake a years-long series of mourning feasts intended to construct a perfected image of the deceased.[40] At the same time, the feasts are essentially a series of exchanges, mainly of food, that serve to discharge any obligations the deceased may have left unfulfilled. In this way, the feasts help to redefine social bonds among the living. For instance, as a widow discharges her husband's remaining debts and obligations, social bonds with those parties become looser. But as she increasingly relies on her kin to help her host the quite elaborate feasts, those kinship bonds become stronger. And, eventually, when the widow discharges all of her husband's obligations, her own identity is decoupled from her husband's, and she becomes eligible to remarry.[41]

Similarly, among Papua New Guineans in the Collingwood Bay vicinity, roots work serves to define and strengthen the identities of the living with reference to the dead. Residents of this area take turns hosting elaborate church festivals, complete with drumming, dancing, and singing.[42] Kin groups travel great distances and spend considerable time covering themselves with clan emblems, often utterly transforming their appearance. The dancers, thus transformed, in some sense are reflections of ancestral spirits. If a dancer makes an impressive showing, it is believed that the ancestors gave him strength, and if he does poorly observers may conclude that the ancestors withheld their support, perhaps out of displeasure with the family. These church festivals, with their origins in older competitive clan feasts, serve to strengthen the bonds between family members and define the boundaries between kin (clan) groups. In other words, this roots work serves to define individual and family identities.

Likewise, the Asabano of Papua New Guinea traditionally conducted a series of mortuary rituals designed to transform the deceased from a potentially troublesome and dangerous ghost into a benevolent spirit member of the household.[43] The Asabano, like many cultures around the world, believed in a divisible human soul. The permanent, benevolent "big soul" was housed in human bone, whereas the troublesome "little soul" resided in the flesh.[44] So when the Asabano wished to incorporate an ancestral spirit into the household, the body of the deceased would be exposed to the elements, aiding in the decomposition of the flesh that housed the troublesome part of the spirit. Then the clean bones containing only the benevolent spirit were collected and housed close to the living, and descendants would make offerings to the spirit, addressing it and including it in the life of the kin group.[45] This transformation of the body from unclean and spiritually dangerous to clean and benevolent is, in effect, a transformation of the social identity of the deceased—from a living member of the community to an active spirit member.

This case illustrates a crucial point for the understanding of roots work worldwide. In cultures around the world, ancestors are socially constructed. Yes, purely biological ancestry is a fact of nature, but all cultures select certain individuals who are singled out for special designation as "ancestors." Consider, for instance, the way the Asabano would traditionally treat the bodies of people they did not wish to transform into ancestral spirits, like their enemies. These bodies would be thrown into the river so the spirits would be permanently removed from the community. The Asabano case illustrates another important aspect of roots work worldwide: the way it can be transformed over time by social change. Specifically, after the arrival of Christianity and colonial rule, the Asabano were no longer allowed to engage in their customary mortuary practices. Instead, they were required to bury the dead in cemeteries. Because the flesh and bones decayed underground and there was no way to separate the "big soul" from the "little soul," people began to fear graveyards and the troublesome spirits believed to dwell there.[46] But eventually, traditional Asabano beliefs melded with Christian teachings, so that today many believe that the "big soul" ascends to heaven and the "little soul" goes to hell.[47]

Similarly, residents of the Chuuk islands in Micronesia also traditionally believed in two souls—a "good" one that could roam free (in dreams and in the afterlife), and a "bad" one that was tied to the physical body.[48] Death for the Chuukese today is seen as a continuation of life's journey, and the dead are thought to experience homesickness in the first days, weeks, or sometimes years after death, until they become settled into the spirit realm. It is during this period that female relatives of the deceased are most likely to experience possession by the "good" spirit. The woman may first experience a feeling of weakness, numbness, or other illness, until the possession manifests in signs such as stiffened limbs, a clenched jaw, or unusual strength. Those who witness the possession will talk with the spirit, and often the spirit will reveal its identity and simply express love and longing for kin, or chastise them for family discord and advise them on solutions to their problems. Family members, in turn, voice their love and longing for the deceased and work to resolve any conflicts or problems identified by the spirit.[49] Such possession experiences, thus, typically serve to reinforce family bonds, to ease the emotional turmoil and family discord that often arise after the death of a loved one, and to reaffirm kin group membership and kin group obligations.

In addition, while burial practices in the islands are quite diverse, at least some Chuukese choose to bury the remains of the deceased very close at hand, with burials beneath or next to the family home. Such "residential burials," which occur in many cultures around the world, arguably not only reinforce a sense of close kinship between the living (and close links between the living and the dead), but also strengthen ties to the family home and family land.[50] In a sense, the place itself exerts a centripetal force, drawing the family together. So on the Chuuk islands, roots work in the form of residential burials and spirit possession helps to bind families more closely together.

As is true with the Asabano in Papua New Guinea, the arrival of Christianity led to certain changes in Chuukese beliefs and practices. Today Christian beliefs in heaven, hell, and (for Catholics) purgatory have been incorporated into Chuukese beliefs about the soul's journey in the afterlife.[51] Likewise, we can see many cultures around the world where older beliefs about ancestral spirits melded with Christian orthodoxy to create new, syncretic forms of religious belief and practice. Such examples are prevalent, for instance, in the New World in locations where large numbers of Africans were enslaved by a Christian ruling class. Cubans, Haitians, Puerto Ricans, and Brazilians of African heritage, for example, all developed syncretic religions that allowed them to hold on to their African cultural identities while still operating within a social structure dominated by Christian beliefs and practices.

Under the brutal and dehumanizing conditions of slavery in the New World, ancestor worship and traditional African religious beliefs and practices became a vital source of cultural and individual identities. White slave owners and colonial administrators who, in many places, were vastly outnumbered by slaves of African descent, lived in constant fear of slave uprisings. For this reason, they developed strategies to reduce the ability of slaves to collectively organize. Captives from the same linguistic and cultural groups were often split up to weaken social bonds and make communication more difficult. Slaves were routinely forbidden to learn to read and write, they were usually stripped of their African names and assigned European names by their captors, and they were forced to adopt Christianity and barred from practicing their African religions. Such practices were designed to strip slaves of their individual and cultural identities and their sense of agency and independence. But slaves continued to secretly worship their ancestors and African deities by adapting their religious rituals and cast of divine beings to those of their captors.

In Cuba, for instance, where most slaves came from West African Yoruba territories, captives developed a new religion, Santería (the "way of the saints"), which blended Catholicism and French spiritism (which focused on communication with the dead through living mediums) with Yoruba beliefs in ancestral spirits and a host of divine entities (*orishas*) who communicate with a supreme being.[52] In Santería, the *orishas* were fused with Catholic saints who had similar traits or expertise. Saint Lazarus, for example, whom the Bible says was raised from death by Jesus, was melded with Babalu Aye, a Yoruba *orisha* strongly associated with illness and healing.[53] So slaves were able to worship Babalu Aye through the figure of Saint Lazarus, appealing simultaneously to both the *orisha* and the Catholic saint to intercede with the supreme being on their behalf. Such religious syncretism allowed slaves to maintain their cultural connections with Africa and strengthened their communal bonds while allowing them to carve out something that was uniquely theirs in an environment that denied them even the most basic freedoms. As one scholar notes, "In this way the slaves took possession of Catholicism and thereby repossessed themselves as active spiritual subjects."[54]

Likewise, in Brazil where the majority of slaves came from Yoruba regions, Yoruba religious beliefs were blended with Catholicism. Specifically, in the syncretized religions of Umbanda and Candomblé, Yoruba *orishas* were melded with Catholic saints and worshipped in ways that appeared broadly consistent with Catholic orthodoxy. Nonetheless, the white Christian ruling elite attempted to maintain its position of dominance in Brazil by attacking African religious practices as primitive, superstitious, and immoral. As a consequence, some traditional rites (such as animal sacrifices) were driven further underground, and some were pushed out of the sacred realm and into secular realms like Carnival. Despite such changes, these new religious forms have provided "a mechanism by which black Africans and Brazilians could distance themselves culturally from the world dominated by the white oppressor," maintain their links to Africa, and assert distinctive cultural identities.[55]

Similarly, in Haiti where the majority of slaves came from the Fon cultures of West Africa, captives blended their own religious system of spirits and deities (*vodun*) with Catholic beliefs and practices.[56] The resulting syncretic religion, Vodun (sometimes written Vodou, Vaudou, or Voodoo) incorporates ancestral spirits and other spirit entities who can be called upon for assistance with health, wealth, love, or other matters. Such assistance may take the form of protection or divine guidance, but adherents also believe that spirits can be employed to attack enemies and rivals. Such "black magic" looms large in Western representations of "voodoo." Indeed, the Catholic Church in Haiti has long branded the practices of Vodun satanic or diabolical (which, ironically, has only served to reconfirm the power of dark spiritual forces among Vodun adherents). Arguably, the beliefs and practices of Vodun are grounded in struggles over both resources and identities.[57] Specifically, since the colonial era, both the natural resources and human capital in Haiti have been so disproportionately controlled by an elite ruling class that for most people, existence is precarious. Poverty, disease, corruption, and violence are widespread. In a climate of competition for scarce resources, it is not surprising that people attribute dramatic and destructive events to dark forces commanded by those who are jealous, greedy, or angry.[58] Nor is it surprising that people who lack material power would seek to rally spirit powers to their aid.

In addition, scholars note that the rather sinister image of "voodoo" in the West is grounded in struggles over identity and power in Haiti. Just as white colonists legitimized their rule by labeling blacks (and African religious beliefs) inferior, mixed-race Haitians have long attempted to set themselves apart from darker-skinned Haitians by criticizing Vodun and its practitioners. In other words, lighter-skinned Haitians have long demonized African religious influences as a way of claiming higher-status identities for themselves.[59] But Vodun has also served to unite Haitians of African descent against oppression. The "spirit of kinship" offered by Vodun arguably helped to fuel the slave revolts that led to national independence and the end of slavery in 1804.[60]

Another syncretic religion emerged in Puerto Rico, where most slaves came from the Kongo region of Africa.[61] Here Kongo ancestor veneration was blended with Catholicism and French spiritism to give rise to Espiritismo. In this syncretic religion, spirit mediums seek guidance and assistance from ancestral spirits, who are asked to intercede with the supreme being. Symbols such as the crucifix do double duty in Espiritismo, evoking the high god and his son, but also serving as a reminder of the enduring spirit and its cyclical journey through multiple incarnations.[62] Unlike the syncretic religions of Cuba and Brazil, however, there is no place for *orishas* in Espiritismo. Scholars argue that in Puerto Rico, with its much smaller population of slaves, some distinctively African religious elements (such as the *orishas*) were downplayed. Instead of emphasizing African spiritual roots, Espiritismo allowed practitioners to claim a uniquely Puerto Rican (and largely white) cultural identity.[63]

Despite many differences between these New World syncretic religions, they are all grounded in the belief that there is life after physical death, that ancestral spirits remain involved in the world of the living, and that spirits can be asked (or even compelled) to act on behalf of the living, particularly their descendants. Such beliefs would have provided a strong sense of family identity, cultural connection, and social cohesion to enslaved Africans in exploitative systems designed to inhibit communal identities. Clearly, roots work can help us to strengthen and redefine our identities amid experiences of loss, hardship, and oppression. Likewise, roots work can serve as an antidote to social changes that challenge our individual and collective identities.

In recent decades, social groups around the world—including families, ethnic groups, and communities of faith, for instance—have faced pressures on their cohesion. The increasing mobility of populations has split families and other groups apart and scattered them far and wide. At the same time, technological developments are changing the ways people within these groups communicate and connect with each other. The genealogists I interviewed frequently listed such factors among their motivations for doing family history research. Families are increasingly fractured by divorce and migration, they explained.[64] People are so fixated on social media that they no longer communicate in authentic and meaningful ways, they say.[65] And what's more, society is changing so fast that traditions are being lost, and globalization is stripping world cultures of their uniqueness.[66] It is this fragmentation, this homogenization, this hollowing out of communal social life that makes us long for something deeper, truer, more uniquely and distinctively our own. And this, they explain, is one reason people turn to genealogy. As Madeline (69, Missouri) succinctly put it, "Our world is moving so fast . . . it is difficult to keep up with changes. Genealogy links us to those who have gone before us, giving us a sense of belonging to something unchanging."

THE SOCIAL ORDER EFFECTS OF ROOTS WORK

The discussion above has shown that roots work, in its varied forms, can psychologically console and comfort us and provide us with a sense of belonging to a larger social group. But in so doing, it also frequently contributes to the ordering of society. Practices such as communing with ancestral spirits, praise singing, and joining patriotic lineage societies such as the DAR, remind participants of their shared norms and values, and help to define and legitimize social ranks and roles. In this way, roots work tends to be a conservative force serving to maintain the status quo. In some circumstances, however, roots work may allow participants to challenge long-standing power relations. Let us consider some examples from among the cultures we have already surveyed, as well as some additional cases.

As discussed above, in many cultures around the world—particularly in East Asia, Melanesia, Sub-Saharan Africa, and the Afro-Caribbean region— ancestral spirits are believed to be active participants in the world of the living. They reward desirable behavior with protection and good luck, and punish undesirable behavior with illness, accident, food shortages, or other calamities.[67] These beliefs exert considerable pressure on the living to behave according to widely shared norms and values. Just as the threat of spending an eternity in hell exerts pressure on believers in predominantly Christian societies to conform to agreed-upon rules of social interaction, the fear of punishment by the ancestors and the promise of rewards encourage believers to obey the rules and fulfill their culturally defined obligations.

This pressure toward conformity is further reinforced by specific features of ancestor veneration in many cultures. First, there is the process of selecting which ancestors to revere. Typically, not everyone who dies in cultures with ancestor veneration will become an "ancestor." Indeed, it is commonly the case that only individuals who lived "good" lives, married, left descendants, and died "good" deaths (for instance, dying in old age of natural causes, not earlier in life or by violence, suicide, or unexplained causes) may become revered ancestors.[68] This fact no doubt provides an incentive to marry, have children, and lead a long and virtuous life. In addition, in many cultures, there is a belief that the well-being of ancestral spirits is in the hands of their descendants.[69] If descendants conduct the proper rituals, the spirits will rest at peace and perhaps progress to higher spiritual states. If descendants fail to conduct the proper rituals, however, spirits will become unhappy, hungry, and unable to settle into the spirit world. In such belief systems, the fate of one's eternal soul is in the hands of one's family members. This provides a powerful incentive to maintain favorable family relationships and close kinship bonds.

Indeed, a key outcome of roots work around the globe is to reinforce family cohesion. This is strikingly clear, for instance, in the Chuuk islands when ancestral spirits speak through the living to direct descendants to care for one another and to resolve family conflicts.[70] However, it is also observed in cultures around the world where descendants are expected to cooperate and pool resources to organize elaborate funerals and ancestor rituals.[71] In order to properly care for the spirits of the dead and to be well regarded by the broader community, family members must put aside disputes and join together in collective action. Arguably, engaging in such collective activities may actually ease some of the tensions that arise with the death of a family member—for instance, tensions over succession or the division of property.

Even in societies like the United States where ancestral spirits are not routinely believed to intervene in the lives of descendants or to depend on the living for their well-being in the afterlife, roots work can encourage conformity to social norms and values. All genealogists must make choices about which ancestors to focus on most intently. It requires considerable time, effort, and money to dig into the details of our forebears' lives. And our motivations for choosing one "ancestor" over another vary. We may choose the one who was most socially prominent, because the records on his life are most plentiful.[72] We may choose the one who appears unusual in some way, in hopes that we will find more colorful stories to pass on to future generations. Or we may choose the one who is most likely to lead us to a Revolutionary War patriot, a founding father or mother of the republic, a descendant of the *Mayflower*. Such choices reflect our cultural values, our priorities, and our preoccupations.

This becomes quite clear in American roots television shows, where the most illustrious and admirable forebears are traced, while less prominent family members are largely ignored, and those with undesirable traits are dismissed as "bad apples" or "black sheep." As we will see in chapter 6, such programs routinely celebrate national values such as hard work, egalitarianism, rugged individualism, and faith, and the selected ancestors are held up as exemplars for us to emulate. So even in the absence of beliefs in active ancestral spirits, roots work can encourage us to conform to communal values and behavioral norms.

In addition to reinforcing shared norms and values, roots work worldwide often serves to legitimize existing social hierarchies.[73] Indeed, classic anthropological studies have shown that genealogies often tell us at least as much about power relations as they tell us about kinship.[74] For instance, current political, economic, or other social considerations can influence who counts as a family member or an "ancestor" at any given time. Families may choose to emphasize (or even fabricate) certain kinship links while downplaying (or denying) others to best suit the needs of the living. This tendency becomes quite clear when we consider the role of lineage praise-singers around the world. While there are significant differences between them, the Griots of Senegal, the Chāraṇ of Western India, and the courtly genealogist-bards of ancient Ireland, Wales, and Scandinavia all specialize(d) in learning and reciting the lineages of illustrious patrons.[75] Public recitations of noble lineages served to legitimize the rule of kings and chiefs, or even sacralize their rule if lineages were traced back to gods, goddesses, or other mythological figures.[76] Today, in a more democratic era, these genealogist-bards (or praise-singers) are less likely to be employed by kings or chiefs to naturalize their rule, and more likely to be employed by wealthy families to arrange an advantageous marriage or recite an illustrious lineage at a wedding.[77] But the genealogist-bards of today serve much the same role as those of old. Their recitations buttress their patrons' claims to high social status.

Rulers and other elites have long recognized the power of roots work to legitimize their privileged status. For instance, bureaucrats in Imperial China (1750 to circa 1920) made a concerted effort to standardize ancestor veneration rituals and beliefs in ways that emphasized the importance of obedience to higher authority (to the father, to the ancestors, to the hierarchy of gods and goddesses, and to the imperial state itself).[78] Not only did this standardization contribute to a "cultural unification" of diverse groups within China, but it also reinforced the obedience of the population to the Chinese state.[79] Likewise, the Japanese state used roots work (ancestor veneration and mandatory genealogical recordkeeping) from the late-nineteenth century through the end of World War II to better monitor and control the population.[80] Genealogical records, in the form of state-mandated family registries (*koseki*), allowed the state to more efficiently tax the population and conscript young men to military service. And ancestor veneration reinforced the importance of unquestioned obedience and loyalty to one's father and to the "father" of the nation, the emperor.

The centrality of paternal authority in China and Japan reflects a broader tendency in roots work worldwide toward reinforcing the power and social position of men. In traditional Chinese ancestor veneration practices, for instance, rituals were typically only performed for male ancestors, and genealogical records were only kept for the male line.[81] In a system where women are simply subsumed into their husbands' lineages, women's individual identities and their perceived social value are undermined.[82] Thus, roots work often contributes to the maintenance of male dominance and the subordination of women. Likewise, among the Igbo in southeastern Nigeria, mainly male ancestors are venerated through masquerades during which dancers don elaborate masks and receive the spirits of dead.[83] Furthermore, only men may wear the ancestral masks and incarnate the spirits; only men are allowed to care for the masks; and only boys and men are allowed to join masking societies, where they are taught to keep all secret knowledge away from women.[84] The exclusion of women from these crucial rituals in the lives of the community and the family both mirrors women's subordination and helps to maintain women's inferior status. While the patriarchal bias of roots work is perhaps less obvious in contemporary American society, American genealogists today readily acknowledge the disproportionate attention given to paternal lines and to male ancestors. This may be due in large part to the fact that more complete records are often available for men than for women, but it also both reflects a long history of male dominance in America, and arguably reinforces patriarchal social relations by obscuring women's contributions to our families, our communities, and our nation.

Just as roots work around the world often serves to legitimize social hierarchies (men over women, nobles over commoners, one race or caste over another), it can also be used by the living as an "investment in social climbing."[85] In particular, elaborate funeral and ancestor veneration rituals often provide an opportunity for families to showcase their wealth and social standing to the broader community.[86] Making a favorable impression on the community may have a number of positive effects on the family. It may help to facilitate business alliances, marriage alliances, and political alliances, and it will likely enhance the reputation of the deceased and increase his (or occasionally her) likelihood of becoming a widely revered ancestral spirit. While elaborate funerals with dancing, entertainment, and custom-made mourning clothes are not common in the United States today, as they are elsewhere in the world, another form of roots work has long served as a rung on the American social ladder—admission to lineage societies. As noted in chapter 2, membership in heritage societies such as the DAR, the SAR, and the Mayflower Society has long signaled respectability, patriotism, and an elite status that set "older" families apart from more recent immigrant populations.

Because roots work routinely reinforces social norms and values, legitimizes power relations, and is used by families to enhance their social status, it often serves to maintain the status quo. However, it can also be used to challenge existing social hierarchies and arrangements. This is seen perhaps most clearly in the Chuuk islands where the spirits of the dead are believed to speak through the living—primarily women.[87] These women frequently voice criticisms of unjust arrangements, and urge more equitable and loving treatment of family members. Whether or not these women actually believe themselves to be possessed, the social effect is the same. Their words can prompt changes in behavior. In the American context, we can also see historically marginalized groups such as African Americans using roots work to write themselves into the nation's history. After centuries of being largely passed over in America's national stories, African Americans are now claiming a place as builders and active members of the nation. And through genealogies reaching back to Africa, they are reclaiming histories that were stolen from them by captivity.

Roots work in diverse cultures around the world tends to reinforce social conformity. It exerts considerable pressure to adhere to communal norms and values, it naturalizes social hierarchies, and it is often used to claim higher status and forge advantageous social alliances. Nonetheless, roots work can also create opportunities for individuals and larger social groups to contest long-standing hierarchies and make demands for more-equitable arrangements. So roots work is, potentially, a pathway toward social change.

THE UNIVERSALITY OF ROOTS WORK: UNDERSTANDING *HOMO GENEALOGICUS*

I have shown in this chapter that cultures around the world engage in various kinds of roots work—activities that help us to define and manage our links to the dead. Although such practices are incredibly diverse, including everything from spirit possessions to the orderly collection of birth, marriage, and death records, it is clear that roots work has similar effects in all the cultures we have discussed. It psychologically consoles us in our grief, provides us with explanations for the inexplicable, and gives us hope both for the dead and for ourselves. Roots work also helps us to (re)define and reinforce our identities, both as individuals and as members of families, ethnic groups, and even nations. Such identities can give us strength and resilience in the face of adversity. In addition, roots work helps to sustain collective norms, values, and social hierarchies. And, while it usually serves to maintain the status quo, it can also open up opportunities to challenge injustices and inequalities.

So what does the existence of roots work in cultures around the world tell us about humans as a species? What does it tell us about what it means to be human? Researchers have long described and attempted to explain cultural universals—practices, beliefs, and social institutions that exist in all known cultures.[88] Scholarship confirms that, among many other shared features, all cultures use language (with consistent elements such as nouns, verbs, and discrete sounds); all cultures use tools; all cultures have rules of social interaction; and in all cultures we can find gestures, music, play, gossip, systems of exchange, myth, spiritual beliefs, families, and rites for the dead in one form or another. While such features exist in all cultures,[89] specific practices vary a great deal. For instance, all cultures use language, but not the *same* language. All cultures have families, but some cultures prefer small nuclear families living in autonomous households, while some prefer large multigenerational extended families living in shared households. And all cultures have rites for the dead, but, as we have seen, such rites take many different forms.

The question, then, becomes how to explain the existence of cultural universals. As one scholar put it, "Given the inherent tendency for disparate peoples to develop disparate cultures, how on earth can some things be the same everywhere?"[90] Three factors are frequently offered to explain the existence of cultural universals. The first is the gradual diffusion of knowledge. We know from physical evidence, for instance, that our very early human ancestors used fire. It is highly likely that as humans migrated across the globe, they took their knowledge of fire-starting and fire use with them. Similarly, it is likely that they took other practices and beliefs with them, which explains the universality (or near universality) of such features. A second factor contributing to the existence of cultural universals is the evolution of the human brain. For instance, the human brain's evolved mechanisms for pattern recognition and symbolic communication may help to explain the universality of art, music, and spirituality. And a third is what one scholar calls "the cultural reflection of physical facts."[91] For instance, the near universal human fear of snakes may largely be a reflection of the real physical danger they represent to us; and the near universal preference for right-handedness (in cultures where there is a preference) likely reflects the prevalence of right-handedness in our species.

Although more research is required, this analysis, based on some three dozen cultures around the world, suggests that roots work, broadly defined, is another cultural universal.[92] If roots work is a cultural universal, it may be, in part, due to a diffusion of cultural beliefs and practices over time. (Indeed, we saw quite clearly above how specific kinds of roots work are prevalent in certain regions such as East Asia, Sub-Saharan Africa, and the Caribbean.) But roots work may also have developed out of both "physical facts"—namely, that death is a universal feature of the human experience—and out of evolved features of the human brain. For instance, our capacity for pattern recognition and symbolic communication may have led us to explain human death in ways that are easily comprehensible and grounded in our lived experiences (the notion of an afterlife that mirrors the physical world; the continued participation of ancestral spirits in family affairs; and systems of reward and punishment for both the living and the dead). In addition, roots work provides certain crucial mechanisms that hold social groups together in all cultures—namely, roots work psychologically consoles and comforts us, helps us to define our identities and binds us more closely to others, and helps to ensure conformity to widely shared norms, values, and social orders. And all of these effects of roots work likely contribute to human survival.

In scientific terminology, humans are classified as *Homo sapiens*, from the Latin terms *homo* (human or "man") and *sapiens* (wise). In other words, one of our defining characteristics as a species is our rationality. In the two and a half centuries since that label was adopted, scholars have suggested that we might just as reasonably call ourselves *Homo faber* (the tool-making animal), *Homo economicus* (the economic animal), or *Homo loquens* (the talking animal), as these are all distinguishing traits of our species. We might (only half-jokingly) add another to that list—*Homo genealogicus*. For our roots work sets us apart from the rest of the animal kingdom.

4

MEMORY WORK IN THE AGE
OF QUANTUM GENEALOGY

A society is what it remembers; we are what we remember;
I am what I remember; the self is a trick of memory.

—Albert Wendt, "Novelists and Historians
and the Art of Remembering"[1]

In the previous chapter, we explored the centrality of "roots work" in cultures around the world. Next, we turn our attention to the many ways memory and "memory work" are being revolutionized by new technologies and new ways of life. Let's begin with a brief foray into fiction. In S. J. Watson's 2011 thriller *Before I Go to Sleep*, the protagonist suffers from a memory disorder. Every morning she awakes not knowing who she is, and not recognizing the people and places that surround her. She spends each day relearning who she is and how to navigate the world. But when she falls asleep, the day's memories are erased, and she awakes the next morning lost to herself again.[2] The amnesiac's tortured existence offers insight into the indispensable role memory plays in our lives. Without memory, we cannot function as competent members of our society, we cannot make and sustain social bonds, and we cannot cultivate a sense of self. Memory, in short, makes us who we are.

It is hardly surprising, then, that we devote a great deal of time to what we might call *memory work*—constructing, ordering, and maintaining memories.[3] This memory work may be individual or collective, and it takes many forms. At the individual level, we do everything from keeping diaries and photo albums (or their twenty-first-century iterations on social media), to reminiscing with friends and family members, displaying family portraits in our homes and offices, writing holiday letters, creating scrapbooks and memory quilts, and researching our family trees, among many other activities. At the collective level, we build museums and memorials and archives, march in Independence Day parades, celebrate religious holidays, attend birthday parties, anniversary celebrations, and funerals, and, at a more prosaic level, compile company reports and annual performance reviews. What these diverse activities have in common is a concern with remembrance.

It is important to note, however, that our memories are not simply discrete chunks of data, tucked away in our skulls, waiting to be called into use. Whether individual or collective, memories are by their very nature always edited versions of our experiences. Certain features take on more prominence while others fade (or are unceremoniously pushed) into the shadows. Selective forgetting is an essential component of memory-making. Moreover, far from simply residing in our minds, memories can also be *externalized* and embedded in the material world—in texts, monuments, works of art and music, topographies, bodies, or even habits bequeathed to us by our forebears.[4] Whether we are aware of it or not, we reside in a memoryscape that shapes our perceptions and experiences, even as our own actions contribute to its constant revision.[5]

At the dawn of the twenty-first century, many scholars have noted that we are in the midst of a "memory boom," as evidenced by our eager consumption of "the past," whether in the form of selfies and hashtags, historical fiction and memoirs, costume dramas and documentaries, heritage theme parks and historical reenactments, or antiques and all things ancestral—homelands, ethnic traditions, pedigree charts, DNA profiles, and much more.[6] The question, however, is why we are now so fervently embracing our pasts. If we can understand this, we will better understand the current boom in family history and the shift to what I call quantum genealogy.

MODERNITY AND MEMORY

Several features of the modern era have revolutionized memory.[7] First and foremost, improvements to print technologies in the nineteenth and early-twentieth centuries led to a dramatic expansion of the written word. The increased availability and affordability of texts drove literacy rates up, and made it possible for ordinary people to record aspects of their own lives—in journals, letters, family Bibles, and wills, for instance. At the same time, with the advent of printed forms and an increasingly literate populace, the state began large-scale record collection, from censuses to birth, marriage, and death records, financial and land records, and all manner of legal records. Through such documents, memory became increasingly externalized in physical form. Of course, none of these activities were entirely new to the modern era. Written records had long been kept by ruling elites, and by religious institutions. However, improved print technologies allowed for the *democratization* of recordkeeping, the inclusion of all classes and social categories (although certainly not equally). Such records have become the bedrock of American genealogy today. Without them, American genealogy as we know it could not exist.

The proliferation of the written word accelerated further with innovations in computing and telecommunications starting in the late twentieth century. Today, with our enthusiasm for texting, tweeting, and blogging, and the ubiquity of talk radio and twenty-four-hour news channels, we are likely producing and consuming more words each day than any generation before us.[8] Some scholars have suggested that social media, in particular, allow us to "curate" our identities and experiences in more detailed and deliberate ways, as we actively edit our memories for public consumption. And although some observers have voiced concerns that the "excessive" sharing of experiences and the "outsourcing" of memory to social media platforms will lead to the degradation of memory and perhaps even a kind of historical amnesia, one recent study indicates that posting to social media allows us both to craft our identities in meaningful ways, and to more effectively remember our own experiences.[9] Likewise, in our media-saturated world, arguably we have access to a greater number of other people's memories now than ever before. That is, by consuming mediated words and images, we readily partake in the memories of others, whether they are friends and family members, public figures, or nameless strangers embroiled in world events (protesters in Tahrir Square, Syrian refugees, or victims of police violence, for instance). Furthermore, this revolutionary expansion of memory has increasingly blurred the boundaries between private and public memories. Hitting the "Share" button transforms personal memories into collective ones.[10]

In addition to modern technologies revolutionizing memory, modern values have reshaped our memory work. In the United States and much of the developed world, modernity has been keenly focused upon the future, and particularly upon progress. The promises of scientific innovation, upward mobility, increased efficiency, larger profits, and seemingly endless expansions and improvements have driven modern life. And this is reflected in our memory work. The memories we externalize through our social media postings, for instance, often present idealized selves and idealized lives filled with smiling people, beautiful places, and markers of success. This phenomenon is so prevalent, in fact, that researchers have be-gun investigating the psychological origins and potentially harmful effects of the "false Facebook-self."[11] When we conceptualize social media postings as memory work, however, such idealized representations of self cannot be reduced to individual psychological pathologies. Rather, they are quite consistent with modern memory-making, in that they are highly edited to emphasize individual success and progress.

Our memory work courts the modern dream of success and progress in other ways as well. For instance, social media have built-in systems of ex-ternal validation. The number of one's "followers," "friends," "likes," and subscribers seems to neatly quantify one's success. And high numbers can further enhance one's social status and attract ever larger audiences. Indeed, we can conceptualize some forms of memory work—particularly more time-consuming forms such as blogging or genealogy—as what sociologist Chris Rojek calls "*serious leisure*."[12] We can broadly define leisure as volun-tary activity we engage in during our free time. But, as Rojek points out, while this time may be "free" of paid labor, our choices of how to use that time are not perfectly free. They are constrained by a multitude of factors. Our disposable income determines our access to certain pursuits. The state may place restrictions on our preferred activities. Corporations may steer us toward certain types of activities, from which they will profit. Religious institutions may encourage us to engage in activities they consider whole-some and to avoid forms of leisure defined as sinful or degenerate. And, of course, social norms more generally shape our ideas about what kinds of leisure are socially acceptable and socially desirable.

Rojek conceptualizes "serious leisure" as leisure activity that serves in part to increase our cultural capital—the socially valued characteristics that enhance our social standing. Arguably, serious leisure is an outgrowth of the modern focus on self-improvement, on progress, on moving ever onward and upward. When we spend our leisure time honing our taste in wine or music, gaining knowledge of current events or popular culture (reading the books "everyone" is reading, watching the films "everyone" is talking about), manicuring our gardens, or traveling to exotic places gathering up snapshots and stories along the way, we are gaining knowl-edge, skills, experiences, and resources that may actually give us economic and social advantages. The qualities we acquire through our serious leisure may enhance other people's opinions of us, and help us to climb further up the social ladder.[13]

Genealogy is a particularly apt example of this serious leisure. In pursuit of their hobby, amateur genealogists acquire specialist skills, knowledge, and vocabulary. They build networks that allow for social recognition of their effort and expertise. And they often construct family history narratives which stress upward mobility and triumph over adversity, and which emphasize links with notable historical figures and events, or with "colorful" characters in their family trees. It is not difficult to imagine how descent from Old World nobility or a Revolutionary War hero might be used to impress others. Indeed, such glory by association has been a motivating factor for family historians since the earliest years of American genealogy. Research on some of the founding figures of New England genealogy, for instance, reveals a keen desire to develop prestigious pedigrees to improve the social and economic standing of their families.[14] And while genealogists today are unlikely to openly express such desires (and indeed deride status-seeking genealogists as "ancestor collectors,")[15] there are other reputational advantages to be gained through this serious leisure. American genealogists today readily display their impressive knowledge—of historical details, of genealogical techniques and technologies, and of prominent figures in the professional genealogical world. They readily employ specialist jargon, which helps to distinguish seasoned experts from newcomers. And they further distinguish themselves among their peers by the historical depth and detail of their family trees. Particularly for retirees who no longer participate in conventional career paths to social distinction (promotions, raises, awards), their serious genealogical labor may win them the recognition and admiration of their peers.

If modernity has revolutionized memory work—by *externalizing*, *democratizing*, *expanding*, and *incentivizing* it with reputational rewards—certain countervailing social forces of late modernity have posed challenges to traditional forms of memory-making. For instance, the average American will move roughly twelve times and change jobs between twelve and twenty times during their lives. In addition, our communities are increasingly ethnically diverse, and we are traveling farther and more often than ever before.[16] And while such changes certainly offer a number of liberating possibilities, they also undercut some older forms of memory-making and identity construction. The more we move, for instance (from one community to another, one job to another, even one marriage to another), the less contact we have with the traditional touchstones of collective memory and identity—the stories, images, places, and experiences we share with others. The more we push beyond long-standing social networks of people who think and act and look much the same way we do, the more distinctions between insider and outsider identities break down. At the same time, rapid changes in science and technology constantly present us with new ways of life and new ways of understanding our world. Such significant social and material changes spark nostalgic longings for the familiar, for a sense of belonging, for unambiguous and secure identities.[17] We reside on constantly shifting ground, and our intense focus on memory work offers an antidote to the dizzying changes that swirl around us.

THE PAST ISN'T WHAT IT USED TO BE

Arguably, even the past itself is changing today. We typically conceive of the past as fixed, frozen. "You can't change the past," as the truism goes. But the past is more than the sum total of all the events that came before this moment. Because we can only know the past from the vantage point of the present, the past is always filtered through the lens of the here and now. It is always, to some degree, socially constructed. Just as memory work is being revolutionized today, the past itself is being transformed.

Certain transformations were made possible by changes to history as an academic discipline in the mid- to late twentieth century. As I noted in chapter 2, amid the civil rights movement, the women's liberation movement, and other similar empowerment movements of the 1960s and 1970s, some historians adopted a so-called bottom-up approach. That is, rather than focusing on the "great men" of history—kings and industrialists, for instance—they sought to understand the experiences and perspectives of ordinary people, particularly those who had been routinely ignored by history, such as women, people of color, or the poor. Over the last half-century, "social history" and "cultural history" have transformed our understandings of the past by making these once silenced voices heard. Some scholars have suggested, in fact, that we have increasingly come to *personalize* history. In other words, amid this new diversity of perspectives, we are better able to imagine our forebears' experiences, better able to see how the events of the past affected our ancestors' (and therefore our own) lives, and better able to situate our ancestors and ourselves within history. We also personalize history in other ways. By employing social media to meticulously document our own lives (the foods we eat, the places we go, the company we keep, our thoughts and emotions), for instance, we are constructing our own pasts, or at the very least, our own archives. The past is no longer simply presented to us in official histories written by academics or political functionaries. Rather, it is being actively constructed, contested, and curated by countless documentarians through Instagram, YouTube, or Twitter. We are, in effect, creating "personal museums" that celebrate and interpret the self.[18]

Genealogists today are curators par excellence of such personal museums. Like traditional museum curators, they collect "artifacts" from far and wide—photographs, baptismal certificates, obituaries, passenger lists, family lore, and heirlooms—often requiring significant effort and expenditure. They then impose order on this motley collection, taking care to chart connections between one person, generation, or artifact and the next, and making choices about which details to leave out. And finally, they display the artifacts in an easily digestible form, such as a family tree, a pedigree chart, or a family history narrative. Unlike the traditional museum collection, however, the ultimate focus of this "personal museum" is the curator/genealogist him- or herself. For genealogy is, first and foremost, a quest for self. Who am *I*? Where did *I* come from? What are the names and dates, the faces and places that culminated in *my* birth? The genealogist is the star exhibit of his or her own museum of identity, the one to whom everyone else is related, and the one on whom everyone else depends to order the past and make sense of one particular slice of the present.

Some scholars have even characterized the contemporary genealogist as (metaphorically) cannibalistic, "harvesting information from dead ancestors to transplant into [his or her] own sense of identity."[19] While some might take issue with the morbid imagery, it is certainly the case that genealogists use what remains of their ancestors (stories, documents, photos) as raw building materials for their own narratives of self. And as these remnants of the past are increasingly digitized and sold through online subscription services like Ancestry.com, the ancestors themselves (what remains of them) become commodities, bits/bytes of information that are bought and sold and conspicuously displayed.[20]

This suggests yet another way the past is being transformed, through increasing *commodification*. Historian Jerome de Groot charts the countless ways history is commercialized and consumed at the dawn of the twenty-first century.[21] Our voracious appetite for everything from *Downton Abbey* to DNA tests demonstrates that we are willing to pay for access to the past. It is important to recognize, however, that not just *any* past will do. The hottest commodities here are often romanticized, sanitized, and simplified constructions of the past. The genteel manor house mystery novel, the tour of a picturesque Southern plantation with the ugly realities of slavery hidden from view, the pie chart informing a genealogist that she is 31 percent East European (the limitations of which we explore in chapter 5). As the market caters to our tastes, our understandings of the past—and the present—are reshaped. While history may be written by the victors, as the aphorism suggests, it is also edited to appeal to consumers.

MORTALITY, IMMORTALITY, AND MEMORY

While modernity has clearly reshaped both memory work and our experiences of the past, a fascination with memory is certainly not radically new. Indeed, some scholars have suggested that a great many (if not all) cultural practices have developed out of a deep-seated human fear of our own mortality and a desperate desire to transcend it. A desire to be remembered. Indeed, Ernest Becker, in his Pulitzer Prize–winning book *The Denial of Death*, asserts that

> the idea of death, the fear of it, haunts the human animal like nothing else; it is a mainspring of human activity—activity designed largely to avoid the fatality of death, to overcome it by denying in some way that it is the final destiny for man. . . . The hope and belief is that the things that man creates in society are of lasting worth and meaning, that they outlive or outshine death and decay, that man and his products count. . . . [S]ociety everywhere is a living myth of the significance of human life, a defiant creation of meaning.[22]

In other words, the "denial of death" thesis suggests that because humans are so terrified at the thought of our own deaths, we create all kinds of seemingly permanent edifices—families, businesses, religions, bodies of scientific knowledge and literature and the arts, monuments, skyscrapers, entire nation-states—that we believe will outlive us. We feel that such efforts buy us a degree of immortality. Likewise, the construction of family trees and pedigree charts might be seen as an attempt to triumph over death. We achieve a kind of immortality by ensuring that our names and select details of our lives will be preserved for generations to come.

If taken to its extremes, this notion that all cultural practices, all social institutions, and all social groups arise out of our fevered (if largely unconscious) quest for immortality, is problematic.[23] It is overly simplistic to reduce all of human activity—over diverse cultures and time periods—to a single psychological drive. Nonetheless, a more tempered version of this thesis offers insights into our motivation to engage in memory work. Zygmunt Bauman, for instance, in *Mortality, Immortality and Other Life Strategies*, observes that the promise of various forms of immortality is tempting "bait" for humans around the globe.[24] That is, the notion that our reputations, our genes, the products of our labor and sacrifice, will live on long after we die motivates us to work hard and to conform to social expectations. As I noted in chapter 3, funerary rituals and other rites of remembrance themselves promote social cohesion and social order, by uniting us in purpose and reminding us that we too will enjoy such forms of immortalization if we live "good" and productive lives.

As Bauman points out, however, the spoils of immortality are unequally distributed. Throughout all of human history, those of greater means have had disproportionate opportunities to achieve immortality—that is, to build their public reputations and be memorialized in texts, monuments, and works of art. "Professional immortality brokers" (such as publicists, biographers, praise-singers, and artists) are often employed by the powerful to bolster their fame and enhance the glory of their family name. And yet, just as modernity democratized memory, it has also democratized immortality. Whereas headstones, portraits, and family trees were once luxuries of the privileged few, they are now within reach of the masses, at least in industrialized nations.

Arguably, death itself has been transformed in modernity. Philippe Ariès suggests that before the scientific revolution (roughly the seventeenth century), death was a part of everyday experience. People were likely to die young and at home. And bodies were typically laid out in the home until they were interred (often one on top of another) in churchyards, which sat at the center of towns and villages. With the dead so close at hand, Ariès argues, people were constantly reminded of the inevitability of death. But as scientific and technological advances allowed us to keep death at bay longer and longer, death became no longer commonplace, but rather seen as somehow abnormal, even embarrassing. It became something we increasingly attempted to hide from view by confining the dying to sterile hospitals and surrendering the dead to professional corpse handlers who transform lifeless bodies into simulations of living ones (through embalming and cosmetic techniques) or into ash (inert and utterly stripped of individual identity), and "quarantining" the dead in often remote and park-like cemeteries.[25] In a modern world obsessed with progress and success, death is the ultimate defeat. And while most of us recognize that death itself is inevitable, we nonetheless are encouraged to make concerted efforts to manage it, by protecting ourselves against the concrete causes of death—say, cancer, heart disease, or traffic accidents—as long as possible.

Finally, as Freud famously observed, humans have "an unmistakable tendency to put death on one side, to eliminate it from life . . . to hush it up."[26] And one of the ways we have muted the sting of death is to wrap it in the concealing shrouds of religion. Belief in an afterlife or in reincarnation, for instance, obscures (indeed denies) the finality of death. Such doctrines promise various forms of immortality and the spiritual transcendence of the physical body. But, yet again, we see the forces of modernity transforming our understandings of mortality. The rise of science and the emergence of highly complex industrialized nation-states have rendered religious institutions less central to the organization of everyday life. People may still hold to spiritual beliefs and still engage in religious practices, but for most people in industrialized societies, such religious beliefs and practices are no longer key to the operations of our professional, personal, and practical lives.[27] This secularization of modern societies has gradually stripped death of its concealing shroud, and left those who can no longer maintain faith in an afterlife seeking new forms of transcendence. Our more intense focus on memory work, on curating our identities through the archives of our "personal museums," on preserving our experiences and thoughts and reputations in external (increasingly digital) form, may be just our most recent bid to cheat death.

THE WORKING DEAD

If we accept that the fear of death is universal among human cultures, we must consider that so too is our elevation of the dead. As we saw in chapter 3, the dead are sometimes feared, sometimes revered, and often both. We are both fascinated and repulsed by the corpse. It is disquietingly anomalous—simultaneously human and not human, simultaneously a cherished loved one and a lifeless object, simultaneously a presence and an absence. And it is the most palpable reminder humans have of our own mortality, our own unimaginable nothingness. In spite of the angst the dead inspire in us, or indeed perhaps *because* of that angst, we put the dead to work in a variety of ways, even as we continue to serve them. As historian Thomas Laqueur has argued, "The living are endlessly inventive in finding new work for the dead."[28] Perhaps most visibly, we employ the dead in our efforts to bind our communities together, to impose order and meaning on a messy and confusing world, and to claim various forms of legitimacy and power.

Let us first consider the ways the dead serve to strengthen our communities. Through our rituals of remembrance for the dead—whether funerals and ancestral veneration, or modern forms of genealogy—rehearsing the names and deeds of the dead binds us to our kin, our ethnic group, or even our nation in several ways. First, the dead bring us together in communal action. Participation in death rituals, for instance, promotes cooperation and collaboration for a perceived greater good. Second, extolling the virtues of the dead reminds us of expected and valued behaviors, so in a sense the dead help to discipline us into conforming to social norms and values. And third, the dead provide a rallying cry to stiffen our resolve, particularly in times of hardship or war. "Remember the Alamo!" "Remember Pearl Harbor!" In such cries, it is our dead who inspire us to act, to fight, to win, so they "shall not have died in vain," as Abraham Lincoln so eloquently proclaimed at Gettysburg.

The dead, moreover, help us to make sense of the world. As literary scholar Robert Pogue Harrison has observed,

> We follow in the footsteps of the dead. . . . Whether we are conscious of it or not we do the will of the ancestors: our commandments come to us from their realm; their precedents are our law; we submit to their dictates. . . . We inherit their obsessions; assume their burdens; carry on their causes; promote their mentalities, ideologies, and very often their superstitions; and often we die trying to vindicate their humiliations.[29]

In other words, we look to the dead to guide us in our understandings and our actions. Those who came before us created our families, our tribes, our religious and moral codes, and the very frameworks we use to interpret our experiences. Striving to protect and preserve what our dead created gives us a sense of purpose and certainty. Indeed, we will risk even death itself to defend the works and the memories of our dead.

So what accounts for our willingness to make such sacrifices? Pogue Harrison argues that "we have no choice. Only the dead can grant us legitimacy. . . . In exchange for legitimacy, which humans need and crave more than anything else, we surrender ourselves to their dominion." Such claims of legitimacy and power take many forms. We evoke the dead to justify, even sanctify, our actions. As noted above, we also exploit the dead to build our own reputations. Family trees are never simply neutral or "innocent." They always both reflect and reproduce power relations. Proving links to the esteemed dead, for instance, may allow us to claim authority, respect, title, glory, and even property—in short, social legitimacy, and often material benefits. In cultures where ancestral spirits are believed to intervene in the affairs of the living, for instance, the happy dead are the bringers of good luck, good health, good harvests, good relations. The angry dead, on the other hand, are the bearers of calamity.[30]

THE ENCHANTED DEAD

In cultures around the world the dead are, in a sense, *enchanted*. In other words, although they are biologically dead, they are still animated with the power to shape the thoughts and actions of the living. And while corpses are almost always regarded as disquieting, even frightening, the specific powers of the dead vary across cultures. These powers are more literal and direct in societies with a belief in active ancestral spirits, and more indirect and diffuse in societies without such beliefs. Even in industrialized societies without beliefs in interventionist ancestors, certain dead—the "special dead," such as saints, martyrs, heroes, and even pop stars—are often believed to manifest extraordinary powers.[31] Their burial sites become places of pilgrimage, where visitors seek healing, comfort, strength, or inspiration. Indeed, so great is the power of the special dead that the living often battle over control of their bodily remains. History is replete with unseemly tussles over the body parts of saints and martyrs, and a lively trade in these (often fraudulent) relics. Currently no fewer than four sites claim to be the final resting place of the head of John the Baptist, for instance.[32] Likewise, the control of bodily remains is a pressing legal and diplomatic issue today, as diverse indigenous groups sue museums around the world for the return of their dead.[33] At the heart of such disputes is the desire of descendants (direct or indirect) to provide their ancestors with culturally appropriate funerary rites, both to ensure the repose of the spirits, and to assert the identity, the dignity, and the essential humanity of a people. For, as Pogue Harrison points out, it is the careful and elaborate care of our dead that distinguishes humans from other creatures. "To be human means above all to bury."[34]

While arguably the dead are enchanted—imbued with power—in cultures around the world, we must also consider the ways modernity has *disenchanted* the dead. Sociologist Max Weber suggested that as the modern world became increasingly ruled by scientific thinking, rational calculation, abstract rules, standardized procedures, and a drive toward efficiency (all combined in a process he called "rationalization"), traditional forms of spiritual belief would fade away. For who needs the will of the gods to explain a natural disaster when science will provide the answers? Who needs to appeal to the deities for healing when modern medicine is so effective? Thus, Weber predicted the "disenchantment" of the modern world, the declining importance of magical or mystical modes of thought and action.[35] And to some degree modernity has disenchanted the dead. Scientists from the Enlightenment era onward transformed the corpse from a ghastly Other to an object of scientific study. And increasingly, science has "deconstructed" death. That is, we now routinely break death down into its more easily understandable and manageable constituent parts, like disease mechanisms and scientifically determined, officially declared "causes of death." And we routinely turn death and the dead over to various specialist institutions—hospitals, funeral homes, probate courts. In so doing, death and the dead have become increasingly disenchanted. That is, some of the mystery has been stripped from them.[36]

But the disenchantment of the dead has been only partial, no doubt because so much about death is still unknown and seemingly unknowable, and because the experience of loss through death is so profound. Moreover, contrary to Weber's predictions, modernity has not led to a uniform disenchantment of the world. Instead, the rise of science and standardized, rationalized processes has often provoked a kind of backlash response. While membership in traditional organized religions has declined in the United States, for instance, "New Age" religions and more individualized forms of spiritual practice including yoga and meditation have enjoyed increased popularity over the last few decades. Disenchantment of the social world, in other words, has led to its re-enchantment. Likewise, the disenchantment of the dead appears to have prompted our attempts at their re-enchantment. Our keen interest in genealogy and memory work, along with our other efforts at conjuring the past, may well be seen as attempts to reanimate—or re-enchant—the dead.

MEMORY WORK AND QUANTUM GENEALOGY

Transformations of memory and memory work, of death and the dead, and of the past itself, provide insights into the way genealogy is practiced in the United States today. As noted in chapter 2, from roughly the 1990s onward American genealogy has been increasingly focused on individual identity narratives, global interconnections, and scientific tools, methods, and data—combining in what I have called quantum genealogy. Let us conclude this chapter by considering how the transformations described above have fueled the rise of these distinctive features of contemporary American genealogy.

The genealogist's individual identity narrative is at the heart of American genealogy today. The title of the staggeringly successful *Who Do You Think You Are?* television show and its spin-off products reveals this keen focus on the genealogist's own construction of self. As literary scholar Claire Lynch points out,

> Thinking about the question [*Who Do You Think You Are?*] carefully, it does not ask who you are in any objective, knowable sense, the kind of information archival records might provide, but who do you *think* you are, who do you doubt yourself to be, who do you hope or imagine

yourself to be. . . . [The show is] not called "who do you think they were," after all. The search ceases to be about knowing those you did not or could not know, and becomes instead a matter of . . . [your] own sense of identity.[37]

Likewise, the leading genealogical research website, Ancestry.com, emphasizes this quest for self-knowledge and for stories of self in its advertisements. "Discover *your* story," one tagline directs us. "Reveal the unique, improbable, and completely remarkable path that led to *you*," another ad promises. Or yet another: "You never know exactly why you are the way you are, but Ancestry.com can show you who you came from, what they did, where they lived, and how it all led to *you*. *Your* story is here."[38]

This focus on creating individual identities both exemplifies and is fueled by the democratization and personalization of history discussed above. Individuals are encouraged to create customized histories with themselves as both the organizing principle and the end point. And such efforts are incentivized, with promises of self-knowledge—discovering "why you are the way you are"—and glory by association. Characters in the ads are shown, for instance, finding previously unknown links to great historical figures, including George Washington and Abraham Lincoln. The genealogical television shows and websites, furthermore, are built upon externalized memories—birth and death records, court records, newspaper clippings, photographs, and so on—and, in turn, allow genealogists to externalize their own memories in a variety of forms, including family history books, trees, posters, websites, and video productions. Indeed, so many customizable family history products are for sale today that we can clearly see commodification at work: commodification of history, of memory, of the ancestors, and of individual identities. In a larger sense, our genealogical quests today both reflect and enact the democratization of immortality described above. As we resuscitate the names and stories of our ancestors—as we re-enchant them—we achieve a form of immortality that was once only available to the powerful and famous. Through the family trees and individual identity narratives we create, we, in some sense, transcend death.

A second feature of twenty-first-century quantum genealogy is its focus on global interconnections. We might see this as a counterweight to the emphasis on the highly individualized historical and identity narratives discussed above. But rather than standing in opposition to such individualization, a focus on global kinship linkages neatly complements the individual identity narrative. Specifically, as genealogists today seek to extend the branches of their family trees around the globe and further back in time (sometimes tens of thousands of years, through the use of DNA evidence), they create stories with an almost mythic quality. That scores of individuals from all corners of the world, over centuries of change, migration, and struggle, somehow intersected to produce the individual genealogist him- or herself seems close to miraculous. The "unique, improbable and completely remarkable path," the magical confluence of events that led to *you*, as Ancestry.com puts it.

So this new global and deep historical focus of genealogy is really about stretching individual identities to encompass as much territory and as much time as possible. This emerges quite clearly in roots tourism, where tour companies promise to take you to your "homeland" or "ancestral hometowns" where you can "walk in the footsteps" of your forebears and perhaps even meet living "cousins." Certainly this expansive use of terms such as *homeland*, *hometown*, and *cousin* greatly extends the typical understanding of these terms. Roots tourists may never have set foot in their "homeland" or "hometown," and may not be able to identify a specific shared ancestor with a newly identified "cousin." But when they purchase a roots tour package (sometimes complete with commemorative family history book or video), they also purchase colorful details to add to their own customized identity narratives. Thus we can understand the global focus of quantum genealogy as both a reflection and an outgrowth of the democratization, personalization, and commodification of history described above. Moreover, we can view this preoccupation with global and deep historical connections as yet another attempt to ensure our own immortality. For finding traces of ourselves all around the world, reaching back through time immemorial, suggests that we are part of an unbroken and unbreakable chain that will endure long after our demise.

Finally, the hallmark of quantum genealogy is its firm commitment to scientific tools, methods, and data. This commitment is a clear reflection of some of the key values and organizing principles of modernity—scientific thinking, rational processes, standardized rules and procedures, and confidence in the potential of science, technology, and rationality to fuel endless progress, and possibly even transcend the awesome mystery of death itself. Certainly scientific and technological innovations—principally in computing and genetics—have allowed for the exponential growth of genealogical research. The massive digitization of documents has provided us with easy access to more family history records than genealogists a generation ago could have ever imagined, and DNA testing has allowed us to construct global kinship networks and deep historical linkages that are virtually impossible to trace through traditional documentary evidence.

Likewise, social media facilitate the sharing of genealogical knowledge, both information on specific families and on genealogical tools and techniques. The abundance of genealogy blogs, podcasts, and YouTube channels is a testament to our drive to both showcase and expand our genealogical understandings. One force that is clearly at work here is commodification. These scientific tools and techniques can be costly, whether we are purchasing one of hundreds of how-to genealogy books, a genealogical credentialing course, the services of a professional researcher, the newest software and hardware products, online database subscriptions, or a host of direct-to-consumer DNA tests. Advertising promises that such products will facilitate more systematic, more valid, and more comprehensive research, which will allow us to create truer and more satisfying family history narratives. In other words, advertisers pledge that if you buy their products, you will add color, depth, certainty, and value to your identity. Such promises should sound familiar. Since the rise of mass marketing in the nineteenth century, advertisers have suggested that our problems—no matter how vexing or intractable—can be solved by buying the correct product.[39] Stains are quickly removed with the right detergent, aging reversed with the right cosmetics or vitamins, love and fortune found with the right toothpaste or car or whiskey. What these genealogical products offer is a solution to one of the most enduring human problems—the problem of identity—of answering the age-old question, "Who am I?"

5

THE NEW BLOOD QUANTUM

Genetic Genealogy and the Creation of Kinship

Genealogy does not simply *trace* kinship; it *creates* kinship. That is, gene-alogy—by identifying individuals and drawing lines between them—reifies kinship, gives it perceived substance. You and I are not considered cousins, for instance, unless we can chart certain connections between our families. In fact, some scholars have suggested that we should think of this process of kinship creation as *kinning*.[1] We can quite clearly see kinning at work in families with adoption or assisted reproduction, where purposive ef-forts are made to incorporate sometimes biologically unrelated children into kinship networks. We can see it at work in family reunions where far-flung relations—some of whom have never met and many of whom share no ge-netic connection—get grafted onto the family tree. Despite clear evidence of the labor that we devote to defining and maintaining kinship, however, we often conceptualize kinship primarily in biological terms—as shared "blood," or genes.[2] This tendency comes to the forefront with the increas-ingly popular practice of genetic genealogy—the use of DNA evidence to define ancestry, to identify kin, and, in a sense, to tell us who we *really* are.

BLOOD, GENETICS, AND IDENTITY

According to my own AncestryDNA results, I am 49 percent British, 30 percent Eastern European, 12 percent Irish, and 9 percent Northwest Rus-sian/Finnish (the latter being an unexpected and still unexplored branch of my family tree). It is highly unlikely, based on these percentages, that American readers would conclude that my "real" ethnicity is Russian/ Finnish, or that, despite my Irish family name and Famine-era Irish ances-tors, I am not entitled to claim Irish heritage. None of these ethnicities (all currently considered "white" in the United States, although this was not always the case) trumps the others. And none of these ethnicities demands that I meet a minimum threshold of ancestry to claim it. Rather, I am at liberty to claim any of these ethnicities, or all of them, as I desire, without fear of challenge or consequence.

But in the United States today, all racial and ethnic categories are not treated equally. Historically, African Americans and Native Americans in particular have been subject to quite different rules of descent, rules that have constrained their ability to claim their full ancestries. And curiously, the special rules of descent applied by officialdom to African Americans and Native Americans have been glaringly contradictory. Under the principle of *hypodescent* (the "one-drop" rule), even a single drop of "African blood"—in other words, even a single black ancestor on your family tree—rendered you legally black. By contrast, you were only entitled to claim Native American identity if you had *enough* "Indian blood," usually one-eighth to one-quarter indigenous heritage, determined through blood quantum calculations. How can we understand these very different ways of thinking about ancestry and identity?

The "one-drop" rule for people of African descent was formalized in the 1665 Virginia court case *Re Mulatto*, in which a man of mixed white and black parentage was ruled to be legally black, and therefore subject to the bonds of chattel slavery.[3] Although some regions had separate laws governing individuals considered mulatto ("half-black"), quadroon ("one-quarter black"), and octoroon ("one-eighth black"), such classifications were difficult to substantiate, which made the administration of these laws problematic.[4] From a legal standpoint, it was far simpler to have clear-cut distinctions between blacks and whites, and the "one-drop" rule made this possible. Subsequent court cases and statutes reaffirmed the "one-drop" principle. For instance, the landmark 1896 Supreme Court decision *Plessy v. Ferguson* defined Homer Adolph Plessy as "colored" by virtue of his one-eighth African heritage.[5] And a 1924 anti-miscegenation law in Virginia defined as "white" only individuals who had "no trace whatsoever of blood other than Caucasian."[6] Although the *Plessy* decision and anti-miscegenation laws were eventually invalidated by the Supreme Court, "one-drop" thinking has persisted. We have only to look at President Barack Obama, who, with a white mother and an African father, is commonly referred to as the first "black" president, or golfer Tiger Woods, who, despite having Thai, Chinese, African American, Native American, and white ancestry, is often simply referred to as a "black" golfer, to see that African heritage is still widely seen to override other ancestries in America today.[7]

By contrast, for more than a hundred years Native Americans have had to prove they have *enough* Indian "blood" to count as Native American. In 1887, the Dawes Act empowered the federal government to divide Indian reservations into 160-acre allotments to be granted to individual Indian families. One intent of the act was to encourage Native Americans to adopt European models of labor, property rights, and family composition, and to help them "acquire the habits of thrift, industry, and individualism needed for assimilation into white culture."[8] Eligibility for the allotments was based, in part, on rough "blood quantum" calculations, formalized and recorded on the Dawes Rolls.[9] When the act failed to have the desired social effects, it was superseded by the 1934 Indian Reorganization Act, which provided a number of special property rights, educational and vocational programs, and some degree of self-rule for Native Americans.

However, it also necessitated the development of clear bureaucratic procedures to determine eligibility for those benefits. This led the Bureau of Indian Affairs (BIA) to adopt a formal process of substantiating and quantifying Native American "blood." Those who could provide the necessary evidence would receive a Certificate of Degree of Indian Blood, but those deemed to be not Indian *enough* were rendered ineligible for the benefits provided by the act. Under the current procedures for defining Indian descent, it is predicted that by the next century approximately 60 percent of the Native American population will fail to meet the blood quantum requirements for full BIA benefits.[10] This raises the possibility of Native Americans eventually being bureaucratically defined out of existence.

So how can we explain these two very different approaches to defining ancestry—that *any trace* of African "blood" makes you black, but only *enough* Native American "blood" can make you Indian? We need to consider some of the economic realities that shaped these definitions. The reality is that the "one-drop" rule for people of African ancestry was economically beneficial to white slaveholders, who could increase their human "stock" by impregnating their female slaves. All resulting children would be legally classified as chattel slaves, to be used or sold as their owners desired. Even after the abolition of slavery, the "one-drop" rule helped to ensure the continued supremacy of whites by offering supposedly biological differences between the races as a justification for discrimination against people of color in education, employment, politics, and other realms of social life. At the same time, anti-miscegenation laws ensured that the children of interracial couples were legally defined as illegitimate, and therefore not entitled to inheritance. These laws prevented the wealth of white parents from passing to children of color, and therefore helped to preserve the economic gap between whites and blacks. So the "one-drop" rule served to reinforce the economic, political, and social advantages of whites.

Likewise, the blood quantum rules for Native Americans conferred (and still confer) advantages on certain groups. For instance, under the Dawes Act, lands that were formerly set aside for Native Americans could be sold off to non-Indians if Indians did not claim them. So the fewer "eligible" Indians the government recognized, the more land was available for non-Indians to buy. This worked to the advantage of white settlers. Likewise, stricter procedures for determining blood quantum under the BIA meant that fewer people of Indian descent were eligible for government benefits, which reduced the financial obligations of the US government to Native Americans, to the advantage of the American taxpayer. And, more recently, with revenues from gaming and land use agreements at stake, some tribes themselves have moved to restrict tribal membership. In the year 2000, for instance, the Oklahoma Seminoles amended their constitution to, in effect, exclude so-called Black Seminoles (or Freedmen) from tribal membership. Black Seminoles, the descendants of slaves who came to live among the Florida Seminoles as early as the seventeenth century, have long been well integrated into the tribe and were included in the Dawes Rolls (albeit, under a distinct classification). But in the wake of a $56 million settlement from the federal government in the 1990s, the tribe changed its membership requirements. Now tribal members must be able to prove at least one-eighth Seminole blood, which effectively strips most Black Seminoles of their tribal affiliation (and the economic benefits that come with it).[11]

The history of the "one-drop" rule and blood quantum calculations clearly illustrates some of the ways definitions of ancestry are shaped by economic, political, and other social considerations, often to the advantage of some and the disadvantage of others. It also demonstrates the power of biology in the American genealogical imagination. Indeed, as noted in chapter 2, from the late nineteenth to the late twentieth century, American genealogy was clearly focused on delineating racial and ethnic distinctions. Race and ethnicity were often conceptualized in biological terms, and traits such as intelligence, morality, and criminality were widely believed to pass down through the blood or genes. Although scholars over the last four decades have persuasively demonstrated that race and ethnicity are socially constructed classifications rather than natural biological categories, rising interest in genetic genealogy seems to suggest a shift back toward biological definitions of race and ethnicity. In some sense, genetic genealogy re-essentializes ancestry by tying it more firmly to biology.[12] As uncomfortable as it may be, we must consider whether ancestral DNA testing is creating something akin to a new blood quantum.

GENETIC GENEALOGY:
THE PROMISES AND THE PROBLEMS

Three kinds of tests are most widely available today for the purposes of genetic genealogy: Y-chromosomal DNA tests, mitochondrial DNA (mtDNA) tests, and autosomal DNA tests.[13] You may remember from your high school biology class that only males have a Y-chromosome. Consequently Y-chromosomal DNA tests trace only the DNA that is passed down through the direct male line, father to son to grandson, and so on. Only males can take this test. We all inherit mtDNA from our mothers, however, so mtDNA tests trace DNA that has been passed down from our long line of grandmothers over the millennia. Both men and women can take this test. And, in addition to our X and Y chromosomes (the sex-determining chromosomes), we also inherit twenty-two pairs of chromosomes (or autosomes) from our parents, half of each pair from each parent. Both men and women can take an autosomal DNA test, to reveal genetic markers passed through both parental lines. Due to significant differences between these three types of DNA tests, each test will likely give you quite a different picture of your ancestry.

Testing firms make a variety of explicit and implicit claims in their promotional materials. While each DNA testing firm offers a different range of products, all of the major companies promise to reveal surprising and enlightening details about the customer's ancestry.[14] Most testing firms provide clients with a numerical breakdown of their "ethnic mix" (29 percent Asian, 14 percent Sub-Saharan African, etc.). Most companies also promise (at least obliquely) to trace the client's "deep" or "ancient" ancestry—reaching back to "thousands of years ago" (Oxford Ancestors, Roots for Real), "150,000 years ago" (GeneBase), or even "as far back as the first peoples who populated the earth," as claimed by one firm (AncestryByDNA). Most companies offer the prospect of finding new relatives, and customer testimonials often stress the enriching potential of these new connections. Some companies offer clients the opportunity to trace the origins of certain physical traits, such as blue eyes, red hair, or specific medical conditions, and to even predict the appearance of such traits in their own children. And some companies stress the emotional dividends of DNA analysis, which include an enhanced "love for self," a "sense of closure," a "sense of pride," and "life-changing discoveries" (African Ancestry and MyHeritageDNA). More generally, DNA analysis is promoted as a way of solving genealogical mysteries, breaking through "brick walls" when documentary evidence is lacking, and discovering one's own unique identity. Genetic genealogy "puts the 'you' in unique," as one ad for AncestryDNA notes.

Despite the significant claims made by DNA testing companies, the question is whether genetic genealogy really delivers what it promises. It is true that genetic genealogy can be a powerful tool, particularly for historically oppressed groups for whom written records are scant. For many African Americans, for instance, whose ancestral ties were broken by the brutalities of slavery, genetic genealogy can offer "the re-possession of a dispossessed past" in the form of genetic links to a particular region, nation, or tribal group in Africa.[15] Scholars have noted, however, that today's DNA tests have some serious limitations. The first of these is that all tests reveal the genetic material of only a few out of our many thousands of ancestors. One bioethicist neatly summarized it this way:

> It is possible for a person to have an eight-times-great-grandmother who was Japanese, an eight-times-great-grandfather who was Zulu and 1,022 other ancestors in the tenth generation who were Irish. Mitochondrial DNA analysis would suggest that the subject *was* Japanese, or at least East Asian; Y chromosome analysis would suggest that the subject *was* Zulu, or at least Sub-Saharan African. Neither would even hint at the Irish origin of 99.8 percent of the subject's ancestors.[16]

Even autosomal DNA tests that chart genetic markers from both parental lines give us a very incomplete picture of the origins of the countless ancestors who came before us. Just because your parent carries the genetic markers associated with Native American heritage, for instance, it does not mean that you will carry those same markers.

It is also crucial to keep in mind that DNA cannot speak for itself. Genetic data must always be interpreted, and interpretations are shaped by many factors, including the size and diversity of the database against which the client's DNA is compared. This is a significant problem for certain populations, because most databases lack a sizable number of samples from indigenous peoples and from less developed regions of the world, including much of Africa. It is perhaps not surprising, therefore, that at least one study that compared two testing firms found that they reported substantially different results more than half of the time.[17] It is not difficult to understand why certain populations are underrepresented in genetic databases. For the most part, genetic genealogy has been the province of affluent Westerners, who are more likely to be of European origin. Unless poorer populations from less developed nations participate in a medical or ethnographic study, they are unlikely to contribute genetic material to a database. And the fewer samples there are from these diverse populations, the less accurate genetic test results will be for everyone, but particularly for people with ancestral ties to these populations. Furthermore, many indigenous groups, in particular, have been reluctant to provide DNA samples to researchers. Groups with a history of dispossession, domination, and abuse by authorities are likely to be skeptical of officialdom. And, indeed, there are concerns among some Native American groups that genetic definitions of Indian heritage might come to override social and cultural definitions of what it means to be a tribal member. This would, in effect, strip indigenous communities of control over tribal membership and put it in the hands of scientists and bureaucrats.[18]

Another significant limitation of current ancestral DNA tests is that, for the most part, interpretations are based on comparisons with the genetic material found in specific regions today. In other words, when I submit a DNA sample, my genetic markers are compared with a contemporary set of samples from Africa, Asia, the British Isles, the New World, and so on, and genetic similarities with contemporary populations are taken as indicators that my ancestors hailed from these regions. As many scholars have pointed out, however, such inferences often simply treat contemporary populations as proxies for ancient populations. The underlying assumption that populations (and their genes) are fairly stable over time downplays or ignores complex histories of contact, colonialism, and migration.[19]

In addition to the inherent limitations of genetic data and the analytical frameworks used to interpret it, scholars observe that DNA results are often misunderstood by consumers. One researcher notes, for instance, that due to rather limited "genetic literacy," the public often assumes that there are specific genes for certain traits—one for race, still others for traits like intelligence or religiosity or sexual orientation. The mass media sometimes contribute to such misperceptions by using headline-friendly terms such as the "god gene" or "gay DNA." This represents a fundamental misunderstanding of the ways numerous genetic factors are associated with complex human traits. Likewise, contrary to popular perceptions (and the promotional materials of some testing firms), there is no such thing as "Native American DNA," only certain genetic markers that tend to be more prevalent among Native Americans.[20] Indeed, many of these same markers are found in Asian, Middle Eastern, Southern Mediterranean, and North

African populations as well. This makes it possible for, say, a modern Egyptian or Turk with no ancestral ties to the New World to test positive for so-called Native American DNA.

We must also remember that scientists have now demonstrated that all humans share 99.9 percent of our genes in common.[21] So in looking for the genetic material that makes us "unique" and supposedly defines our essential identity, we are really only focusing on one-tenth of 1 percent of our genetic makeup. Imagine that the two patterns below represent two people (see figure 5.1). If you look carefully, you will see that they are 99.9 percent identical. Based on the minuscule differences between them, would you be inclined to describe one as a Circle and one as a Diamond, and to assume that the Circle will display all the traits associated with Circles, while the Diamond displays a distinct Diamond-ness? Probably not. And yet this is, in effect, what we do with genetic genealogy. We focus on quite small and rather superficial differences between human populations and draw largely insupportable conclusions about such things as temperament, character, and ability. One genealogist I interviewed, for instance, explained his unique aptitude for family history research with reference to such essentialized traits. "My German roots make me anal-retentive to detail," he said, "while the Italian side makes me passionate about it!" (Glen, 44, Indiana).

As one biologist recently observed, "If companies stated all of these very real provisos, caveats, and uncertainties, most customers would likely be left scratching their heads and wondering what new information they

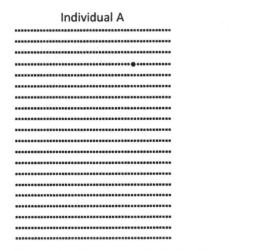

Figure 5.1.   Human Genetic Similarities

had actually learned from ancestry tracing."[22] So, while DNA is today often perceived as an indelible, unfalsifiable, and scientifically objective record of our ancestral pasts—etched, as it were, into our very cells—genetic genealogy provides us with, at best, highly selective and incomplete renderings of our complex ancestries. And if this is the best we can expect, what is the worst that might arise from our increased tendency to geneticize identity?

THE DUAL POTENTIAL OF GENETIC GENEALOGY

Just like so many technologies—combustion engines, nuclear fusion, drones—ancestral DNA analysis, by its very nature, has both positive and negative potentials. On the positive side, genetic genealogy promotes a liberating and inclusive vision of human diversity and human interconnectedness. Indeed, many leading ancestral DNA testing firms use images of world maps and smiling, attractive people of diverse backgrounds to illustrate the potential of genetic analysis to link clients to kinship networks that span the globe. One promotion for AncestryDNA, for instance, features images of "cousins" who are phenotypically Irish (fair-skinned with red hair), Mediterranean, South Asian, African, and multiethnic, all superimposed on a world map that identifies their places of origin.[23] Such imagery places a positive value on ethnic diversity and suggests that, no matter what our outward appearance or socially defined race or ethnicity, we are all genetically connected. This is what we might call the *universalizing* potential of genetic genealogy, and it is a message that runs contrary to notions of racial exclusivity, purity, or superiority. After all, if we are all of "mixed" origins, racism and racial hierarchies are rendered meaningless.

This universalizing potential is seen quite clearly in the genetic genealogy popularized by Henry Louis Gates Jr., Harvard African American studies professor turned public television host. In his television shows—*African American Lives* (2006–8), *Faces of America* (2010), and *Finding Your Roots* (2012–17)—Gates uses a combination of archival records and DNA evidence to trace the ancestry of his celebrity guests. He suggests that DNA is both "a kind of Rosetta Stone for deciphering one's true identity" and the substance that "binds us all together."[24] In *Faces of America*, season 1, for instance, his celebrity guests include luminaries of diverse origins—African, Italian, Native American, Jamaican-British, Syrian-Swedish, Chinese, Japanese, West European, Irish Catholic, Eastern European Jewish, Turkish Muslim, and Hispanic. At the end of the series, Gates reveals to his guests how "astonishingly closely related" we all are by charting unexpected genetic connections between the celebrities he has included in the show. Indeed, he finds that eleven out of twelve people featured in the series had a "cousin" in the group.[25] The term *cousin* here is used in its broadest sense, since some links are at the ninth cousin level (where DNA results are often quite inconclusive—even at the level of fifth cousins, roughly 50 percent of matches are "false positives"),[26] or at the haplogroup level, which traces ancient populations with shared gene mutations rather than specific identifiable ancestors. Nonetheless, many guests are visibly moved by these revelations. "How extraordinarily liberating it is to have another way of thinking about yourself," remarks author Malcolm Gladwell. "This uncovering, it forces you to contemplate your own history. That's why I think it's so powerful. . . . The more ways you can define yourself, the better off you are."[27]

Perhaps nowhere is the universalizing potential of genetic genealogy more clearly visible than in attempts to link all of humanity in a single family tree. Author A. J. Jacobs has advocated such efforts in a series of articles and podcasts, a TED talk, and a 2015 event billed as the Global Family Reunion, "the biggest, most extraordinary and most inclusive family reunion in history."[28] While Jacobs does not solely promote DNA analysis, genetic connections are at the very core of his project. The knowledge that we all share a common ancestry, he argues, the knowledge that we are all "literally biological cousins," will make us feel more connected to others around the globe. This will help to create a "kinder world," a more just and democratic world, in which bigotry and exclusion can no longer be sustained. The more interconnected we feel, he argues, the better off we will be.

Just beneath the surface of such idealistic visions of a globe united by shared DNA, however, are some problematic implications of genetic genealogy—what we might call its *reductive* and *exclusionary* potential. Test results that quantify our "ethnic mix" ultimately reduce our identities to biology—to sequences of chemical bases. This reinforces the socially problematic (and scientifically insupportable) notion that race and ethnicity are simply natural, biological facts, and ignores the significance of social and historical ties to kin and community. Although geneticists themselves are generally careful to avoid terms such as *race* and *ethnicity* in favor of terms like *biogeographical ancestry*, the ethnic breakdowns provided by DNA testing companies typically bear close resemblance to long-standing racial and ethnic categories. So 51 percent West African, for instance, is understood by consumers as 51 percent black. Exemplifying this tendency, in the television series *Finding Your Roots*, Henry Louis Gates tells his guests that DNA tests can now tell us "just how black, red, and white our ancestors really have been over the past five hundred years."[29]

Such quantification of race and ethnicity looks uncomfortably close to both blood quantum calculations for Native Americans and older categories such as mulatto, quadroon, and octoroon for people of African descent. As discussed above, such biological definitions of ethnic and racial identity can have devastating consequences, particularly for oppressed groups. Indeed, some scholars have noted that our growing preoccupation with genetic definitions of identity could represent a "backdoor to eugenics."[30] As noted in chapter 2, eugenics—an attempt to improve human genetic stock through selective breeding—was widely embraced in early-twentieth century Amer ica and elsewhere, including most notoriously in Nazi Germany. Eugenics was premised on the notion that both desirable and undesirable traits—high or low intelligence, morality or criminality, industriousness or laziness, for instance—were transmitted genetically. Therefore, reproduction between supposedly superior individuals would strengthen the "racial stock" of a lineage or a nation, and reproduction with supposedly inferior individuals would compromise and weaken this racial stock. In its mildest form, eugenics both reflected and contributed to misunderstandings of the genetic basis of complex human traits and behaviors. More insidiously, in the American context, it helped to sustain Jim Crow segregation, discrimination, and violence; it provided justification for the forced sterilization of those deemed genetically inferior; and it was used to prevent genetically "undesirable" immigrants from gaining entry to the nation. Of course, at its worst, eugenics was used by Nazis to justify the interment and murder of those who were believed to weaken the nation's Aryan racial stock—including Jews, political dissidents, and the disabled, among others.

Let me clarify that I am not equating genetic genealogy with Nazism or genocide. Nor am I suggesting that those who do ancestral DNA testing (including me) do so out of a desire to prove their racial purity or superiority. Nonetheless, we would do well to recognize the deleterious potential of geneticizing identity, so we might guard against it. Indeed, in recent years we have begun to see some real-world illustrations of such dangers. As genetic science has advanced and genetic testing has become more affordable, a number of countries—Australia, Canada, Estonia, Norway, Singapore, South Africa, Sweden, Tonga, Iceland, and the UK among them—have undertaken national genetic mapping projects. The "People of the British Isles" study and the "Icelandic Genome Project," for instance, have aimed to explore the genetic composition of their national populations.[31] The British Isles study set out to chart both ancient and current genetic patterns in the region. And the Icelandic study has the additional aim of providing medical researchers with a strikingly comprehensive "biobank" of genetic material from a relatively isolated population. What is clear from such projects, however, is, first, that long-standing notions of who "belongs" and who really "counts" in the nation shape the gathering and interpretation of genetic data. And, second, no matter how well-intentioned such studies are, they can have unintended and often unfortunate side effects.

In the British Isles study, for instance, a distinction was made between the national "genetic heritage" and contemporary genetic diversity. In order to explore "genetic heritage," researchers decided to sample only people who currently resided in rural areas, and whose families had lived in those areas for three or more generations. The rationale behind such selective sampling was that this population was the least likely to have produced offspring with outsiders and newcomers, so their DNA would be most representative of the ancient inhabitants of the British Isles. This genetic profile could then be compared and contrasted with the more diverse genetic profile of urban populations. While the logic is clear, the result was that conclusions about the "genetic heritage" of the nation were based almost exclusively on genetic samples from rural whites. While this may seem innocuous enough, such a research design inevitably reinforces ideas about "us" and "them," about pure and mixed "blood," about ancient/original/rightful inhabitants of the land and encroaching newcomers.

Perhaps not surprisingly, then, DNA results were subsequently used by the far-right British National Party (BNP) to demand that whites be granted special protections and privileges as the "indigenous" people of Britain.[32] To the BNP, with its roots in the neo-Nazi National Front, this national genetic study provided support for their white supremacist, anti-immigrant sentiments. Similarly, a recent study by researchers from UCLA found that American white supremacists are using ancestral DNA testing to "prove" their racial purity. Interestingly, however, when the tests show unexpected racial and ethnic admixtures, they often challenge the scientific validity of the results or engage in conspiracy theories about, for instance, Jewish control of the genetic testing industry.[33]

The Icelandic Genome Project raises similar issues of national belonging. Iceland is in a unique position to contribute to genetic research. It has a population of only about three hundred thousand people, most of whom are descended from a relatively small group of original settlers, and it has experienced low levels of immigration since its founding in the ninth century. With such a homogenous and isolated population, it is easier for medical researchers to identify gene mutations associated with certain health conditions, including cancer and Alzheimer's disease. (It also makes it more difficult to find a romantic partner, however. Because Icelanders have been relatively isolated, it can be hard to find someone who is not related to you. A new phone app now makes it possible for Icelanders to simply bump their smartphones together to check and see if they are too closely related to date!)[34] As an added bonus, a national archive, the so-called Book of Iceland, contains extensive genealogical records on virtually the entire population dating back to 1703.[35] This allows medical researchers to more effectively trace the prevalence of certain disorders among family members. To date, approximately one-third of Icelanders have provided genetic samples to the project.

Publicity around the project has raised popular awareness of—and pride in—the nation's unique genetic heritage. While more recent immigrants have also been included in the study, researchers note that they are widely regarded as outsiders, not "real" Icelanders. Some scholars, in fact, have raised concerns that the current fascination with Icelandic genetic uniqueness echoes early-twentieth-century efforts to protect the racial purity of the nation.[36] If taken too far, they warn, Icelanders may come to envision the nation less as a community of citizens bound together by shared values and laws and culture, and more as a natural biological body, united by shared DNA. Defining the nation in genetic terms—what we might call *genonationalism*—would potentially exclude more recent immigrants from full membership in the nation. As one scholar observed, "Genetic accounts of the native and non-native, however careful to avoid overtly geneticizing ethnicity, are never immune from being interpreted as evidence for who has most and fewest rights to belong, legally as well as symbolically."[37]

So for all the promises of genetic genealogy to reveal who we *really* are, to push our pedigrees further back in time than earlier generations of genealogists could have ever imagined, and to unite all of humanity as a single, happy family, geneticizing kinship also has potentially negative political, legal, economic, and other social effects.[38] This leaves us with the pressing question of why we are increasingly drawn to genetic genealogy. What is driving our hunger for the secrets of our DNA?

GENETIC GENEALOGY AND
THE HUNGER FOR SUBSTANCE

Jessica Kolopenuk, a scholar of Cree heritage, has used the traditional figure of the *wiindigo* to explore the increasing popularity of genetic genealogy today. "According to Nehiyaw, Anishinaabe, and other Indigenous tribal beliefs," she explains, "the *wiindigo* or *wetiko* is understood to be a figure that personifies cannibalistic greed and hunger and, when left unstopped, is perpetually driven by its emptiness caused by disconnection."[39] This fearsome demon feels so empty, so cut off from human relationships, that it has an insatiable hunger for human flesh. Kolopenuk suggests that genetic genealogy companies are the modern equivalent of the *wiindigo*. They prey on people's growing sense of social isolation and dislocation, their longing to understand who they are, and they lure people into surrendering bits of their human "flesh" (DNA samples) that both the company and the customers themselves "feast" on. For the testing firms, this feast takes the form of profits. For customers, the feast takes the form of pride and confidence in their own newfound identities. Indeed, they can "dine out" on their ancestral heritage, particularly if it carries prestige or novelty value. This is especially problematic, she argues, for customers who claim to have "Native American DNA" when they have no social or cultural links to Native peoples. In effect, she says, this is just the latest theft from indigenous peoples—the theft of their identities, the theft of their right to self-definition.

Whether or not one agrees with Kolopenuk's metaphor of a flesh-eating demon for what she characterizes as an exploitative "genetic-genealogical machine," her larger point is a compelling one—that our increasing interest in genetic genealogy arises, in part, from a sense of alienation, dislocation, and rootlessness that is a hallmark of modern industrialized societies.[40] Uncertainties about who we *really* are may be even further intensified, as argued earlier, by the virtualization of social life (through digital technologies), the relativization of knowledge (through more critical perspectives in the academy), people's increased mobility (moving from city to city, job to job, even marriage to marriage), and the secularization of industrial societies. All of these developments can lead us to seek our "authentic" or essential selves. To belong to something greater than ourselves, an unbroken line of descent. To identify some concrete, indisputable, and indelible substance that defines us. Our genes seem to offer the substance we crave.

We must also consider that in a world in which certain boundaries are growing less distinct—boundaries between racial and ethnic groups as our nations become more diverse, boundaries between nations themselves as rapid transport and telecommunications make our borders more porous, boundaries between real and imaginary experiences with the rise of virtual technologies, even the boundaries between seemingly "natural" and fixed categories of gender, which are now increasingly challenged by the transgender rights movement—genetic genealogy offers the promise of clear boundaries of identity. The "ethnic mix" pie chart provided by many testing firms is an apt visual representation of boundary-marking. Each "slice" in the multicolored pie represents a seemingly distinct ethnicity—blue for Irish, yellow for Norse, and so on—with clearly demarcated boundaries between them. But, no doubt for the sake of simplicity, such representations ignore significant histories of contact and movement between these populations. There is no gradual overlap between the yellow Irish slice and the blue Norse slice—no slightly greenish area between the two. Just a hard line that provides a satisfyingly simple quantification of my identity—15 percent this, 21 percent that. As noted above, however, such neatly demarcated percentages are little more than pleasant illusions. Ancestral DNA tests capture only a small part of our full ancestral heritage. But in an age of increasingly blurry boundaries, clear-cut and well-bounded categories have their appeal.

Additionally, genetic genealogy allows today's genealogists to create boundaries of a different type, boundaries based on specialist knowledge. As noted in chapter 2, genealogy as a field has long struggled with its own identity. In particular, academic historians and professional archivists have often viewed genealogists as status-seeking hacks and hobbyists, lacking in the skills and motivation to engage in sound research. Perhaps in an effort to prove its own worth, genealogy has become increasingly professionalized in recent decades. Genealogists can expand their knowledge and skills and bolster their reputations within the genealogical community by attaining any number of certificates and affiliations.[41] Conference speakers proudly display such credentials in a veritable alphabet soup below their names in conference programs—CG, CGL, FASG, FNGS.[42] And while formal certifications in genetic genealogy are unusual, genealogists routinely mark themselves as knowledgeable insiders through their use of jargon and identifiers from the field. Conference participants talk about STRs (short tandem repeats) and SNPs (or "snips," single nucleotide polymorphisms). They identify themselves by haplogroup—J-M172, E1b1a—or by ancient matrilineal "clan"—Clan of Tara, Clan of Jasmine, and so on.[43] And they sometimes make light of those who are less knowledgeable about genetics. One genetic genealogy blogger joked, for instance, about the number of people who mistakenly refer to haplogroups as everything from "hologroups" to "Holygroups" to "helpgroups."[44]

So what "boundaries" are being created here? Scholarship on "boundary work" in the sciences demonstrates that scientists often attempt to bolster their intellectual authority and create a favorable public image for their field in part by setting up contrasts (or boundaries) between science and nonscience/pseudoscience.[45] One of the ways they do this is by framing rivals in unflattering ways, often defining them as outsiders or amateurs. By extension, when genetic genealogists employ technical jargon and identi-fiers from the field and make light of those who do not understand or use such concepts appropriately, they are defining the boundary between knowledgeable insider and ill-informed outsider, between the serious ge-netic genealogist and the amateur hack, between rigorous scientific research and slapdash ancestor hunting. In this way, their apparent expertise in ge-netic genealogy allows them to bolster their own authority and credibility among their fellow genealogists.

GENETIC GENEALOGY AND THE CREATION OF KINSHIP

I opened this chapter with the observation that genealogy does not simply *trace* kinship; it *creates* kinship. Although we often imagine kinship as a bio-logical fact—a traceable network of connections through blood and genes and reproductive partnerships—families are, by their very nature, socially constructed entities. They must be imagined. They must be socially recog-nized. And that imagination and recognition arise, in part, from our roots work—the purposive classification and rehearsal of connections between individuals. One question facing us today is what impact genetic geneal-ogy—and genetic science more generally—will have on the ways we think about family and kinship and all the rights and obligations that typically come with family membership.

In one recent conference session on genetic genealogy, the presenter gave audience members a warning. "If you don't want to find a skeleton in the closet," she said, "don't open the closet." Ancestral DNA testing can have unexpected and sometimes discomfiting results. Researchers might discover an unknown adoption, a "non-paternity event" (in which the presumed father was not the biological father), evidence of incest or rape, evidence that disproves cherished family lore, or an unexpected racial or ethnic heritage. Another genetic genealogist related the story of a "white Southern gentleman" of her acquaintance who was distressed to discover his African haplogroup. While the man had told her he was personally "okay with it," he felt he needed to hide the discovery from the rest of his family.

So genetic genealogy raises a number of pressing questions. First, what does it mean for our identities—for our sense of self—if our genetic profile does not match our perceived family heritage? If I grew up as a proud Ital-ian American, only to find that I have few or none of the genetic mark-ers associated with Italian ancestry, does that make me *less* Italian? If my full sibling has a higher percentage of those markers than I do, does that make her *more* Italian than I am? If I grew up believing the people I called "Mother" and "Father" were my biological parents, only to discover that I was adopted, would they no longer be my family? If I grew up, like the "white Southern gentleman" above, enjoying all the privileges of whiteness in the American South, what would it mean for my social position if my African ancestry became known?[46] While ancestral DNA test results do not change who I am physically, nor do they change my lived history, they can profoundly challenge my sense of who I am, and change the way others regard and treat me.[47]

Second, how might genetic results alter our rights and obligations as family members? If I prove not to have a genetic link to my parents or siblings, does that mean I have less of an obligation to assist and care for them in times of hardship? Does it mean I am less entitled to their support in return? In the eyes of the courts, this may be true. Familial DNA tests are commonly used in child support and custody cases, in disputes over inheritance, and even in immigration cases (where a visa applicant must prove a family link to a legal resident of the United States).[48] But legal definitions and social definitions of kinship are often quite different. This can be seen quite clearly in families headed by same-sex couples. While gay and lesbian couples have long formed families—maintaining committed partnerships and raising children—historically these families were not legally recognized in the United States.[49] Until the Supreme Court ruled in June of 2015 that states could not bar same-sex marriage, gay and lesbian partners in many states could be legally denied insurance and tax benefits, inheritance, medical visitation, and child custody rights. With changing legal definitions of marriage, however, notions of family are also being transformed.

Scholars have documented, for instance, the ways same-sex partners actively create kinship through their reproductive choices. A lesbian couple choosing a sperm donor or a gay couple choosing a surrogate may devote considerable time to selecting someone whose physical appearance, talents, and interests most closely resemble those of the couple (or of the parent who will not be contributing DNA to the child). And couples often prefer to use the same donor or surrogate for subsequent conceptions to give their children biological full siblings. Such "natural" similarities and links are seen by couples as ways of strengthening family bonds, and integrating their children more easily into kinship networks. Likewise, we see that in adoptive families—no matter what the sexual orientation of the parents—concerted efforts are made to integrate the child into the past, present, and future of the kinship network. The child might be dressed in a baptismal gown that has been handed down through the generations, or given a family name. They might be taken to visit an ancestral village or taught to participate in family traditions. Relatives might even remark on the child's resemblance to an adoptive parent or grandparent. Such practices, in a sense, transform the child from outsider to insider, from stranger to kin.[50]

It remains to be seen how genealogy as a field of practice will adapt to changing family forms, changing definitions of kinship, and changes in assisted reproduction. Consider, for instance, the primary file format used by American genealogists today to transfer genealogical data from one digital location to another, the GEDCOM (short for Genealogical Data Communication). The GEDCOM was originally developed by the Church of Jesus Christ of Latter-day Saints (the LDS), and perhaps not surprisingly, it reflects certain religious norms. For instance, the file format does not easily accommodate genealogical information on same-sex partners, cohabiting partners, or other kin who differ from those typically found in the normative LDS family. Twenty-first-century genealogists will have to consider how diverse kinship bonds can be more readily integrated into our family trees. Likewise, as genetic science and reproductive technologies advance, genealogists will increasingly be challenged to find ways of charting new kinds of family bonds. How should we reckon the heritage of a child conceived with a donated egg and sperm, implanted through in vitro fertilization, and gestated through a surrogate? A child, in other words with five "parents"—DNA from two biological parents, plus two adoptive parents and a gestational parent. How should we reckon the heritage of children—still a small number around the world—who have DNA from three parents? This occurs when the DNA of two biological parents is combined with a donor's mitochondria to prevent the transmission of certain serious genetic disorders.[51]

The way we each answer such questions reveals deeply ingrained notions about family, ancestry, and identity. Moreover, the way we answer these questions can have a meaningful impact both on individuals and on societies. More inclusive and expansive definitions of family, ancestry, and identity have the potential to unify us in cooperation, mutual understanding, and acceptance. More reductive and exclusionary definitions have the potential to further divide us and pit us against each other in battles over the right to define who belongs and who doesn't, which families count and which don't, and which ancestries are valued more than others.

6

WHO DO WE THINK WE ARE?

Televised Roots Quests

Biographical television programming is nothing new. In the 1950s and '60s, *This Is Your Life* captivated audiences with the life stories of celebrities and everyday heroes. In the 1970s, the television miniseries *Roots*, based on Alex Haley's novel, drew more than 130 million viewers, one of the most-watched television events of all time. And today, networks including the History Channel, A&E, and E! present biographies of the rich, the famous, and the infamous. But in 2004, a new take on biographical television emerged with the BBC's genealogical quest series *Who Do You Think You Are?* (2004–17), which featured celebrities tracking down their family roots with the assistance of genealogists and historians. The show proved so popular that producers in Canada (2007–8), Australia (2008–16), and the United States (2010–18) launched their own versions of the series. And similar shows, including PBS's *Faces of America* (2010) and *Finding Your Roots* (2012–17) and BYU-TV's *The Generations Project* (2010–12) soon followed.

Roots TV has become phenomenally successful, sparking spin-off products (including the *Who Do You Think You Are? Encyclopedia of Genealogy* and the *Finding Your Roots Official Companion* volume) and live events (such as *Who Do You Think You Are? Live!* and the *Genealogy Roadshow*, which was also televised on PBS, 2013–16). Many of the genealogists I interviewed are devoted viewers of one or more roots TV shows, and many observe that the shows have played a major role in drawing more people to the pursuit of family history. Nonetheless, seasoned genealogists are often critical of the shows for what they see as superficial and sensationalized depictions of their avocation.

In this chapter we will first analyze roots television shows—how they are structured, what messages they commonly convey, and what they appear to offer to participating guests. Then we will examine the complicated relationship genealogists have with roots TV, and why they find televised roots quests both so fascinating and so fraught. And finally we will consider the ways televised roots quests—and the shift toward virtualized, digitized, mass-mediated forms of social life—may be changing the ways we present and perceive ourselves and our family connections.

THE ANATOMY OF THE TELEVISED ROOTS QUEST

There are some notable differences between specific American roots television series.[1] Most obviously, while each episode of *Who Do You Think You Are?* features one celebrity guest (usually a prominent actor or musician), the PBS shows focus on multiple celebrity guests in each episode, and the BYU-TV show *The Generations Project* features noncelebrity guests. Despite such differences, the shows tend to follow a fairly standard format. Episodes typically consist of three main "acts," what we might call the Hook, the Journey, and the Homecoming. Each episode opens with the Hook—in other words, the mystery, existential question, or dilemma at the heart of the guest's roots quest. The bulk of the show is then devoted to the Journey, which often involves physical journeys to other cities, states, and countries in search of genealogical evidence. And the episode concludes with a Homecoming scene, as guests reflect on what they have learned from their quests, sometimes sharing these lessons with family members. Let's examine each of these "acts" in further detail:

- The Hook
- The Journey
  - Breadcrumbs
  - Shocks
  - Spin
- The Homecoming

The Hook

In the opening sequence of each episode, the audience is drawn in, or "hooked," by what is framed as a dramatic mystery or problem. Episodes are often structured as if they were detective stories. Susan Sarandon, for instance, goes in search of a "mysterious grandmother" who disappeared without a trace. Kim Cattrall follows the trail of a grandfather who left home one day, never to be heard of again. Marisa Tomei seeks answers to uncomfortable questions about her great-grandfather's shooting death. Even when specific puzzles are not apparent at the beginning of an episode, there is often a promise of sensational revelations. When Hollywood couple Kevin Bacon and Kyra Sedgwick begin their roots quest, the narrator asks, "What secrets will we reveal? What mysteries will we solve? What will we learn about how their ancestors shaped who they are today?"[2]

This notion that the experiences and traits of our ancestors can help to explain our own character and life choices strongly underpins televised roots quests of all types. At the heart of these quests are basic existential questions: "Who am I?" and "Why am I the person I am?" Country singer Tim McGraw wants to find out "who he truly is." Actress Vanessa Williams is looking for "another piece of the puzzle to my life and who I am." And other guests seek to understand their own particular traits. Ashley Judd wants to understand why she has always been so passionate about human rights and equality. Martin Sheen wonders why he has always been so committed to promoting peace and social justice. Rob Lowe wants to know why he has always been so "in love with Americana, patriotism, and politics." And, as is always the case in televised roots quests, all of the featured guests find ancestors with these same traits—a champion of religious freedom, a political dissident taking a stand against fascism, a soldier in the Revolutionary War.[3] Perhaps not surprisingly, guests typically focus only on the positive traits that have been passed down through the generations—traits such as perseverance, patriotism, courage, or an entrepreneurial spirit. When the genealogical record reveals criminals, bigots, murderers, and wastrels in the family tree, they are often dismissed as bad apples or the victims of circumstance. Actor Kevin Bacon playfully acknowledges this tendency when records reveal that one of his ancestors was a slaveholder. "Well, he was a bad egg," Bacon says wryly. "I never liked the guy."[4]

In many episodes, guests talk about having a "blank" or a "void" inside of them because they don't know where they came from. They feel an "eternal longing" for their past, for their ancestors. They crave a sense of belonging. As Native American author Louise Erdrich observes in one episode, "We [Americans] want connection. And it's partly because of what we call our melting pot. I don't think we really want to melt into an amorphous mass. We want to be ourselves. We want to feel a certain belonging." And, inevitably, the televised roots quest delivers. At the end of his genealogical journey, actor Matthew Broderick notes, "Something has been filled in that I didn't know was blank." Actress Brooke Shields remarks that "this has been an amazing exploration . . . being able to find your place in the grand scheme of things. There's something empowering about it." In another show, a woman struggling with low self-esteem arising from childhood abuse finds affirmation of her value in the stories of her ancestors. "I have a lot to be proud of," she says. "I'm a Somebody." Yet another guest reflects on her life-changing genealogical quest. "I feel like I come from someplace now. And I didn't realize that I even cared about that before."[5]

In addition to "hooking" the audience through mysteries and existential questions, some episodes draw audiences into the guests' emotional dilemmas, their need to heal, forgive, or find "closure" through their roots quests. Danielle is a law student who hopes to find the inspiration and confidence to see her through her studies. Andrea suffers from serious health problems and needs to find the strength to make significant changes to her life. Natalie, whose infant son died tragically, needs to heal emotionally so she can take care of her other three children. Jill wants to let go of her anger toward her neglectful, alcoholic father. And the televised roots quest never fails to deliver. Danielle finds an inspirational ancestor. Andrea connects with her Irish heritage and feels "alive . . . energized . . . rooted." Natalie finds "the strength to prevail" when she learns of an ancestor who also lost a child. And after investigating the story of her father's troubled life, Jill says, "I don't feel angry anymore. I feel lighter. I feel freer. I feel peaceful. . . . I know who my father is now."[6]

The Journey

Once the "hook" of the episode is established, the guest's "journey" begins. Sometimes this is an armchair journey, as a host methodically reveals family stories. And sometimes it is a literal journey, with guests following in their ancestors' "footsteps," seeking out traces of their lives. Rosie O'Donnell travels to Quebec and Ireland; Brooke Shields, to Italy and France; Lisa Kudrow, to Belarus and Poland; Matthew Broderick, to Washington, DC, Gettysburg, Atlanta, and France. Along the way, genealogists, historians, archivists, local residents, and even newly discovered relatives offer genealogical breadcrumbs for the guest to follow. Such evidence is presented gradually, vividly, and dramatically for maximum emotional impact on both the guest and the audience. Shock revelations, "cliffhanger" questions, and cathartic tears heighten the suspense, empathy, sorrow, and triumph.

One common feature of the televised roots journey is the creative interpretation of genealogical evidence, or what we might call the "spinning" of the genealogical record. The reality of family history research is that records are inevitably incomplete. Gaps, inconsistencies, and errors abound, and dead ends (or "brick walls," as genealogists call them) are commonplace. Consequently, guests and hosts in televised roots quests must interpret the evidence to the best of their ability to create a meaningful narrative of a family's journey through time and space. What is striking is the almost universal tendency to put a positive spin on the record, even when evidence for that interpretation is scant or contradictory.

Musician Harry Connick Jr., for instance, recounts his childhood growing up as a skinny white kid in New Orleans, enamored with jazz music and black jazz musicians. "It frustrated me to not be black," he says. "I wanted to be fat and black because all of my heroes were fat and black," and most of his best friends were black. When he finds that his Irish immigrant ancestor enlisted and served for three years in the Confederate Army, he looks uncomfortable. "It's kind of shameful to even admit that," he says. "That sucks." He then tries to imagine all the reasons why his ancestor may have enlisted. "I'm just hoping that there was some other motive besides [defending slavery]." Maybe there were no other jobs available. Maybe he was just trying to support his family. The show then cuts to a local historian who talks about the economic hardships in New Orleans during the Civil War, the shortages of coal and flour, the bread riots, the Northern embargoes. "It was a destitute time."

Connick seizes on this with visible relief. "See, I told you he wasn't really fighting for the South!" he exclaims. "He went in there and said, 'Listen, I'm doing this to feed my family.'" Although no specific evidence supports this charitable interpretation of his ancestor's motivations, it is one that clearly assuages Connick's sense of inherited guilt. The show's host, African American scholar Henry Louis Gates Jr., offers further comfort to his guest. "You're not responsible for your ancestors," he tells Connick. "It's impossible to know what any of us would've done in the face of these difficult moral decisions."[7]

In another episode, actor Blair Underwood finds an ancestor who was confined to an all-black mental institution in 1900. Newspaper accounts from the period describe the man wandering the streets in strange clothing, pronouncing himself to be the second messiah, killing a cow, pledging to kill all the cows he could find, and finally attempting to shoot a man who tried to seize him. Further investigation shows that this ancestor had a number of violent encounters with white farmers, and had even been shot on three separate occasions, seemingly in disputes over property. In trying to explain this ancestor's tumultuous life and "eccentric" behavior, the show interviews a historian who suggests that the man may have been a "conjurer" in the African tradition—a traditional healer and community leader whom whites would have found threatening.

Underwood embraces this interpretation, deciding that his ancestor was a man with "internal strength and fortitude . . . a maverick that thinks outside the box and lives by his own credo . . . a man that could not be broken." Underwood concludes from scant evidence that his ancestor likely vowed to kill as many cows as he could because his white neighbor's cattle were wandering onto his land and destroying his crops. He was just trying to keep his family safe and defend his rights and his property. So it wasn't that his ancestor was mentally ill, but rather that white authorities thought the best way to control this formidable black man was to lock him up in a mental institution. "I am very proud [of him]," he notes.[8]

The focus of an episode from another roots series was Gloria, a woman trying to come to terms with her difficult childhood. Her father was "very strict and crude," a racist, a drunk, and a bully. And her grandfather was said to have died in shameful circumstances. With the help of researchers she finds that her grandfather had a hard childhood as well. He left home in his youth, worked in terrible conditions at the local mills, and drank very heavily until one night he died in a hotel, likely of a combination of heat exhaustion and alcohol abuse. She expresses empathy for him and says she can understand why he might have wanted to get "a little bit tipsy" to "wind down" from a hard day, working to provide for his family. "Yeah, he did drink too much," she says. "But it's sad he died so young. He didn't live long enough to know his grandchildren. . . . I really think he would've been a good granddaddy. . . . He did the best he could."

Next she finds out that her great-grandfather, nicknamed Tom the Drunk, had shot and killed a black man for allegedly stealing his whiskey. The story leaves her visibly troubled. When she then finds that her great-great-grandfather was a Baptist minister, she sheds tears of relief. "It makes me feel good [because] . . . I've heard so much bad stuff." She visits his church and senses his "good spirit" there. She proclaims him a "righteous man" and knows that he awaits her in Heaven. When it is revealed that this minister threw his wife out of the house and prevented her from ever seeing her children again—which seems to have scarred them and eventually led them to alcohol—she works hard to find a charitable explanation. With no evidence beyond her own faith in the minister's righteousness, she concludes that he must have thrown his wife out for good reasons, and that he was simply trying to protect his children.[9]

When yet another guest, Ty, begins his roots quest, he expresses misgivings about exploring the roles his German ancestors played in World

War II. "I want to be German," he says. "I feel German . . . [but] I am nervous." During his visit to Germany, he meets living relatives who knew his grandfather. They confirm that he joined the Hitler Youth, but assure Ty that it was all in fun. Young people were manipulated into thinking it was for the good of the country, they say. Ty also finds that his grandfather enlisted in the German Navy during the war, but relatives suggest that he was never really committed to the Nazi Party. "It seems like my grandfather was a pretty cool guy," Ty concludes. "I mean, he was part of Hitler's Youth, but as I understand it, so was everybody else in the country. . . . It feels like they were just kind of swept up in this whole movement."

Moving further back in time, Ty discovers a long-ago Jewish ancestor who had converted to Christianity. He welcomes the discovery of his Jewish heritage and attempts to find out how Jewish ancestry affected his relatives during the war. He finds that while his direct forebears denied their Jewish "blood," and passed as "Aryan," some of his distant cousins were forced to flee Nazi persecution. He says that while he had feared revelations about Nazis in his family tree, this roots journey gave him something else. "Instead of being the perpetrator of all of these events, I kind of experienced the side of what it was like being persecuted in a small way. . . . So it's understanding what it was like from a Jewish perspective."[10]

What all of these cases, and many more, have in common is a creative and favorable interpretation of incomplete records—a charitable filling in of blanks in the family history to create a positive narrative of the family's past. A Confederate soldier becomes a family man who joined up out of economic necessity. A man adjudicated mentally ill, a self-professed messiah with a history of violence, becomes a community leader whose spirituality and defense of African American rights posed a threat to the white establishment. Generations of abusive alcoholic men are explained away by the hardships they endured. The apparent cruelty of a husband banishing his wife from her home and children is reframed as a righteous attempt to protect those children. And the choices of a Nazi ancestor are both moderated by the notion that "everybody" was doing it, and counterbalanced by the discovery of persecuted Jews in the family tree. We all want family stories to be proud of. We all want to bask in the reflected glory of our ancestors' triumphs over adversity, their ingenuity, their integrity. We all want to see a little of ourselves—the best parts of ourselves—being passed down to us through the generations. And the genealogical record, as flawed and incomplete as it always is, gives us the flexibility to craft palatable and even affirming stories out of the scraps of our ancestors' lives.

The Homecoming

Once the audience has been hooked, the journey has been taken, the evidence has been strung out tantalizingly over the episode like bread-crumbs, once the shocks have been experienced, and guests, hosts, and experts have put a favorable spin on the genealogical record, the featured guests turn homeward and reflect on their experiences. Some guests find an explanation for their own traits. Tim McGraw finds a long line of "self-made" men who were always "pushing forward, pushing the envelope," just as he has done through his musical career. Politician and civil rights activist John Lewis finds ancestors who were politically active from the earliest days of African American suffrage. "So maybe, just maybe, it's part of my DNA," he says, "my bloodline, or whatever you want to call it."[11]

Other guests find affirmation of their own choices in the stories of their ancestors. Actress Edie Falco, who adopted her children, discovers an orphan in her family tree. "It really clarified for me what family really means," she said, "which has very little to do with what country your great-great-great-great-grandfather lived in and more about what emotional clouds you were surrounded in as you grew up. . . . It made me feel so much more solid about having adopted kids. And it really is more about the people who have loved you and cared for you."[12]

Some guests reflect on the trials their ancestors endured and feel profoundly grateful for their own more privileged lives. Director Mike Nichols, hearing of family members who fled from Nazi persecution, concludes, "I'm beyond lucky. . . . And what a putz [I am] to ever have complained about anything for even a moment." Musician Lionel Richie tells his family of the brave freedom fighters in their family tree. "You should be very proud to know that that's in your family history. [And] to understand how fortunate we are now. We are here because of their struggle." And comedian Rosie O'Donnell reflects on the suffering of her Irish Famine–era ancestors. If they could endure and triumph, she knows she can put the emotional hardships of her past behind her. "We all have the choice to focus on the horror or the redemption," she observes. "And the gift is to focus on the redemption."[13]

Some guests reflect on the ways our ancestors' choices and experiences have shaped us. "We are the sum of all people that have lived before us," actress Meryl Streep observes. "Everything that they learned, everything that wounded them, everything that made them stronger, everything that made them happy, we contain in our little corporeal selves." Other guests emphasize the key role family stories play in shaping our sense of self. Actress Gwyneth Paltrow notes that "we need to take responsibility for all of our stories and teach our children about where we come from in both good ways and the bad. Because the most meaningful thing about our histories is what we learn from them." And rabbi Angela Buchdahl asserts, "I think our families choose the stories that we want to tell about ourselves. Because that is who we want to be. But those stories that we share, I think, more than any DNA or anything else, shape who we are."[14]

The homecoming often ends with a platitude or observation that is broadly applicable to the viewing audience. "It's important to know where you've been to know where you're going," observes actress Eva Longoria. "We have to learn from the past so we can make the future better," actor Steve Buscemi notes. "I feel we have come full circle," actress Kim Cattrall says. "[Finding my missing grandfather] was really more about finding the family that I do have." "I hope my children understand that they're on the shoulders of great people," director Spike Lee offers. "History's very important. I am who I am today based upon my ancestors."

AND THE MORAL OF THE STORY IS . . .

In some ways, the televised roots quest can be seen as a twenty-first-century morality tale. The protagonists embark on their journeys, and encounter characters and events that exemplify good and evil, justice and injustice, strength and weakness. And from these encounters, the protagonists take moral lessons—lessons about what is most important in life; lessons about how to live their lives; lessons about what it means to be a good parent, child, sibling, or spouse, a good citizen, a good American. The general lessons that emerge most commonly from the shows include the importance of family and the bonds of love and community; the importance of peace, empathy, acceptance, and the humane treatment of others, but also of resistance and even violence in the struggle for justice; and the importance of understanding history and the sacrifices of your ancestors in order to make the most of your life on Earth. But American televised roots quests also convey the importance of certain national values—specifically, multiculturalism, the American Dream, religious faith, and progress.

Multiculturalism

Living in a settler society, most Americans today come from immigrant stock. It is hardly surprising, then, that American roots television celebrates the multicultural diversity of the nation. While the majority of guests featured on American roots series are white, producers make clear attempts to include a range of racial, religious, and national backgrounds in their storylines.[15] A consistent theme across the series is that as a nation, our diversity makes us stronger. As political commentator Linda Chavez put it when exploring her family history on PBS,

> I've always thought that the story of America was the story of peoples coming here from all different parts of the world—some voluntarily, some involuntarily—and that what made this country such a great country is that we did have this mixing of peoples. . . . We bring into *our* culture bits and pieces of so many different strains of other traditions and cultures, and that's made us stronger.

Featured guests from all of the roots shows analyzed here express similarly positive views of America's multicultural social fabric. Indeed, almost without exception guests welcome the discovery of unexpected ethnoracial ancestries in their family tree. "Cool!" German American Ty says when he uncovers a Jewish ancestor. "Awesome!" actress Michelle Rodriguez exclaims when DNA results reveal that she is "21 percent African." At the same time, guests express disappointment at not being sufficiently multicultural. "What?! I'm appalled," Rodriguez says when she learns that in addition to her significant African heritage, she is "72 percent European." "I'm so, like, not impressed. . . . I wanted to be Native American." Likewise, when actor Robert Downey Jr. is told that his DNA results identify him as "100 percent white," he says, "I have to admit I'm a little bit disappointed, because I thought I had some African American influence in my blood."

At the start of the twentieth century, Americans often used genealogy to document their racial purity, to set themselves apart from certain undesirable classes of immigrants and inferiors, and claim a privileged place in the social hierarchy. At the start of the twenty-first century, however, many Americans clearly hope for a diverse cast of characters in their family tree. Not only does such diversity add interest and "color" to your family history, but it also renders you quintessentially American, the product of fortuitous and fortifying admixtures.

The American Dream

Closely linked to the celebration of American multiculturalism in roots television is the celebration of the "American Dream." While that dream takes slightly different forms in each episode, it usually encompasses notions of liberty, equality, and opportunity. As guests explore their family histories, they frequently reflect on the kinds of oppression their ancestors were fleeing in the Old World—religious, political, and economic oppression—and on their ancestors' gradual or sometimes dramatic rise from rags to riches. This often leads them to reflect on how fortunate they are to live in America, where all things are possible if you only work hard enough.

Actress Rita Wilson wants to know more about her Greek immigrant father. She travels to Greece and Eastern Europe and discovers the series of hardships and poignant losses that led her father to "escape" to America. Toward the end of her journey she recalls that her father said "God bless America" every day. And now she knows why. It was because her father had lived the "American Dream." It was because even amid his suffering in Europe, he knew that a better life awaited him in America, where "anything is possible." Likewise, when scholar Henry Louis Gates Jr. interviews politician John Lewis, Gates observes that "only in America" could Lewis have risen from being the son of an impoverished sharecropper to a senior member of Congress. "Yeah. Only in America," Lewis agrees. Similarly, musician Reba McEntire finds an ancestor who came to America as an indentured servant when he was just a child. Although she initially feels anger toward the boy's father for sending him away, she later sees that indentured servitude was likely the boy's best and only chance to move up the social ladder as he did. "Only in America" would that be possible, a historian tells her. Such assertions suggest that the United States is unparalleled in the opportunities and freedoms it offers. (Unfortunately, the economic data do not support this assumption.)[16]

Pastor Rick Warren finds that his pilgrim ancestors dreamed of building a "Christian utopia" in the New World. And while he sees that dream as unrealistic, he asserts that the United States is certainly unique in its "commitment to justice, the commitment to truth, the commitment to love. No nation is as generous as America. None. Nobody even comes close." Similarly, comedian Stephen Colbert notes, "When I was a kid I thought [being American] just meant being the best. . . . That we're number one. . . . It's the greatest country in the world. . . . I could intellectually deconstruct that idea, but I have zero desire to do so." What these comments have in common (besides being articulated by men who are both "100 percent white," according to the DNA results Gates gives them) is the notion not only that America is unique in terms of the opportunities it offers, but that it is the greatest, most generous, most just, and most loving nation in the world. (Again, such notions are not supported by objective data.)[17]

The upside of notions of the American Dream and American exceptionalism is that they are a source of national pride and may in fact encourage a strong work ethic that drives economic growth and an attention to issues of justice that provides a counterbalance to powerful political and corporate interests. The downside to these notions, however, is that they often obscure long-standing inequalities (including those based on race, class, and gender) that are deeply embedded in the social structure. If we believe in the American Dream—that America is a land of freedom, equality, and opportunity, and that anyone can go from rags to riches if they work hard enough—then any group that lags behind in earnings or education or political voice must not be trying hard enough.[18] And if we believe in American exceptionalism—that we are truly the greatest, most just, and most humane nation on Earth—then there is little reason to face our social problems, because whatever they may be, we can be confident that we are still doing things better than anyone else is.

Such thinking often inflects the interpretations of guests on roots television shows. Danielle, for instance, investigates the life of a slave ancestor who was eventually able to buy himself and his wife and children out of slavery. "He was able to escape . . . at least mentally escape, from the idea of slavery," she observes. "A lot of that slave mentality is not knowing who you are as an individual and not having any kind of aspirations for yourself. If you see yourself as property, you'll continue to be property." Her ancestor didn't think of himself as a slave, but as a man, she explains. That's what set him apart from "every other slave who remained in slavery through the end of the Civil War." While this interpretation of events gives Danielle a sense of personal "strength," "determination," and "confidence," it does imply that what kept other people enslaved was primarily their self-defeating attitudes, their lack of ambition, their poor self-esteem. The notion of the American Dream here obscures the reality that slavery was enforced with chains and guns and whips, and with an entire economic, legal, and social system designed to reduce people of African descent to the status of chattel. So while Danielle's "spin" on the historical record may make her feel proud and confident, it reduces slavery to a state of mind and, in effect, blames slaves for their own captivity.

Faith

Bound up with the American Dream and American exceptionalism is the notion of religious faith as a central component of the American experience. As guests explore the stories of their immigrant ancestors, they frequently contrast experiences of religious persecution in the Old World with what they see as one of the unique promises of America—religious liberty. Actress Ashley Judd captures this succinctly when she learns that her pilgrim ancestor was a religious radical who had been targeted by English officials for his beliefs. "The American idea inheres in his story," she says. "Everything is implicated. All of our basic freedoms that we, you know, value, and in many instances take for granted in America, inhere: freedom of speech, freedom of religion, separation of church and state." Her father agrees on the significance of her findings. "The thread that you have followed is the fabric of our country," he observes. Indeed, religious liberty is considered such an essential feature of American life that *Finding Your Roots* devotes an entire episode to examining the family histories of three contemporary religious leaders and considering what those histories tell us about "the spiritual foundations of this country, our unrelenting struggle for religious freedom and tolerance."[19]

In addition to reflecting on issues of religious persecution and religious liberty, guests often have direct and personal experiences of spirituality in the course of their televised roots quests. Many guests feel the presence of their ancestors. This is particularly pronounced on BYU-TV's *The Generations Project*, a show with ties to the Mormon Church. When one guest, Boyd, visits an ancestor's burial site, he says, "I'm sure she's here other than just bones. I feel her spirit." Another guest, native Hawaiian Maile, dedicates herself to uncovering the details of her ancestors' lives because "they help us, they guide us, they give us the knowledge they had, and they're hoping we don't forget them." And in another episode, Emily follows certain "impressions"—images and sensations—that she feels the ancestors are sending to her. She talks directly to the spirits and opens herself up to their messages. "If you have anything to say I'd like to hear it," she tells them. "I'd like to validate your experience." And, indeed, the messages she receives prompts her to arrange for one of her ancestors to be disinterred and reburied in a different location where she believes he will be able to rest in peace.[20]

Even on the less spiritually inflected *Who Do You Think You Are?* guests frequently comment that they can feel the presence of their ancestors. Actress Rita Wilson talks to her father's spirit when she enters his childhood home—"Dad, I'm home"—and again, at the end of her genealogical journey. "Wherever you are, Dad, I love you." Former Miss America Vanessa Williams says she can feel her father's presence. She knows he is taking this journey with her. And after uncovering the stories of his slave ancestors, football legend Emmitt Smith is visibly moved. "I can hear my ancestors," he says. "I can feel it. I can hear it, that they're crying out, 'Thank you. Thank you. My soul is not lost.'" And now they can "move on to heaven."[21]

Moreover, on all of the roots television series analyzed here, guests have what can be described as "uncanny" experiences. That is, they uncover striking similarities and eerie patterns in their families' stories. Emmitt Smith and Rita Wilson find certain significant numbers repeating in their families over the generations. Brooke Shields, Susan Sarandon, and Reba McEntire find explanations for why they have been inexplicably drawn to certain places. And director Spike Lee is stunned to discover that one of his ancestors was named "Mars," because Lee had created a fictional character of that name for one of his films. "It was not an accident," he says. "That was the spirit of Mars that made that happen."

Progress

A final overarching theme of American televised roots quests is progress, particularly on issues such as human rights, civil rights, and women's rights. Guests express disapproval, disgust, and sorrow for past injustices—Indian removals, the Salem witch trials, slavery, segregation, the Holocaust. "I get so angry." "That's kind of nauseating." "I find this really actually physically upsetting." It "stabbed me in the heart." And they feel disappointed and ashamed when they find that their ancestors helped to perpetrate these injustices as conquistadors, slave owners, Confederate soldiers, Nazis. It is "horrific and it's sad . . . it's a shock" to find out. "Oh that's brutal. . . . I'd like to think I was part of a more peaceful ancestry."[22] Such expressions of shock and distaste, of course, separate the guests from the objectionable actions of their ancestors and to some extent absolve them of any guilt by association.

A common response when encountering unpalatable historical facts is for guests to express relief and gratitude that they live in today's America, where such horrors are a thing of the past. Oppression based on race, religion, gender, or class is generally regarded as a feature of the "bad old days," something that has thankfully been overcome. Only occasionally do guests remark upon ongoing injustices. Almost without exception, it is people of color who do so. Roi recounts his own painful experiences of racial discrimination and racist violence. Sometimes he feels he is being "swallowed by hatred" and anger, he says. In the course of his roots quest, he finds free blacks in his family tree going back to seventeenth-century America, and he discovers significant white ancestry as well. He is shocked to find "how white I am! I am white!" And he reconciles with his imprisoned father. "I feel like I'm healing," he says. And he is ready to let go of his anger and "rise above" the racism and injustice he still encounters.[23]

In one episode of *Finding Your Roots*, three prominent African American guests, former secretary of state Condoleezza Rice, actor Samuel L. Jackson, and Brown University president Ruth Simmons, discuss their own perspectives on race in America. All three grew up in the segregated South where they "knew what their place was." Racist indignities were an everyday occurrence and racist violence was a constant threat. But at the same time, whites and blacks were so rigidly separated that, as Rice puts it, "racism was both everything and nothing at all." That is, she had relatively little contact with whites, so relatively few direct experiences of racism. All three rose from humble beginnings, as the descendants of slaves, to the top of their professions. "I wouldn't have thought it possible for a person of my background to become president of Brown University," Simmons observes. But despite their successes, and despite progress over time, they suggest that issues related to slavery and racism have yet to be resolved. "I've always thought that this is the kind of unhealed wound in America, that we have trouble talking about what really happened during slavery," Rice notes. "We have trouble talking about the scars of that. That's the unspoken and unfinished business of race in America."

With the exception of these few more critical perspectives on race and racism in America today, however, most episodes celebrate the progress we have made. Guests and hosts alike marvel at how far we have come, and express relief that all people are treated equally and fairly now, no matter what their race, religion, national origin, class, gender, or sexual orientation. Host Henry Louis Gates captures this sentiment neatly when he observes that "while our ancestors came to this land in different ships, we're all in the same boat now." In other words, we are all on equal footing now. We are all Americans.

TELEVISED ROOTS QUESTS: "FABULOUS" AND FLAWED

We have seen that TV roots quests serve to explain the guests' character traits, affirm their life choices, give them a sense of belonging and connection, and address their emotional needs by providing ways for them to explore their pain, sorrow, anger, love, and profound gratitude. The shows also allow and even encourage guests to interpret (or "spin") their family histories in the most positive ways, by emphasizing the heroes and largely ignoring or explaining away the villains in their family tree. At the same time, these programs articulate American ideals such as multiculturalism, the American Dream, religious faith, and progress. But what do genealogists themselves make of these virtual quests?

Roots television shows are a frequent topic of conversation among American genealogists.[24] Wherever genies gather together, they can be heard discussing recent episodes. They find the shows engrossing, "fun," and "fabulous," and they eagerly await the next episode or season.

Professional genealogists featured on the shows are treated like celebrities at genealogy conferences, their presence creating a palpable buzz of excitement. The shows make family history look glamorous and thrilling, genealogists say, and that draws many new people to the pursuit. While this is generally seen as a good thing, they note that there are also some drawbacks.

The main criticism genealogists have of the shows is that they make the research process look "too easy." They laugh as they discuss episodes where the guest goes hundreds of years back in their family tree with what looks like a few quick clicks on the computer. In reality, such results typically require months or even years of painstaking research. The problem with such depictions, they say, is that people believe that they can quickly create a family tree by simply clicking on a "shaking leaf" (the symbol Ancestry.com uses to indicate possibly relevant records). Such misperceptions can lead to frustration for novice genealogists, or, much worse, to shoddy research that can eventually "infect" other people's family trees with faulty data.

Likewise, genealogists point out that the shows clearly "cherry-pick" the guest's family tree, focusing in on only the most colorful characters and storylines. While this makes for a more interesting show, it also ignores the vast majority of the guest's ancestors, all the "Plain Joes" along the way. This kind of selective "ancestor collecting" strikes serious genealogists as superficial and inferior to the more comprehensive research they do.

Despite the criticisms frequently leveled at the shows by seasoned genealogists, one genie doing research at the Family History Library in Salt Lake City noted, "I wish the director would meet *me* at the door with my prepared family history!" Television hosts often present their guests with professionally prepared books or scrolls spanning hundreds of years and including copies of records, letters, photographs, and newspaper clippings—a genealogist's dream come true. In this way roots TV, like so many other television shows, is in the business of selling dreams. Televised roots quests provide aspirational models, and to some degree, the shows shape the way genealogists think about and go about their own family history research.

One indication of the shows' influence on real-world genealogists is the growing importance of research trips to Old World destinations (a topic we will cover in more detail in chapter 8). Most roots TV shows take guests on picturesque journeys to their "homelands" in search of genealogical clues. These travel segments typically feature visits to ancestral homes, farms, villages, churches, and cemeteries to "pay respect" to the dead, and to "walk in the footsteps" of the ancestors. And, where possible, the shows include tearful "reunions" between the guest and distant relatives they have never met. In interviews with genealogists across the nation, many people recounted similar roots journeys—trips to England, Ireland, Scotland, Wales, Germany, Poland, Sweden, Norway, Denmark, Luxembourg, Italy, and countless other destinations, both international and domestic. (Some had even taken genealogical cruises—combining on-board how-to seminars with scenic ports of call and all-you-can-eat buffets.) And, almost without exception, these journeys are described as deeply meaningful and moving. Real-world genealogists use the same language heard in roots TV to talk about their experiences—their desire to "walk in the footsteps" of their ancestors, "pay respect" to those who came before them, be "reunited" with long-lost and previously unknown family members.

The family histories recounted by real-world genealogists also tend to reflect many of the same features seen in roots television programing—the lure of historical mysteries, the yearning to connect with history and kin, the desire for "colorful" ancestors, and the importance of the American Dream, religious faith, and progress over the generations. Stories of hardship, hard work, and upward mobility and expressions of profound gratitude for the sacrifices of one's forebears feature prominently in genealogists' family narratives. And there is a tendency to linger on the stories of ancestors who are most "colorful," either in terms of their choices and experiences, or in terms of their unexpected ethnic or racial background. Some genealogists even produce videos and books documenting their roots journeys, like those presented to the featured guests on roots television shows. Sessions at genealogical conferences are often focused on how to create polished family history books, websites, and digital presentations, and conference vendors sell everything from software to hardware and professional services that allow genealogists to create their own *Who Do You Think You Are?*–style productions.

But this brings us to a chicken-or-egg dilemma. Are real-world genealogists modeling their roots quests after the television shows, or are the television shows simply modeling the research process followed by real-world genealogists? The likeliest answer is that it is a combination of the two. Roots television producers are guided by the practices of real-world genealogists, but they insert certain dramatic elements—broader historical narratives, scenic locations, emotional encounters—that make for more-interesting viewing. And this, in turn, encourages real-world genealogists to incorporate similar elements into their own research.

The mass media do not simply mirror society. They selectively "edit" reality, imposing order on chaotic experience, creating coherent narratives out of messy and multiple perspectives. In so doing, they help to construct reality—that is, they profoundly shape our perceptions of reality, and potentially our actions in the real world. Arguably, roots television shows are reshaping the ways genealogists and the general public alike view family history, and perhaps more broadly reshaping notions of who we think we are.

VIRTUAL REALITIES, VIRTUAL IDENTITIES, AND VIRTUAL KINSHIP

Our fascination with virtual reality, and our anxieties about it, are by no means new. Ray Bradbury's 1951 short story "The Veldt" centers on two children who become so enamored with the virtual savannah in their high-tech nursery that they lure their parents inside to be devoured by lions. Philip K. Dick's 1966 tale "We Can Remember It for You Wholesale" features a corporation that implants "extra-factual memories" in their clients' brains to provide them with pleasurable illusions. And the 1999 blockbuster film *The Matrix* and its sequels present a dystopian future in which most humans unknowingly dwell in a virtual world created by machines.

While virtual reality technologies have developed more slowly than some futurists and science fiction writers imagined, we are undeniably spending increasing amounts of time in virtual domains.[25] The average American watches roughly five hours of television each day and spends almost two hours a day on social media. And recreational media use is even higher among teens, who spend an average of nine hours each day on their screens. This exceeds the amount of time most of us spend eating, sleeping, or socializing with others face-to-face. Consider that Facebook now claims 1.4 billion users worldwide, the top ten social media outlets together reach 3.8 billion users, and in excess of 200 million people today engage in online gaming, often within virtual communities.[26] Through this digital media, it is now easier than ever to create multiple projections of self — one through Instagram photos, one through a gaming avatar, one through blogs or tweets. But along with these multiple expressions of identity, there is also a growing awareness that none of these expressions is complete, natural, or fully authentic. Rather, each identity is constructed or staged for an audience. This virtualization of identity is likely fueling interest in genealogy by making us long for seemingly more authentic, more elemental, more rooted identities.

Without a doubt, the rise of digital technologies and virtual realities is adding fuel to the current genealogy boom in other ways as well. As public records and archival materials are increasingly digitized, genealogists today can access more family history records than previous generations of researchers ever dreamed of. And genealogists are keenly aware that the growing accessibility of records is attracting many newcomers to the pursuit. As one professional genealogist I interviewed explained,

> A major contributing factor in family history's popularity today is the fact that literally billions of records are available online today. Records that were hidden away and frankly too hard to access or afford in the past are now at hand. . . . When I first became involved in family history in the 1970s, genealogy was pretty much limited to the elite—those who could afford to travel all over and spend large amounts of money to get copies of records or to hire a professional researcher. . . . Today's excitement over genealogy and family history has exploded—mainly because of what Ancestry.com has been able to provide online. . . . Additionally, through the commercials and the sponsorship of the *Who Do You Think You Are?* series, Ancestry.com has made it clear to people of all ages and backgrounds that finding family is not only possible, but beneficial and incredibly enjoyable. (Charlotte, 70, Illinois)

In short, developments in the digital realm are fueling the genealogy boom in multiple ways. The proliferation of virtual identities and virtual interactions prompts us to long for more stable, more coherent, and seemingly more authentic identities. At the same time, digitized records make research easier, faster, and cheaper than ever before. There are also now more ways to share genealogical research with others, whether through websites or through self-published books, blogs, videos, or podcasts. And commercials for online services such as Ancestry.com and roots television shows make family history research seem easy, fun, and enriching.

As many scholars have pointed out, the economic reality of television content is that it is "bait" designed to keep consumers watching so they will be exposed to product advertisements.[27] But television sells more than goods and services. It sells values, ways of life, and ideals of beauty and normalcy. It sells dreams of faraway places, of wealth and romance and excitement. Likewise, roots TV sells dreams of mysterious ancestors, of ancient ties, of cultural and historical influences etched indelibly into our cells and pulling us inexorably toward "home." It sells dreams of family—of struggle, survival, and progress, of painful separation and joyful reunion. And perhaps above all else, roots TV sells us dreams of a fully realized, fully recognized, newly enlightened self.

7

IN SEARCH OF THE
"LIVING DEAD"

Ancestors, Zombies,
and American Roots Quests

One breed of the "living dead" has become frighteningly popular in America. In recent decades zombies have been stalking our televisions, movie screens, and bookshelves in record numbers. Media franchises such as *The Walking Dead* and *World War Z* have attracted a rabid fan base and spawned a host of imitators.[1] We can now participate in zombie walks and zombie conventions, celebrate World Zombie Day, play a zombie video game, or revisit literary and cinematic classics through parodies such as *Pride and Prejudice and Zombies* or *Shaun of the Dead*. The rising fortunes of the zombie in popular culture raise some questions that we will return to at the end of this chapter: Why zombies? And why now? In other words, what makes zombies the monster of choice for early-twenty-first-century America? And how might the current zombie boom be related to our rising interest in genealogy?

But first we need to consider another sort of "living dead"—our ancestors. As we have already seen, in cultures with systems of ancestor worship, the dead are believed to live on in spirit form. They are thought to have the power to intervene in the affairs of the living, and they are seen as active participants in their families and their communities. They are, as one scholar put it, the "living dead"—physically deceased, but socially alive.[2] Their descendants talk to them, feed them, entertain them, and try to keep them happy so they will continue to protect, guide, and bring good fortune to their living kin. While Americans typically don't believe in such interventionist spirits, we do engage with our dead in some similar ways. We may not routinely address the spirits of the dead as if they are still among the living, offer them their favorite chocolates or cigarettes, stage elaborate festivals to amuse them, or "incarnate" them through possession rituals. But we do occasionally talk to the dead, asking for guidance, and expressing our emotions. We also routinely make floral offerings at gravesites, and stage Masses and other rites of remembrance, including those on Memorial Day, Veterans Day, and All Saints' Day. And, increasingly, we devote significant time, energy, and money to bringing the dead "back to life" through genealogy. Today's genealogists don't simply collect names and dates to plug into pedigree charts. Rather, they craft vivid narratives to reanimate the ancestors, so they might "live on" in our memories. In so doing, genealogists confer a kind of immortality on the ancestors.

For members of the Church of Jesus Christ of Latter-day Saints (LDS), the Mormons, such immortality is not merely metaphorical. Rather, genealogy is part of a more pressing spiritual mission to gather in the spirits of the ancestors to baptize them in the Church and thus ensure their salvation. And this religious mission has made the Church a major player in America's genealogy boom. In this chapter, we will examine certain spiritual dimensions of American genealogy today. Specifically, we will look at the ways amateur and professional genealogists articulate their own spiritual missions and experiences, and how those experiences are both facilitated and shaped by the LDS Church. Finally, we will return to zombies, our less appealing "living dead," to consider how their current popularity relates to our genealogical obsessions.

"THEY'RE HOPING WE DON'T FORGET THEM": THE SACRALIZATION OF AMERICAN GENEALOGY

As discussed in previous chapters, twenty-first-century American genealogy has become increasingly focused on scientific methods and technologies. The digital acquisition, storage, and organization of family history materials is now the norm among American genealogists. And many are using DNA tests to push their family histories further back in time and imbue them with the apparent certainty of biological "facts." This increased reliance on science and technology has not stripped genealogy of its deeper meanings, however. Indeed, genealogy takes on keen spiritual significance for some family historians. Many genealogists describe their spiritual motivations for engaging in family history research, and some report having mystical experiences in the course of their roots quests. So in some sense, even as genealogy is becoming more technologized, it is being sacralized (made sacred) by its associations with the divine, the eternal soul, and the afterlife.

"I love the feeling I get when an ancestor seems to call to me," one genealogist noted (Virginia, 75, Michigan). "I feel so drawn to certain individuals, and find they inhabit my dreams day and night. There is no rational explanation, but it is a real part of why I keep going." Likewise, when asked why she does family history research, Jillian (60, Indiana) answered, "For me the reasons are intangible and hard to explain. I am connected to people I have never met. It's a spiritual journey for me. I feel like I've been chosen to be the steward of the past." She believes that the spirits of the ancestors guide us in ways we are unaware of, and she is following their lead. Judy (55, Maryland) reported being more directly guided by the spirits, specifically by the spirit of her deceased father. After her father died, she worked tirelessly for a year trying to track down one of his patriot ancestors, only to fail repeatedly. In the meantime, she was putting off the completion of one final task her father had set her. Then, the very day she completed that task, she also located the ancestor's birth record. She believes that her father was communicating his displeasure with her from beyond the grave by preventing her from finding a long-lost family record. As soon as she complied with his final wishes, he let her find the record.

Genealogical conference speakers sometimes relate similar stories of interventions by the spirits. One presenter finished her how-to session with a personal story. Many years ago her family had been fractured by conflict. Then one day, going through some old things, she felt her great-grandmother calling her, guiding her toward a box. There she found a long-forgotten family treasure, hand-stitched and passed down through the generations, along with a name scrawled on a piece of paper. That artifact and that name helped to bring the family back together again. "Listen to your ancestors," she directed the audience, adding that they are not in our computers, not in the technologies we use for our research. "But I do believe they are speaking to us," she concluded. The room erupted in applause. And as the lights came up at the end of the presentation, several audience members could be seen wiping tears from their eyes and embracing their companions.

It is not surprising that such a story clearly moved those in attendance. It resonates with the genealogist's deepest desires. There is little doubt that after months or even years of searching for traces of an ancestor, more than a few genealogists have fantasized about the dead reaching out to them to say, "Here I am. This is where I was born. This was where I died. This is what happened." Moreover, as noted in chapter 6, mystical experiences are often featured on roots TV shows. Hollywood stars and noncelebrity guests alike say they feel the presence of the dead, feel that they are guided by the dead, feel that the dead approve of their roots quest. As one featured guest, Maile, put it, "[The ancestors] help us, they guide us, they give us the knowledge they had, and they're hoping we don't forget them." It is difficult to determine how strongly genealogists' perceptions are shaped by television narratives, but widespread pop-cultural representations of encounters with the dead—both in roots TV, and also in a whole host of television shows and movies from *The Sixth Sense*, to *The Ghost Whisperer* and *The Medium*—may make genealogists more open to the possibility of communication with the dead, and give them a lens through which to interpret their experiences. So they interpret a lucky find in the archive or a fortuitous stumble in a graveyard as spiritual intervention.

As anthropologist Bronisław Malinowski observed long ago, we humans are much more likely to engage in forms of magical thinking and magical ritual when the outcomes of the activity we are engaged in are uncertain and to some extent beyond our control. Fishermen, gamblers, and baseball players, for example, have been shown to engage in various kinds of everyday magic—wearing a certain pair of socks, carrying a talisman, avoiding certain foods or actions, for instance—in order to attract good luck and repel bad luck.[3] This goes some way toward helping us understand why some genealogists report magical or mystical experiences, uncanny coincidences, and the sense of being guided by unseen forces during the course of their research. Family history records are often elusive. Over time they get moved, misfiled, misplaced, destroyed. Every trip to an archive, every descent into the records room of a county courthouse, is an unpredictable venture. So finding that long-sought-after record can seem nothing short of miraculous, a gift from benevolent spirits.

In addition to these personal spiritual encounters, some genealogists observe that engaging in family history gives them a profound sense of connection to the ancestors, to the past, and, more generally, to something that is larger than any of us. "There is almost a kind of spirituality in being connected to other generations," one genealogist observed (Richard, 69, Indiana). And this is more important than ever, he explained, because Americans are losing their historical memory and their cultural distinctiveness. Doing genealogy "feels divine," remarked Steven (39, Illinois). It makes him feel connected to others in "ways that outlast your own experiences." Likewise, Madeline (69, Missouri) noted that "genealogy links us to those who have gone before us, giving us a sense of belonging to something unchanging," or perhaps belonging to what Lawrence (56, Tennessee) called "one family that lasts forever."

This yearning to belong to something larger than oneself, something permanent and eternal, is understandable in the context of an increasingly secular society. As we saw in chapter 2, according to many measures, America is becoming a more secular society. While 36 percent of Americans attend religious services at least once per week, another 30 percent rarely or never attend services. And this trend is more pronounced among younger generations, with only 17 percent of those aged eighteen to twenty-nine attending services each week. Sixty percent of those who rarely or never attend services still say they are fairly or absolutely certain of the existence of God, but 52 percent of those who rarely or never attend say they don't believe in heaven, or don't know whether they believe. And of the rapidly increasing segment of the population that is religiously unaffiliated (one-third of all adults under thirty), only 27 percent express a firm belief in "God or a universal spirit."[4] While the United States still has a high level of religiosity compared with other industrialized nations, secularization does tend to increase with modernization and industrialization.[5]

When people lose confidence in the existence of the divine, in the persistence of the soul, in the promise of an afterlife, they may seek alternative forms of transcendence and immortality. As sociologist Zygmunt Bauman points out, the well-heeled have always had the means to transcend time and mortality to some degree, by preserving their names, their deeds, their words, and their likenesses in monuments, portraits, and books.[6] This kind of "immortality" became more accessible to the masses in the twentieth century with the spread of literacy, official records, cameras, and, most recently, social media. And we might add genealogy to this list. As a professional genealogist, Glen (44, Indiana) spends between 150 and 200 hours a month doing family history research. He describes himself as a scientist, carefully analyzing evidence and applying deductive logic until he is able to solve the genealogical problem at hand. Reflecting on the value and the broad appeal of genealogy today, he observes, "It gives us a certain amount of immortality." He may not be able to talk to his ancestors directly, he explains, but he can still get to know them through records and accounts from the period. "Wouldn't it be nice to know someone in the distant future can do the same about you and your life when you are long gone from this Earth?" This is the "immortality" Glen, with his scientific mind, aspires to. Not the immortality of an eternal soul, but the immortality of well-organized records, a carefully documented and constructed narrative, a detailed account of his life that will allow his descendants to know him long after he is "gone from this Earth."

"TURN THE HEART OF THE CHILDREN TO THEIR FATHERS": THE LDS GENEALOGICAL MISSION

For one subset of the genealogical community, family history research is a route to more literal immortality, to salvation, and to an everlasting after-life—members of the Church of Jesus Christ of Latter-day Saints (LDS), also known as the Mormons, or the Saints. "I am a Mormon and I firmly believe that I will meet these ancestors one day. And I'd rather know something about them in this life so the conversation will be a little better in the next," observed Theo (32, Utah). "Knowing my family on the other side wants me to find them keeps me going," says Celia (60, California). "I want to know these people when I get to the other side." Celia and Theo are not alone in their spiritual motivations for engaging in family history research. Soon after the founding of the Church, the faithful were instructed on their divine obligation to compile "a book containing the records of our dead."[7] This genealogical mission has put the Mormon Church at the heart of America's family history boom today.

The Mormon Church was founded in 1830 by Joseph Smith. According to Church teachings, the Angel Moroni visited Smith in the 1820s and led him to golden plates bearing the contents of what would become the Book of Mormon. A core tenet of Mormonism is that Jesus Christ established the Church during his lifetime, but that his followers gradually strayed from its spirit, and Smith was chosen to help restore the true gospel and establish "the only true and living church upon the whole earth." The genealogical mission of the Church can be traced back to an 1840 proclamation by Smith. He enjoined the faithful to posthumously baptize the dead in the Church to ensure their salvation. Even though generations of ancestors had not had the opportunity to hear the true gospel that was revealed to Smith, through a process of proxy baptism—with living members standing in for the dead—their names would be "recorded in heaven."[8] This process was relatively straightforward for the known dead, those remembered by their living kin. But gathering in more distant ancestors required more concerted genealogical efforts.

Smith urged Church members toward genealogy with an Old Testament verse: "Behold, I will send you Elijah the prophet before the coming of the great and dreadful day of the Lord: And he shall turn the heart of the fathers to the children, and the heart of the children to the fathers, lest I come and smite the earth with a curse" (Malachi 4: 5–6). It was through genealogy that Mormons would turn their hearts to their fathers (their ancestors). Family history would unite the living with the dead who came before them. And if Church members failed to "weld a link" with their dead—ideally all the way back to Adam and Eve—the Earth would be cursed. Smith considered this genealogical mission so crucial that shortly before his death he declared, "The greatest responsibility in this world that God has laid upon us is to seek after our dead."[9]

Generations of Church leaders helped to ensure that the divine genealogical mission revealed by Smith moved forward. In 1877, Smith's successor Brigham Young preached that the unbaptized dead were "prisoners," and that Mormons had a sacred duty to set them free. To this end, Church members embarked upon genealogical "missions"—journeys to far-flung locations within the United States and abroad to gather genealogical data—beginning in the 1880s. And in 1894, Church president Wilford Woodruff proclaimed,

> We want the Latter-day Saints from this time to trace their genealogies as far as they can and to be sealed to their fathers and mothers. Have children sealed to their parents, and run this chain through as far as you can get it. . . . This is the will of the Lord to his people.[10]

In particular, he urged followers to engage in more systematic and more thorough genealogical research. Woodruff's directive prompted the establishment of the Genealogical Society of Utah, also in 1894. The society's mission was to facilitate sound genealogical research by gathering and maintaining genealogical records, to educate LDS members on genealogical research methods, and to provide the Church with the names of individuals who could be posthumously baptized. Gradually the society built up its library collections, offered research assistance and clerical support for patrons, developed standardized genealogical forms and instruction manuals, published regular newspaper columns and newsletters, and established contact with a network of genealogists within the United States and abroad to help gather in ancestors from distant locations.[11]

In 1912 Nephi Anderson, a librarian and editor for the Genealogical Society of Utah, articulated his vision for the society:

> I see the records of the dead and their histories gathered from every nation under heaven to one great central library in Zion—the largest and best equipped for its particular work in the world. Branch libraries may be established in the nations, but in Zion will be the record of last resort and final authority. Trained genealogists will find constant work in all nations having unpublished records, searching among the archives for families and family connections. Then, as temples multiply, and the

work enlarges to its ultimate proportions, this Society, or some organization growing out of this Society, will have in its care some elaborate, but perfect system of exact registration and checking, so that the work in the temples may be conducted without confusion or duplication. And so throughout the years, reaching into the Millennium of peace, this work of salvation will go on, until every worthy soul that can be found from earthly records will have been searched out and officiated for; and then the unseen world will come to our aid, the broken links will be joined, the tangled threads will be placed in order, and the purposes of God in placing salvation within the reach of all will have been consummated.[12]

Anderson's vision has proven remarkably prescient. The LDS Church has been at the forefront of efforts to copy, digitize, index, centralize, and make accessible genealogical records from around the world. Its ambitious program of microfilming civil and religious records was begun in 1938, and eventually necessitated the building of the massive Granite Mountain Records Vault in Utah, with its sixty-five thousand square feet of temperature- and humidity-controlled storage space.[13] The Genealogical Society of Utah, under its new name FamilySearch, claims to be "the largest genealogy organization in the world," with databases including more than five and a half billion records, a network of almost five thousand research centers stretched across the globe, and access to materials from some ten thousand archives in more than one hundred countries.[14] FamilySearch digitally scans some 80 million new records each year, and is currently digitizing 2.4 million rolls of microfilm.[15] And access to this massive collection of family history records is free and open to all, Mormons and non-Mormons alike.

The centerpiece of the LDS genealogical mission is the Family History library in Salt Lake City, which proclaims itself "the world's largest genealogical library," with more than six hundred thousand books, serials, and maps and billions of digital and microfilm records available to patrons. The library hosts more than seven hundred thousand visitors annually, and serves an estimated forty-five million patrons each year, including online visitors and visitors to its network of family history research centers around the world.[16] Most of these family history researchers will save the information they find in a digital file format created by LDS computer programmers. Indeed, the GEDCOM (Genealogical Data Communications) is now the standard file format used by genealogists throughout the United States to store, organize, and exchange genealogical data.[17] Even genealogical organizations and genealogical software developers unaffiliated with the Mormon Church have adopted the GEDCOM as the industry standard.

While the Family History Library, FamilySearch, and the Family History Department of the Church are all nonprofit entities, they are increasingly partnering with commercial enterprises such as Ancestry.com, MyHeritage .com, and FindMyPast.com to make LDS family history resources more accessible to eager consumers.[18] At the same time, *The Generations Project*, an LDS roots television series, reinforces the importance of family history research for personal enrichment and identity, for psychological healing, for family unity, and for spiritual connection between the living and the dead.

In short, with its divine mandate to engage in genealogical research, the Mormon Church has helped to shape the American genealogical landscape today. Its vast store of records, its infrastructure, its technological innovations and products, and its institutional linkages make it a leader in the field of family history research. And it devotes substantial resources to publicizing the ways genealogy can enrich the lives of Mormons and non-Mormons alike.

Behind the LDS Genealogical Mission

The Mormon genealogical mission has been so assertively articulated and pursued that it is worth pausing for a moment to consider the factors that have shaped this mission over time. The first of these is the LDS doctrine of *progressive revelation*; that is, the belief that God continues to reveal His will to His chosen servants. This has led to the gradual adoption of new practices and beliefs among Mormons, as Church leaders convey new revelations. One such revelation was reported by Joseph Smith in 1840 when he enjoined his followers to baptize their dead. Setting aside the question of whether this commandment came from God or simply from Smith himself, the effect was the same. In an era of high infant and child mortality, grieving parents were no doubt comforted by the notion that their children would live on in heaven, and that families would be reunited one day in the realm of the spirits. So the practice of posthumous baptism proved very popular in this context, and established the foundations for what would become concerted efforts to identify and baptize all the dead in one's family (and indeed, in the whole human family) into the true Church.[19]

Another revelation conveyed by Smith during this period had a profound effect on Mormon identity and ways of life for generations to come—the revelation endorsing "plural marriage" (specifically, polygyny).[20] Following Smith's directive, a long line of Church leaders encouraged men to fulfill their spiritual duties by taking multiple wives. This system would, leaders claimed, safeguard morality, reduce licentious behavior and prostitution, liberate women from excessive sexual and reproductive labor, and ultimately strengthen and expand the Mormon stock.[21] The unintended side effect of polygyny, however, was widespread condemnation of the practice by non-Mormons. In the 1880s the US government began cracking down on what was seen by outsiders as an immoral and highly objectionable system. Faced with the impending seizure of Church assets, and tempted by the promise of statehood for Utah if the Mormons did away with their "peculiar practice," Church president Wilford Woodruff presented a new revelation to the faithful in 1890. Polygyny was no longer God's command-ment, and the Church would no longer sanction the practice.[22]

It was shortly after the Church officially disendorsed plural marriage that President Woodruff exhorted the faithful to redouble their genealogical efforts. The energy that had once been committed to enlarging and perfect-ing the Mormon community through plural marriage was now shifted to enlarging and perfecting the community through gathering in the dead and posthumously baptizing them in the faith.[23] Additionally, the experience of being a persecuted, marginalized, and demonized community no doubt fu-eled Mormon desires to document their lineages, write themselves into the history of the republic, and establish their legitimacy in the eyes of the nation.

There was another pressing reason to step up LDS genealogical efforts. Previous generations of researchers had somewhat haphazardly drawn up their lineages and submitted names of the dead for baptism and other rituals (such as spiritually "sealing" the dead into eternal families). Not only did this lead to many factual errors in recording names and family relationships, but it often led to the same dead individual being baptized many times, and perhaps being mistakenly sealed into different lineages. Woodruff's call for more systematic and more narrowly focused research on one's direct family line, along with more centralized recordkeeping, would reduce, and ideally eliminate, errors and duplication of temple rituals. In addition, Woodruff's revelation helped to address another nagging complexity of LDS genealogy. That is, for years many Mormon families had chosen to be "adopted" into the lineages of high-ranking Church leaders, with the belief that joining a "priestly" lineage would confer spiritual benefits on their families. This had led to confusion when charting actual lineages. President Woodruff, an avid genealogist himself, found this problematic. When he directed the faithful to practice more systematic research, he aimed to put the "tangled threads" of family history back in their rightful order.[24]

As the Church expanded its reach in the twentieth century, more changes to LDS genealogy were in store. Specifically, one aspect of LDS lineage reckoning became increasingly problematic in the post–civil rights era, and that was its racialist underpinnings. According to Joseph Smith and other early Church leaders, Mormons were the descendants of one of the twelve tribes of Israel, the highest, most divinely favored of the tribes. The other tribes could be ranked from highest (including modern Jews and Native Americans) to the lowest, people of African descent, whose dark skin was seen as a visible marker of the Curse of Ham. God's supposed punishment of the descendants of Noah's disgraced son Ham was cited by Church leaders to justify excluding people of African descent from full participation in the Church. While this position certainly accorded with widespread racist views in nineteenth-century America and with eugenicist thinking in the early twentieth century, it grew increasingly untenable. First, the Holocaust exposed the genocidal potential of racialist hierarchies. Second, the civil rights movement substantially advanced the principle of racial equality. And third, the Mormon Church was expanding more rapidly in Africa, Latin America, and the Pacific Islands than in predominantly white nations around the globe. All of these developments necessitated changes in LDS lineage thinking. Gradually references to the literal tribes of Israel and to the pure "believing blood" of Mormons faded from view, and in 1978 a new revelation declared that any man, regardless of descent, was eligible for Mormon "priesthood." Church president Howard W. Hunter further solidified the Church position when he stated in the 1990s that despite differences of race and nationality, "we are all of one blood"; we are all the children of God.[25]

In 1999, the LDS launched its FamilySearch.org website, attracting an estimated one hundred million hits in a single day. "Looking at this from the standpoint of a person of faith, our belief is that God placed computer technology on Earth for a good purpose, and this is a good purpose," an LDS official commented.[26] The striking success and continued expansion of FamilySearch has brought the Mormon family history mission to mainstream America and garnered positive publicity for the once maligned Church. FamilySearch website materials and displays at the Family History Library in Salt Lake City use careful language and imagery to emphasize noncontroversial values and goals—the desire to understand where we come from, the universal importance of family, and the interrelatedness of diverse branches of humanity. Not surprisingly, references to more controversial beliefs and practices (such as the proxy baptism of non-Mormons, or historical polygyny and racialist hierarchies) are conspicuously absent from these materials.

Imagining "The Great Heavenly Family of God"

On a bone-chilling January morning, I stood waiting in a crowd of hearty souls who were braving the 2-degree Fahrenheit weather to be at the Family History Library in Salt Lake City when it opened. With delightful promptness the doors were unlocked as the clock struck eight, and the excited (though half-frozen) group hustled inside. Although the signs on the building's exterior had featured an all-white cast of characters beaming under slogans such as "Find yourself in family history" or "Share, discover, learn," the images inside told a different story. All of the smiling faces on the "Welcome" sign in the library's first floor were phenotypically non-white—people of African, Asian, and indigenous origins. The orientation area included colorful panels organized by region—North America, Latin America, Europe, the British Isles, Asia, the Pacific Islands, and Africa—each displaying images of happy families, iconic landmarks, and cultural artifacts. "We are eager to help you discover your heritage among the families of the world," a sign informed patrons.

Another display offered reasons for engaging in family history research. Smiling, attractive headshots and historical photographs were arranged under keywords such as "Connection" or "Mystery." And below the photographs, unnamed patrons provided brief testimonials about their motivations for tracing their family roots.

> Connection: "I felt a strong connection with my family and it has helped me bring peace to my life."
>
> Mystery: "I love a good mystery. . . . I discovered a few family secrets with fascinating characters."
>
> Heritage: "Each time I discover something new about my family, I gain a better understanding of where I came from and who I am."
>
> History: "As I discover more about my family, I feel a strong sense of their personal historical significance."
>
> Perspective: "[I've] developed a better understanding of who I am and what makes me this way."
>
> Dreams: "Learning [about my ancestor] made me feel good about myself, like I was carrying on his dream. I felt a link, a really personal link. I felt like I knew him."

The panels are carefully balanced by gender and ethnicity. Three men and three women; three phenotypically white folks and three people of color. The themes of inclusiveness and the universal appeal of family history are repeated throughout the library's displays.

One display in the library engages specifically with the Mormon genealogical mission. Under the caption "Why Members of the Church of Jesus Christ of Latter-day Saints Care about Family History," we see a stained-glass image of Elijah along with his injunction to turn the hearts of the children to their fathers. We see sepia photographs of historic Mormon temples and of Church president (and genealogist) Wilford Woodruff, and images of beatific families from around the world, some seemingly bathed in heavenly light. "Members of the Church of Jesus Christ of Latter-day Saints believe that Jesus Christ, families, temples, and family history are interconnected," the display explains. "One family at a time, all can eventually be brought together into the great heavenly family of God."

This message is further emphasized in heroic paintings by Theodore S. Gorka (*Genealogy*) and Judith Mehr (*The Eternal Family through Christ*). Both show contemporary Mormons with legions of their ancestors behind them, some in historical costumes—pilgrims, nobles, shepherds, scholars—some in heavenly robes. "All of the ancestors want their descendants to remember them," a placard accompanying Gorka's painting explains. And yet, in contrast to the careful ethnic and racial inclusiveness of the library's other displays, these paintings imagine a decidedly Caucasian "eternal family." All but four of the approximately eighty-seven people portrayed in the paintings are white. When white patrons are tracing their family histories, the paintings seem to suggest, they are unlikely to find any nonwhite ancestors.

So what can we learn from such materials? More than seven hundred thousand visitors walk through the doors of the Family History Library each year, and its displays serve as the public face of LDS genealogy. They offer noncontroversial goals and values of family history research—deepening family connections, achieving a sense of peace and self-knowledge, fulfilling dreams, and solving fascinating mysteries. They are also decidedly inclusive in terms of race, ethnicity, and national origin. Indeed, most displays appear to overrepresent people of color relative to the global LDS community. According to Church statistics, roughly 61 percent of Mormons reside in North America and Europe (areas with predominantly white populations), with only 39 percent being drawn from South America, Asia, Oceania and the Pacific, or Africa (areas with predominantly nonwhite populations).

While the correspondence between geographic region and race/ethnicity is far from perfect, this suggests that the majority of Mormons are white. In the United States, for instance, 86 percent of Mormons are white, and 93 percent are US-born.[27] Yet in Family History Library displays, only 47 percent of all the people pictured were phenotypically white. More than half were people of color. The underlying message is not difficult to decipher: Mormonism is a global religion, an inclusive and welcoming community which embraces universally accepted values and ideals. Mormonism is mainstream. The LDS genealogical mission has arguably helped to advance the mainstreaming of a once stigmatized religion.

While the content of Family History Library displays provides glimpses into the Church's spiritual and public relations goals, we must also consider what the displays leave out. Amid the celebratory depictions of racial and ethnic diversity, there is (not surprisingly) no hint of the notions of pure "blood" and divinely ranked lineages that were once used to bar certain peoples of color from full participation in the Church. Nor is there any reference to the controversies that have dogged the Church in recent decades with revelations that Church members were posthumously baptizing Holocaust victims (including Anne Frank and the parents of Simon Wiesenthal) and revered figures such as Mahatma Gandhi without the knowledge or consent of their living kin. Although the Church prohibited such baptisms in 1991, LDS "whistleblowers" suggest that the practice continues today.[28]

The displays also strongly emphasize traditional heterosexual marriage and nuclear families that are blessed with many children. Images of brides and grooms, and couples surrounded by cherubic children, feature prominently in the displays. Absent are any references to same-sex couples or to Church policies on homosexuality. In recent years the Church has softened its condemnation of homosexuality by reaching out to LGBT Mormons through its "Mormon and Gay" website, and by declaring that same-sex attraction is not sinful—only acting on that attraction is sinful. Church policy shifted in 2016, however, with a declaration that those living in same-sex relationships were apostates and subject to excommunication, and any children of same-sex couples would be denied religious rites until they turned eighteen, rejected homosexuality, and separated themselves from their parents.[29] Such attitudes toward LGBT individuals are reflected in LDS genealogical practice. The LDS-created GEDCOM file format for storing genealogical data does not allow users to easily record same-sex partnerships or other intimate relationships outside of traditional homosexual unions. It also does not easily accommodate some non-Western forms of kinship and family formation, including systems of matrilineal descent (descent through only the mother's lineage) or polyandry (a system in which one woman is married to several husbands). One scholar has argued that forcing family trees into a standardized format to suit LDS religious notions is problematic for families that do not fit neatly into that mold. "Just as it is uncivilized to break open ancient tombs and to disturb the relics of the occupants, so it is disrespectful, and ultimately truth-destroying, to rearrange the lineaments of the families of the dead to suit an ideological template."[30]

ZOMBIES AND ROOTS QUESTS:
A SIGN OF THE TIMES?

I opened this chapter with zombies and raised the possibility that there may be links between our present fascination with zombies and our concurrent preoccupation with tracing our roots. In order to explore some of these links, we must first consider why zombies have become the pop-cultural monster of choice in early-twenty-first-century America. As one psychologist has observed,

> When [the] psyche brings forth monsters, it is always wise to take a close look. When the active imagination of global culture fixates on a particular kind of monster, there's a veritable treasure trove of hidden meaning and valuable psychological information to be unearthed.[31]

In other words, the monsters that haunt our imaginations, our folktales, our literature, our television sets and movie screens, tell us something about our deepest fears and desires. With zombie-themed movies and TV shows, books, video games, music, events, and merchandise (zombie coffee mug, anyone?), the living dead have become a multibillion-dollar industry.[32] So why zombies? And why now?

Scholars have suggested that the ascendance of zombies in the twenty-first century is a reflection of growing anxieties over social changes and perceived threats—terrorism, financial collapse, social breakdown, globalization, immigration, rapacious capitalism, mindless consumerism, the degradation of the environment, global pandemics, overdependence on technology, inept government institutions, and even "silent killers" such as cancer and heart disease.[33] Zombies are apt "stand-ins" for such diverse perils.[34] Like the terrorist of fevered nightmares, zombies strike when you least expect them, bent upon destruction, immune to reason, and utterly lacking any compassion or humane impulses. They are mindless killing machines. Like feared foreign Others, they arrive in hordes, overwhelming society, preying on innocents, leading to a breakdown of the social order. Like pandemics and financial meltdowns, zombies spread with stunning rapidity.[35] They are forces beyond our control, striking indiscriminately and close to home. No one is immune from their predation, except perhaps corrupt elites who can seal themselves into luxury bunkers. Like illnesses such as cancer and heart disease, they can lurk undetected among us and steal our loved ones away without warning. Moreover, the arrival of zombies reveals the fragility and inadequacy of our social ecosystem. Our elected leaders and paid defenders—soldiers and police officers—are powerless against legions of the undead. Roads and bridges quickly become clogged with rubble, stores are looted and burned, water and electricity and telecommunications networks cease to function, and only the hardiest (and most well-armed) survivalists can manage to eke out a precarious existence amid such ruin and danger. Authors deploy zombies as remarkably flexible metaphors for whatever they find troubling—phenomena as diverse as class and racial inequality, debates over abortion and global warming, the outsourcing of jobs to low-wage countries, political corruption, or our obsession with youthfulness, beauty, and plastic surgery.[36]

In addition to reflecting such specific twenty-first-century anxieties, zombies also capture age-old existential anxieties over our mortality and what it means to be human. After all, zombies are both us and not us. They are both living and dead. They are both the loved ones who share our homes and the rapacious cannibals who stalk us. Their bodies are human in appearance—as gruesome as that appearance may be—but they generally lack those qualities that define our humanity: higher-order thought, language, and sentiment. They are, in a sense, humanity at its worst—ravenous, selfish, unthinking, unfeeling, and brutal.

Likewise, as zombie bodies decompose before our eyes, they are reminders that our own bodies are destined to disintegrate under the weight of time. They are reminders of our own mortality. While this is surely intended to be unsettling to us—particularly the extravagant gore that is a staple of zombie stories—it is also strangely comforting in that it suggests the possibility of existence after death. In an era when fewer Americans have confidence in an afterlife, zombies may be a reflection of our wishful thinking, our hope that death is not the ultimate end. At the same time, the debased and repulsive state of zombies serves as a (dis)comforting reminder that there are, indeed, fates worse than death.

So how is the fascination with zombies related to the fascination with genealogy in twenty-first-century America? Of course, as argued above, both focus on the "living dead," whether in the form of shambling monsters or ancestors "reanimated" through narratives and documentation. But more significantly, both fascinations may be seen as a reflection of our anxieties and desires—anxieties about our own mortality, and about the inevitable loss of our loved ones. Anxieties about social changes that are altering the world as we know it and confronting us with new threats—to our jobs, our health, our ways of life. Anxieties about the existence of the divine, the eternal soul, and the afterlife. And anxieties about a "fate worse than death."

In zombie stories, the fate worse than death is, of course, becoming a zombie, because zombification results in the ultimate horror—a loss of self and free will. One's body and mind are taken over. One's memories are obliterated; even the deepest human bonds between lovers, friends, and family members mean nothing to the zombie's voracious appetite for human flesh.[37] And while one's body lives on in some form, it also rots and oozes and reeks of decay, becoming that which we fear most—death. In genealogy, by contrast, the fate worse than death is being forgotten. Many genealogists talk about rescuing ancestors from obscurity, unearthing their names and the details of their lives, and putting "flesh and bone" on their forebears (Calvin, 66, Florida). And even as they resuscitate memories of the dead, genealogists are ensuring their own legacy, so future generations will remember them when they are "long gone from this Earth" (Glen, 44, Indiana). For LDS genealogists, in particular, genealogy and the sacred rites performed for the ancestors not only resuscitate memories of the dead, but help to ensure their salvation and their place in heaven. Genealogy is thus a rescue mission for lost souls.

For LDS and non-LDS researchers alike, genealogy in twenty-first-century America is often imbued with spiritual meanings. Whether motivated by a desire to save the dead through posthumous baptism, a desire to connect with and memorialize one's ancestors, a desire to better understand ourselves and ensure that others will keep our names and experiences "alive" long after we die, genealogists today engage with some of the biggest and most enduring questions of human existence. Who are we? Why are we here? What happens when we die? As increasing numbers of Americans step away from organized religions, we look elsewhere for insights into such existential questions. And as scholars increasingly assert that reality and morality are socially constructed and relative, we seek greater clarity and greater certainty on these enduring questions. Literature and popular culture—including zombie narratives—give us one way to explore the nature of life and death, the nature of human connections, and the consequences of our actions, both during our lifetimes and beyond. Genealogy offers another vantage point on these enduring and discomfiting questions.

8

IMAGINED HOMES

Roots Tourism and the Quest for Self

All that is gold does not glitter,
Not all those who wander are lost;
The old that is strong does not wither,
Deep roots are not reached by the frost.[1]

This verse appears in a somewhat cryptic letter from the wizard Gandalf to the Hobbit Frodo Baggins in the first volume of J. R. R. Tolkien's epic *The Lord of the Rings* series. Frodo gradually discovers the meaning of the verse during the course of his long and treacherous quest. The "gold" that does not glitter seems to be Aragorn, a rugged Ranger of the North who turns out to play a crucial role in saving Middle-earth and restoring one of its ancient kingdoms. The "old" that does not wither is Aragorn's noble lineage, the deep roots of which have withstood the ravages of time and war. And those who wander but are not lost may include not only the peripatetic Rangers, but also Frodo Baggins himself as he embarks on a journey into the realm of evil, armed with little more than a pure heart. Frodo's quest—like so many great quests of literature and myth—is not only a journey across space and time, but a journey into the self. In the course of his journey, the timid Hobbit discovers surprising reserves of courage and fortitude, and in the process he strengthens long-standing bonds of friendship and kinship, and forges new and deeply meaningful relationships.

The Hobbits, it should be noted, are keen genealogists, as anyone who has ever read the rather exhaustive accounts of the lineages of the Bagginses and the Boffins, the Tooks and the Brandybucks, the Grubbs and Chubbs and Burrowses and Hornblowers, the Bolgers, the Bracegirdles, the Goodbodies, and the Brockhouses of the books will attest. And Frodo Baggins's dramatic journey offers an apt point of departure for a discussion of

139

genealogical tourism. After all, twenty-first-century genealogists are, for the most part, looking for the "gold that does not glitter," the unsung ancestors whose names and lives have been forgotten. They are looking for the roots that do not wither. The deeper the roots, the stronger the tree. And while they may wander far and wide, through archives and cemeteries, through courthouse basements and Old World villages, they are not lost. Rather, they are on a quest, indefatigably seeking their ancestors, forging new links with far-flung kin, and gaining new insights into who they are. They are on a quest for self.

Roots tourism—also sometimes called *legacy tourism* or *diaspora tourism*—is a bourgeoning industry, particularly in Old World locations from which large numbers of people migrated (or were taken against their will) to New World destinations.[2] For US tourists, some of the most popular overseas roots destinations include Ireland and the United Kingdom, Germany, Italy, Eastern Europe, Scandinavia, and West Africa. And the revenue from roots tourism can be considerable. Overseas tourism to Ireland, for example, generates in excess of 4 percent of the nation's GDP (€5.3 billion in 2016), and employs almost 300,000 people out of a population of 4.8 million. It is estimated that roughly 1 million of these overseas tourists each year come, in part, to investigate their roots, and that number is steadily growing. Visitors from North America (mostly the United States and Canada) increased by almost 22 percent in 2016. And US visitors to the genealogical section of the National Library of Ireland now routinely outnumber visitors from any other nation—including Ireland itself.[3]

Likewise, the West African nation of Ghana hosts more than one million international tourists each year, the largest number coming from the United States. In excess of seven hundred thousand people are employed in tourism-related jobs, out of a national population of twenty-eight million. And foreign tourist dollars account for roughly 8 percent of the nation's foreign currency earnings.[4] Among the primary target markets for Ghanaian tourist providers are wealthy African Americans who are searching for their ancestral roots. For, while these tourists may not be able to document Ghanaian ancestry, many enslaved Africans passed through Ghana's slave ports on their forced journey to the Americas. A growing number of sites, spectacles, and activities now cater to roots tourists' desires to better understand their ancestors' experiences, to connect with "Mother Africa," and to define themselves in relation to a past that predates the traumas of slavery.

In this chapter, we will examine the phenomenon of roots tourism. Specifically, we will ask what motivates genealogists to engage in such roots quests. We will see how roots tourism experiences are structured by tourism providers in two particular contexts, Ireland and Ghana. Finally, in the concluding chapter, we will consider how touristic roots quests are shaped by key features of what we might call our age of rootlessness—globalization and its challenges to our conceptions of time and space; the saturation of the mass media and virtual realities; increasing secularization; new genetic and technological advances; and the commodification of identities.

"UNBELIEVABLE FEELINGS!!"

Roots tourism often entails a considerable investment of time and money. In order to make the most of an overseas roots trip, for instance, genealogists need to do extensive research on Old World lineages before they even step on a plane. Indeed, some tour companies promote add-on packages that offer consultations with professional genealogists who will help roots tourists identify ancestral villages, churches, homes, and even living relatives. Tours are often fully or partially customized to travelers' lineages, and typically cost several thousand dollars per person. So why do genealogists embark on such expensive and time-consuming journeys?

When asked about their roots travels, most genealogists reported quite similar motivations: They wanted to walk where their ancestors walked, see what their ancestors saw, feel what their ancestors felt.

> We walked the streets where my grandmother had walked 140 or so years before and saw some of the sights she had seen growing up. Unbelievable feelings!! . . . I went to the hometown of my great-grandfather, who immigrated with his parents and siblings to New York City. . . . The town historian took me around the area towns, churches, and again, I was able to walk where they walked. Again those indescribable feelings. (Luanne, 80, Texas)

> My most exciting trip was to Ireland where I was able to look at the original parish records where my ancestors were married in 1831 and where my immigrant great-great-grandmother was baptized several years later. To walk around the quiet and beautiful countryside where she walked as a child and to see what they and other emigrants had to leave behind to come to the squalid big cities of America gave me a whole new outlook on life. (Charlotte, 70, Illinois)

> I was able to see the actual buildings and farms my [ancestral] families lived in. . . . Though no graves survived that I could find, understanding the culture a bit and the actual topography where they resided helped me feel quite connected to them. (Diane, 66, Minnesota)

A highlight of my trip was . . . handling documents from 226 years ago. I already had the digital copies of the documents from FamilySearch but being able to pick up a note or deed signed by my fifth-great-grandfather or -grandmother gave me a feeling of physical connection I will never forget. (Virginia, 75, Michigan)

This desire to stand where your ancestors stood, to touch the stones of their houses, to feel the same dirt beneath your feet, reveals what one historian has called the "psychogeographic presumption"—the notion that being in a place where something happened or where someone once stood gives us a special kind of connection to those events or that person. It gives us an understanding beyond the documents, beyond the facts. It gives us a physical and emotional connection to those people and events, and to history more generally.[5] This allows us to personalize history, and to engage with history at a "gut" level. Indeed, the "aura" of authenticity that such Old World locations exude, provokes in many roots tourists an almost mystical sense of connection with their ancestors.[6]

This same sense of direct and personal connection to the past is a common part of roots television programming, in which guests "follow in the footsteps" of their forebears. Lisa Kudrow visits her grandmother's village in Eastern Europe. "This is the view that she saw," Kudrow says. "This is what I pictured. This is exactly what I pictured. It's unbelievable." Later, when she finds the site where Nazis massacred most of the villagers, she weeps. "Those poor parents with their children," she says, wiping tears away. "That's what is so hard. I get so angry when I start thinking about the children." Rita Wilson and Lionel Richie both remark on how "moving" it is to tread the same ground as their forebears. And Rosie O'Donnell visits an Irish workhouse similar to the one in which her destitute Famine-era ancestors lived. Her emotional reaction to the cold, dark rooms is powerful. "I'm mildly scared," she admits. "I don't know if I necessarily believe in ghosts, but I can definitely tell you, you can feel something. . . . It's sad. Overwhelmingly sad. Like I literally have a stomachache." The physical proximity to such suffering helps her to better understand her ancestors and come to terms with tragedies in her own life. She explains that now she knows why Irish people often do not show their emotions—because they had to "shut down" emotionally to survive these horrors. And she now knows that she can survive the devastating losses she suffered as a child, just as her brave ancestors survived their trials.

Roots travelers (both on television and in real life) report feeling "transported" by their genealogical travel—not only across distance, but across time. "Historical research is a time-travel experience for me," notes

Virginia (75, Michigan). In fact, the images of her ancestors' world were so vivid in her mind that when she visited their hometown she felt quite shocked to find a modern city rather than "log cabins and blockhouses and sheep grazing." Emily, a guest on BYU-TV's *The Generations Project,* is likewise transported by learning about her ancestor's world—filled with wagons, horses, sweat, cigars, and buffalo blankets. "That does it!" Emily exclaims. "I can totally smell him!"

Some genealogists are further motivated by the promise of discovering previously unknown living relatives. Barbara (63, Massachusetts) recounts her journey to Great Britain to trace her father's lineage. There she visited a family farm that is still in operation, and met distant relatives who were equally enthusiastic about genealogy. She remains in contact with these new "cousins," and some of them have now visited her in the United States. She looks forward to future journeys elsewhere in the world to trace other family lines. Likewise, Deidre (58, Texas) travels both within the United States and internationally in search of her roots. She makes a point of eating the foods her ancestors would have eaten or staying near the places they lived and trying to imagine what it was like for them. She always tries to find living relatives who share a "common past" with her, because her own mother grew up in an orphanage and never knew what it was like to have those family connections. Finding your family's past, she observes, is "somehow reassuring."

Some genealogists, however, take a more leisurely approach to their roots travel. They try to work genealogical investigations into many of the trips they take, whether for business or for pleasure. They spend a few hours in a library, courthouse, or cemetery between work or family obligations. Sometimes this kind of casual research pays off with an unexpected find, but often the pleasure is in the search and in the destination itself. Serena (50, New York) notes that she and her mother took some time out during their trip to Italy to visit Sicily, where some of their ancestors had lived. She was hoping to find out "why they came over, where they lived, and who was still in Palermo. At the time we went we were hoping to see the house the family lived in. [But] no luck. . . . What we got out of the time was the pleasure of walking the same streets as my great-grandparents and the experience of what to do the next time." Clearly for some genealogists, roots travel is mainly a pleasurable extension of their hobby. Genealogy gives them an "excuse" to travel (Calvin, 66, Florida), and a sense of purpose and structure in their travels. Other travelers wander the streets shopping, eating, and taking in the sights, while genealogists are off sleuthing and digging up hidden stories to pass on through the generations.

No matter what the genealogist's stated motivations for embarking on such journeys, roots tourism can be usefully conceptualized as a pilgrimage of sorts. Consider the essential features of religious pilgrimages. According to Turner and Turner's classic formulation, pilgrimage begins with a separation from the Familiar (from home, from everyday routines, from one's usual roles and obligations). It entails a journey to a Far Place. Often the strains of this journey (whether physical, emotional, or even bureaucratic or fiscal strains) establish its significance by elevating it above the mundane. Once the pilgrimage site is reached, pilgrims seek "a direct experience with the sacred" that will transform them in some way. And finally, the pilgrim returns (transformed) to the Familiar and is reintegrated into the routines of everyday living.

Two crucial features of pilgrimage are its suspension of everyday ways of life, and its goal of transformation. Specifically, as pilgrims we move from our ordinary time and place to a site that, in some ways, transcends time and space. Pilgrims to Lourdes, for instance, are not just visiting a town in France in the present day. They are stepping out of time to the evening in 1858 when the Virgin Mary is said to have appeared to a peasant girl, and they are stepping into the realm of the sacred. And the ultimate goal of the pilgrimage is personal transformation—whether in the form of physical healing (the goal of many of the five million pilgrims who travel each year to Lourdes), spiritual purification, the achievement of "wholeness in oneself," or the strengthening of connections to the divine or to a larger community of faith, thought, or identity (what Turner and Turner call *communitas*).[7]

Roots tourists follow this same trajectory. They leave home, separating themselves from familiar routines and spaces. They undertake a journey to a "far place," often an expensive and time-consuming journey. At ancestral sites, they seek not only further knowledge about the ancestors (names, dates, and locations, for instance), but also an emotional and even a physical connection with them. They are profoundly moved by walking the same paths and breathing the same air as their ancestors (even though that dirt and air have certainly changed over hundreds of years). They hope not only to strengthen connections with their ancestors, but also to forge new links with undiscovered kin, and thus to situate themselves within kinship networks that transcend space and time. And, ultimately, they hope to return home with a greater self-knowledge.

As a number of scholars have demonstrated, such "homecoming" pilgrimages are particularly popular with citizens of settler societies such as the United States, Canada, and Australia. Most of the residents of such societies have ancestral roots in other nations, and generations of assimilation, mobility, and marriage across older ethnic and social lines have left many without a clear sense of ancestral rootedness. In visiting the "homeland" (a complex term given that many tourists have never set foot in these lands before), many roots tourists are seeking an "authentic" experience. They may imagine societies like living museums, largely untouched by modernity, peopled by rustic folk living in quaint cottages. While the locals with their cell phones, satellite TV, and Starbucks coffee might not share the same nostalgic vision of their own lives, to roots tourists the seeming antiquity of the homeland is ancestral heritage made tangible, and the homeland offers deep historical anchors that simply are not in evidence in most comparatively young settler societies.[8]

Consider the case of roots tourists to Scotland. Paul Basu's research following groups of Scottish "homeland" tourists found that they were keenly interested in "clanship."[9] Tourists—mainly from overseas—linked their surnames to particular territories, stories, and symbols (such as tartans), and reported a strong sense of connection with both their ancestral lands and their newfound clan members. While the tourists' profound feelings of personal affirmation and kinship are not in doubt, Basu points out that many clan symbols, territories, and origin myths were only elaborated relatively recently (starting in the nineteenth century), and that, in any case, clan membership was not an index of one's literal lineage. Indeed, he points out that clan membership is often taken much more seriously by North Americans than it is by Scots themselves, who tend to find the visitors' fascination with clan rather curious. He argues that roots tourists of Scottish descent use the "romantic ideology of Highland clanship" to "re-root" their identities in a perceived ancestral homeland, to achieve the kind of "unproblematic territorial belonging" that is not possible for most people in settler societies. Imaginatively pegging one's identity to a particular "homeland" is, after all, simpler than engaging with the more complex identities most of us have in multiethnic societies.[10]

IRISH GATHERINGS AND AFRICAN HOMECOMINGS

Roots tourists' expectations and experiences are shaped by a wide variety of factors, including promotions from tourism providers and state tourism agencies, and features of the tourist sites themselves. After all, Old World sites cannot speak for themselves; they must be interpreted for (and by) the visitor—for instance, through signage, monuments, records, or the narratives of a local guide. All such interpretations direct the tourist's gaze toward certain features, events, and people, and, inevitably, away from others.[11] So even in Old World locations the past isn't simply a feature that can be touched or seen; rather, the past is actively constructed both by and for roots tourists.

Let's consider some of the ways roots quests are structured in two different settings—Ireland and Ghana.

Ireland: Gathering Roots Tourists

Irish roots tourism promotions typically cater to the kinds of motivations detailed above—traveling back through time, treading ancestral grounds, and feeling an authentic connection to those who came before. "Walk in the footsteps of your ancestors," one company directs us. "Experience where they lived and how they lived." Another provider tells us to "walk the paths they once walked, visit the old homestead, chat with the locals; do all of the things that you cannot do at a computer screen and bring back the emotional element, so often lacking in today's family research." One tour company promises that "you will truly experience Ireland, your ancestors' homeland." And another informs us that "in 95 percent of cases [we can] identify the exact home where your family lived as far back as early 1800s in Ireland."[12]

Despite such claims, Irish genealogical research is, in fact, notoriously difficult—complicated by a general dearth of civil records before the twentieth century, the tragic loss of many records in the 1922 Public Record Office fire, and a convoluted system of bureaucratic districts—including counties, townlands, parishes, baronies, unions, dioceses, and provinces, with often overlapping and shifting boundaries. But tourists who are unable to document their Irish roots need not go home empty-handed. For vendors across the nation sell a vast array of surname-themed souvenirs, from key chains, mugs, and T-shirts to faux-parchment "surname history" scrolls complete with noble crests that presumably few tourists could legitimately claim, particularly those millions of overseas Irish who are descendants of poor Famine-era migrants (see photo 8.1). So if you know just one Irish surname in your family tree—or even an approximation of a single surname—you can take home a prepackaged token of your ancestry.

In order to understand roots tourism in Ireland today, we need to reach back in time to the mid-nineteenth century. Ireland had a population of roughly 8 million people at the start of the Great Famine (1845–52) when a blight destroyed most of the potato harvest. While the well-off found other sources of sustenance (and indeed, Ireland continued to *export* food during the Famine), the poor who had subsisted almost exclusively

Photo 8.1.   Irish surname-themed souvenirs.

on potatoes fell desperately short of food. It is estimated that around 1 million people died during the Famine, and another 1.5 million emigrated during the crisis. In addition, more than 1 million people had emigrated from Ireland in the decades before the Great Famine, and an even greater number left in the decades following the crisis. In the United States alone, for instance, more than 3 million Irish immigrants arrived between 1840 and 1890. And by 1900, "there were more Irish in Brooklyn and Manhattan than in Dublin, and more in the United States than in the nation of Ireland."[13] It is estimated that today there are some 70 million people of Irish descent around the globe, a figure that dwarfs Ireland's current population of under 5 million people.

It is little wonder, then, that the Irish government has been promoting the potential of "diaspora capital"—spending and investment by people of Irish descent—as a way of bolstering a flagging economy.[14] Of course, in the early years of the twenty-first century a strong Irish economy had earned it a reputation as the "Celtic Tiger." But the global economic collapse of 2008 took a heavy toll on the nation, leading to high unemployment, high rates of household debt, and a conspicuous number of abandoned half-built housing developments (or "ghost estates") dotting the Irish landscape, the victims of an overinflated real estate market. In this context, Irish governmental bodies have been attempting to lure foreign investors of Irish descent back to the "homeland." In 2011, for instance the Department of Foreign Affairs and Trade announced a plan to issue handsomely produced Certificates of Irish Heritage to those descended from an Irish ancestor. The evidence required was quite minimal (just a single source on a single Irish forebear), and the government publicized the program by presenting certificates to high-profile recipients such as Barack Obama, Bill Clinton, and Tom Cruise. According to the government agency issuing the certificates, the intent behind them was

> to acknowledge and mark the deep connection to Ireland felt by many people of Irish descent. Whether by visiting Ireland, researching family history . . . or contribut[ing] to our social and economic development, these enduring connections are a source of strength and opportunity for all of us.[15]

Despite this effort to bring Ireland's sons and daughters (or at least their money) back home, the certificate program attracted little interest around the world, and was discontinued in 2015 for lack of demand.[16] However, two additional governmental agencies, Tourism Ireland and Fáilte Ireland (the National Tourism Development Authority), launched another initiative in 2013 to bring overseas Irish back home, a yearlong event dubbed "The Gathering" (see photo 8.2). Events were held all across the country—from large festivals to small family reunions and genealogy workshops, to a fiftieth-anniversary commemoration of President John F. Kennedy's visit. Kennedy's quote featured prominently in promotional materials: "I want to express my pleasure at being back from whence I came" (see photo 8.3).

Photo 8.2.   A Dublin Airport building advertising "The Gathering."

Photo 8.3.   A building advertising the fiftieth anniversary of President John F. Kennedy's 1963 visit to New Ross, County Wexford.

In order to understand the ways Irish roots tourists' experiences are shaped by a variety of factors, it is useful to examine some of the specific sites they visit. For the sake of contrast, I'll consider two sites on the heavily trafficked tourist trail (the Dunbrody Famine Ship and Emigrant Experience in New Ross, County Wexford, about two hours south of Dublin, and the Cobh Heritage Centre just outside of Cork, the country's second-largest city), and two sites that are further afield and off the well-worn roots tourism track (the Skibbereen Heritage Centre in far southwest County Cork, and Strokestown Park House and Famine Museum in County Roscommon in the rural midlands). All four of these well-developed sites cater to roots tourists, and at the time of my visits all four offered either a range of genealogical how-to books or an on-site genealogist who was available for consultations with visitors. While there are significant differences between the sites, particularly in their coverage of local events, all four engage with the overarching and overlapping themes of the Great Famine and Irish emigration.

In their exploration of the Great Famine and Irish emigration, all four sites describe the poverty and suffering that was widespread during the Famine years. Hand-drawn illustrations from newspapers of the day are used to capture the horrors of mass starvation (see figure 8.1) and the resulting throngs of emigrants (see figure 8.2). To some degree all of the sites also discuss the social inequalities in Ireland at the time, often by contrasting images of plump, ruddy-cheeked, dandified elites with images of emaciated, filthy peasants dressed in rags. And all of the sites at least mention the role that religious (anti-Catholic) discrimination played in the oppression of a destitute peasantry.

However, there were some significant differences between displays at popular sites on the well-beaten roots tourist track and displays in more out-of-the-way locations (see figure 8.3).[17] The first is that sites off the usual tourist route put much greater emphasis on the poverty, extreme suffering, and extreme inequalities in Famine-era Ireland. Sites on the usual tourist route, by contrast, place more emphasis on the opportunities, successes, and happy reunions resulting from Irish emigration. Indeed, sites off the beaten path take a much more critical stance more generally. This is seen quite clearly in portrayals of those in power (the "elites"), including landlords, estate managers, bankers, politicians, sea captains, and the clergy. Both heavily trafficked and more remote sites include some positive portrayals of elites. The tourist-heavy Dunbrody Famine Ship, for instance, includes multiple references to benevolent businesspeople, philanthropists, and a sea captain so kind, generous, and compassionate that his passengers reportedly wept in gratitude.

Figure 8.1. Bridget O'Donnel and Children (*Illustrated London News*, December 22, 1849)

Figure 8.2. Emigrants' Arrival at Cork (*Illustrated London News*, May 10, 1851)

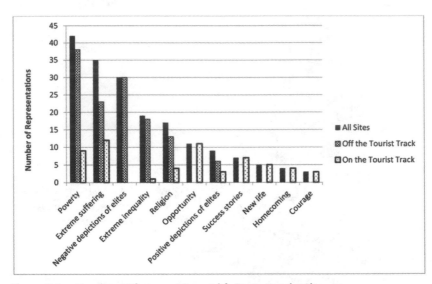

Figure 8.3.   Dominant Themes at Four Irish Roots Tourist Sites

By contrast, only the less trafficked sites include significant criticisms of ruling elites. Strokestown Famine Museum gives significant coverage to the cold calculations and brutal methods landlords and estate managers used to carry out mass evictions. Distant policymakers are portrayed as more devoted to the principles of free trade and profit maximization than to preserving the lives of starving Irish peasants. The rich are shown feasting and dancing, gambling and drinking, while all around them "ghastly yellow-looking spectres" grovel in the filth, and "half-starved, half-naked children" lie dying, their mothers "writhing in agony" and helplessness.[18] Visitors are shown few happy endings here, few stories of shining success through emigration. Instead, these less trafficked sites focus on the horrors and injustices of famine and mass emigration. At sites on the popular tourist track, however, much greater attention is given to feel-good success stories of the opportunities emigrants found, of their courage and fortitude in building their new lives abroad, and of touching reunions when the emigrants or their descendants return to their Irish homeland.

So what factors account for the quite different ways these sites represent the Famine and Irish emigration? In particular, why do sites off the typical roots tourist track take a more critical stance than sites that cater to larger numbers of international visitors? Let's consider four factors that account for these differences. First, sponsorship and donor arrangements. As other scholars have documented, the sponsors of historic sites and museums often exert conservative pressure on the content of exhibits.[19] After all, sponsors generally want some payoff for their sizable donations—and that payoff comes mainly in the form of a positive public image for the donor. Therefore, donors are generally interested in avoiding controversy and criticism and celebrating widely shared values and viewpoints and feel-good narratives. While detailed private and public sponsorship information is hard to come by, all of the sites examined here include prominent partner organizations on their web pages. The two sites on the heavily trafficked roots tourism route (Dunbrody and Cobh) indicate partnerships with Fáilte Ireland (the National Tourism Development Authority), while the two sites off the beaten path (Strokestown and Skibbereen) have partnerships with the Irish Heritage Trust and the Heritage Service, respectively, and the Skibbereen site was developed through both local partnerships and an urban regeneration grant from the European Union.[20] It is possible that sponsorship by a national tourist authority directly or indirectly encourages the heavily trafficked sites to shy away from more overt social critique and focus more on the eventual triumphs of Irish emigrants, while sponsorship by local, international, and heritage organizations may allow the sites to engage in more overt critiques of historical injustices.

A second factor to consider is audience. Because the Dunbrody Famine Ship and the Cobh Heritage Centre are located on main tourist routes with other attractions in close proximity, they attract large groups of tourists on coach tours or cruise ships. These groups typically go through the sites relatively quickly and then move on to other attractions. Such audiences might not be particularly receptive to detailed and nuanced social critiques. Visitors to the more far-flung Skibbereen or Roscommon, by contrast, have few other attractions vying for their attention. Curators at the more distant sites may see this as an opportunity for more in-depth and more critical coverage of famine and emigration. A fairly straightforward economic imperative is in evidence here. In more tourist-heavy venues with multiple attractions nearby, site managers need to keep the tourists happy or they will move on. And the happier they are, the longer they will stay, the more they will spend in the gift shop and cafe, and the more likely they will be to recommend the site to others. More distant sites are likely to depend more on regional visitors and school groups (as suggested, for instance, by the extensive schoolteacher's resources that Strokestown makes available on its website). Because these visitors represent more of a "captive" audience without other attractions to lure them away, these sites may be under less pressure to present patrons with a brisk and cheerful experience.

We must also consider a third factor: local and regional differences. That is, different regions of Ireland had quite different historical experiences of the Famine and emigration. Southwest Cork, near Skibbereen, was one of the hardest-hit regions with the highest death toll. In fact, the decimation of the population left such deep and lasting scars that "Revenge for Skibbereen!" became a rallying cry of the nationalist independence movement in the early twentieth century. Roscommon, the location of Strokestown House, saw massive land clearances, and, according to the museum itself, Roscommon became a byword for brutal evictions by greedy landlords. Cobh, just outside the city of Cork, saw its share of desperate violence during the Famine, with bread riots and hordes of would-be emigrants gathering (sometimes dying) on the docks while waiting to board ships bound for the United States and Canada. But Cobh was also the largest port in the south of Ireland. It was a bustling place of international commerce, and when famine aid arrived, this is where it came ashore. So conditions were perhaps not as dire as in remote Skibbereen or Roscommon. And New Ross in County Wexford, south of Dublin, was better off still. Yes, people suffered from hunger, and many had little option but to board ships for North America. But many migrants were able to at least pay for their ticket and some meager provisions. The worst ravages of the Famine were farther afield.[21] So different experiences of the Great Famine and the emigration process may help to explain the more critical approach to history in more deeply traumatized regions.

Finally, we must remember that in heritage sites around the globe, history is not simply present but is actively constructed. And that construction is a two-way street, with both tourism providers and tourists themselves helping to create a shared vision of the past. As anthropologist Ann Reed points out in her study of roots tourism in Ghana, roots tourists do not arrive in their ancestral homelands as "blank slates." Rather, they come with a whole host of understandings, assumptions, and expectations based on their exposure to written historical accounts, popular fiction and films, tourism marketing campaigns, and even the stories and snapshots of friends and family who made the trip before them.[22] Likewise, tourism providers and site managers solicit feedback from guests in the form of visitor-book comments, surveys, or (increasingly) online reviews, and they sometimes modify their services and narratives based on such comments.

Online reviews for the four sites discussed here are revealing.[23] Visitors to the heavily trafficked Cobh Heritage Centre and Dunbrody Famine Ship commonly stress the pleasant nature of their experience. Site amenities including cafes, toilets, and parking feature prominently, as does the friendliness of staff. Many note that despite learning about difficult and sad top-ics, their experience was "fun" and "entertaining." And while some guests talk of gaining a better understanding of the terrible conditions during the Famine and on immigrant ships, the tendency is to see the emigrants' suf-fering as the beginning of a journey to a better life, to new opportunities, to "fresher fields."

> An interesting view at the history of Cork and in particular the leaving of Ireland in search of better lives in America. (Online review of Cobh Heritage Centre)

> My wife and I spent a few hours touring this museum and were both surprised at the entertainment value. It gives a very good explanation of Ireland and why people immigrated to North America. (Online review of Cobh Heritage Centre)

> An excellent tour made great by enthusiastic and informed guides and actresses. The ship really gives you a sense of the terrible conditions our ancestors had to undergo to escape the famine. Sad but funny in parts. (Online review of Dunbrody Famine Ship and Emigrant Experience)

> Wow! They've done a fantastic job of creating an entertaining historic experience. (Online review of Dunbrody Famine Ship and Emigrant Experience)

Reviews of the two sites off the tourist track reveal quite different visitor experiences—much more somber, with a firm focus on the educational and moral value of the sites rather than on any entertainment value.

> Great overview and insight [in]to one of Ireland's terrible tragedies. You leave with a great sadness in your heart. (Online review of Skibbereen Heritage Centre)

> What you see and read and hear is absolutely awful and depressing. Such was the hardship and death of many thousands. (Online review of Skib-bereen Heritage Centre)

> I believe it is important for all to learn the truth about the famine. While the primary cause was the potato blight, much of the suffering was caused by humans. How could the British government export food from an area that was experiencing famine? How could officials enact the policies that they did? As with holocaust, we must understand and not forget. (Online review of Skibbereen Heritage Centre)

> I was so angry leaving the museum, angry at those who could have stopped, prevented and helped those who needed it (but didn't). You can really feel the pain, heartache and tragedy that Ireland suffered as a result of the Famine. (Online review of Strokestown Famine Museum)

One review, in particular, illustrates the ways visitor feedback informs the presentation of the past at heritage sites. One unhappy visitor to the Skibbereen site writes, "Displays very interesting but could have more variety. There must be more to Skib than the famine!" The general manager of the heritage site responds in turn, "You are absolutely right, there is more to Skibb than the Famine, but *we focus on what our visitors are most interested in*" [emphasis added]. So roots tourists arrive in their homeland destinations with preconceptions and expectations, and tourism providers attempt to supply them with what they are "most interested in." It is a self-reinforcing cycle that is unlikely to challenge widely circulating narratives—whether these focus on selfish or benevolent elites, on hardy, long-suffering peasants, or on the lands of opportunity that received Ireland's desperate emigrants. No matter which story casts your Irish ancestors in the most positive light, you are likely to find it on your roots quest.

Ghana: Returning to Doors of No Return

Ireland is by no means unique in the ways it courts and caters to roots tourists, getting them to open their pocketbooks by giving them what they want. A number of scholars have documented the thriving roots tourism industry in Ghana.[24] There are many similarities between roots tourism in Ghana and Ireland, but also some significant differences that help to illuminate the nature of roots quests more generally.

As in Ireland, government officials in Ghana have recognized the potential of diaspora capital to attract much-needed foreign currency and foreign investment. In the early 1990s, Ghana established its Ministry of Tourism (later renamed the Ministry of Tourism and Diaspora Relations), and launched PANAFEST, a biennial celebration of pan-African identity and unity that attracts diaspora Africans from around the world. In addition, the government also established Emancipation Day as a national holiday commemorating the end of the Transatlantic Slave Trade and the emancipation of slaves in the New World, and set about developing a number of heritage sites and programs to draw affluent diaspora Africans back "home." One local leader captured the promise of wealthy "returnees" in a public prayer at a PANAFEST event:

Almighty God, years ago some of our brothers and sisters were sold into slavery. Today we pray that they have come back to their ancestral land . . . Almighty God, guide them so that their monies will be well-invested for the development of Ghana.[25]

Ghana promotes itself as the "Gateway to the African motherland" because it was the point of departure for a significant number of African captives on their forced journey to New World slavery. Bayo Holsey has noted that while only about 13 percent of slaves bound for North America passed through Ghana, it has become the center of slave heritage tourism in part because it has a number of surviving structures from the period ("slave castles" and "slave forts"), and in part because it is a relatively stable, English-speaking country, which is particularly attractive to affluent Western tourists.[26]

Although Ghana's roots tourism industry invites diaspora Africans from all over the world to return "home," it has made a special effort to attract African Americans, who are perceived to be both affluent and strongly motivated to trace their roots. Reed's study of roots tourists in Ghana found that African American visitors are seeking "something deeper and more meaningful" than the casual tourist.[27] They often envision their journey as a serious undertaking—a quest for a sense of belonging, for emotional healing, for reunion with Mother Africa, a quest to pay respects to the ancestors, and even to bring peace to those restless spirits. And tourism providers cater to these expectations and desires by offering moving tales, spectacles, and rituals that evoke both the ancestors and a sense of African kinship and community.

Two key sites in the roots tourism circuit in Ghana are Elmina Castle and Cape Coast Castle, two forts once used to imprison captives of the slave trade. A sign at the entrance to Cape Coast Castle and a similar one at the entrance of Elmina Castle capture some of the central goals of Ghana's roots tourists:

> In everlasting memory
> Of the anguish of our ancestors.
> May those who died rest in peace.
> May those who return find their roots.
> May humanity never again perpetuate
> Such injustice against humanity.
> We, the living, vow to uphold this.[28]

The larger goals, in other words, are to memorialize the suffering of the ancestors, to ensure the peaceful repose of the dead, and to prevent such atrocities from happening in the future. "Visiting the slave trade sights is an absolute must," remarked one visitor. "Sort of like the Holocaust Museum in Jerusalem or the 911 Museum in NYC." "This is a must to remind [us of] the terrible history and the legacies, to avoid a repetition," commented another.[29] But signage at the sites also includes the more personal goal of roots tourists—to "find their roots." And both personal and larger humanitarian and moral goals are addressed through activities in and around the castles.

Tour guides lead groups through the castles, providing them with not only the historical "facts," but also vivid (often quite imaginative and unsubstantiated) details of the experiences of captives. Many tours appear designed to provoke strong emotional reactions—fear, anger, sadness, disgust. Tourists are sometimes led into a dimly lit dungeon, where the guide extinguishes the single bulb and instructs them to imagine the smell of hundreds of unwashed bodies pressed together, the smell of excrement and sweat and rotting flesh in the summer heat. Some guides tell grisly tales of beatings, torture, and rape. And on occasion, troupes of local performers reenact a slave march, with some of the performers in chains and others dressed as European slave traders. Tourists are routinely shown to a "Door of No Return," from which captives are said to have stepped onto slave ships bound for the New World. They are asked to retrace the captives' steps by passing through the fateful door. But then some tourists—especially African American tourists—are led to another door, a "Door of Return," which they step back through, symbolizing their own "return" to Africa. Rituals of return can also include dancing, drumming, singing, and words of welcome offered by local chiefs. These experiences are so powerful that visitors frequently weep, report that they feel the spirits of the ancestors, or express anger and even hatred of the perpetrators of these atrocities.[30]

> Be prepared to feel some intense emotions while going through this experience. (Online review of Elmina Castle)

> The place had me in tears to know and feel my ancestors' pain. (Online review of Cape Coast Castle)

> As an African American with a penchant for history, physically stepping on the stones where my ancestors were [led] into the trade or to their death was an experience that I simply cannot describe. . . . Be prepared for a heavy experience that will bring new depth to understanding the slave trade. (Online review of Elmina Castle)

> Let's be real, this was not a fun tour to take. It was painful and tragic to listen to the history of this place. More so because it was likely a place

that my family lineage may have passed through at some point. Loved that the "Door of Return" is now . . . for people like me . . . BRING TISSUES!!! (Online review of Cape Coast Castle)[31]

In the context of such heightened emotions, it is perhaps not surprising that tour providers tend to divide visitors into racially segregated groups, with African Americans and black African visitors in one group and white visitors in another. Guides report past incidents of racial conflict on these emotionally charged tours, and their aim is to minimize the potential for such clashes.[32]

In addition to segregating their tours, guides report adjusting the content of their tours to cater to the interests of particular groups. As one guide told Reed,

> First we must know the group . . . and we will know what to deliver. Some people will like to know more, hammer more on the activities that went on after the slave trade; some people will want to know the role played by the Europeans. Some people will want [to know] why few people have been buried over here. Now a group of African Americans are not interested to see some of these who are buried there. So such areas, sometimes we don't even mention. . . . So, always we look at the people [on tour]—not because we are trying to hide certain things, but . . . when they want to know more on that sort, we talk more on that.[33]

Despite such attempts to create historical narratives that will appeal to particular groups, guides find it difficult to satisfy all visitors. Reed reports that African Americans sometimes complain that the true horrors of slavery are not adequately addressed at the castles, and that the role of white perpetrators is downplayed. Europeans sometimes complain that whites are demonized and inaccurately represented as the sole perpetrators of the atrocities, when in fact many black Africans were participants in the slave trade. Ghanaian visitors sometimes complain that the tour narratives are designed to cater only to foreign visitors' interests. And foreign visitors sometimes think that Ghanaian minds seem to be "colonized"—that they cannot see their own continued oppression at the hands of the white Westerners who distort the true history of slavery. Clearly, Ghana's slave castles are the site of struggles over both history and identity.

In a broader sense, roots tourism ventures in Ghana highlight such conflicting views of history and identity. For instance, African American roots tourists often think of themselves as "returnees." They do not consider themselves mere "tourists," but long-absent sons and daughters of Africa coming "home" at last. They are therefore sometimes upset and offended to be called *oburoni*, a term which literally means "one who comes from beyond the horizon," but is more generally applied to foreigners and white people.[34] In the eyes of many Ghanaians, African Americans have more in common with affluent white Europeans and North Americans than with the poor Africans they want to claim as "kin." After all, most African Americans do not speak the local languages or conform to local forms of etiquette. They stay in international hotels, eat at expensive restaurants, and travel in air-conditioned buses, and they do not come bearing gifts, as *real* kin would do. African Americans expecting to be welcomed as long-lost family members face a rude awakening when they are asked for money (by vendors, by children in the streets, or by officials seeking investors) and expected to pay more than Ghanaians for admission to tourist sites.[35] As one unhappy visitor to Elmina Castle commented,

> Although I am technically from the Diaspora and my ancestors were the slaves they bought and sold, [they] tried to charge 40.00 GH¢ [Ghanaian cedis].[36] . . . This particular tourist attraction is not like any other attraction. It involves very sensitive history for folks of color and all those living in the Diaspora. . . . It is a slap in the face when someone comes back to learn of the slave trade and is hit with a foreign fee even though once upon a time their people were from here.[37]

Likewise, there is a tension between the ways Ghanaians and foreign tourists experience sites such as the slave castles. To many foreign tourists, especially the descendants of slaves, these are sacred sites, sites of profound suffering and death, the epicenter of the African Holocaust. They therefore expect to enter places of somber, respectful reflection and education about the transatlantic slave trade. As one visitor to Cape Coast Castle remarked, "Standing in a dungeon where slaves were kept was difficult but powerful. I felt like I was standing on sacred ground."[38] Perhaps not unexpectedly, controversy erupted when authorities introduced a cafe to the Cape Coast Castle site and a gift shop within Elmina Castle. "Hallowed ground!" one visitor wrote in a guest book. "How can you eat and sell at the graveyard of our ancestors!" "You will not be allowed to make a 'Disneyland' from our pain and suffering!" wrote another.[39] After careful consideration, government authorities determined that the amenities were not in keeping with the sober memorialization of the slave trade, and they were quietly removed. (Incidentally, such controversies did not plague Irish Famine tourism sites. Cafes and gift shops were regular and expected features at such sites, leading at one site to the jarring image of a brightly colored poster advertising ice cream at the entrance to a Famine museum.)

Ghanaians, by contrast, come to the sites with different expectations. The castles have stood for hundreds of years and have served as military forts, trading outposts, schools, hospitals, prisons, administrative centers, and more. In the long history of the castles, their involvement in the slave trade was only one significant episode among many. So Ghanaian visitors may be disappointed if guides emphasize the history of the slave trade over other aspects of the site. In addition, many Ghanaians are reluctant to discuss the slave trade. Some of their ancestors, after all, were willing participants in the trade. Some of their ancestors may also have been domestic slaves themselves who were later absorbed into the families of their owners. In either case, it is thought that such embarrassing histories are better forgotten. As one former tour guide told Reed,

> African Americans take the slave stories very serious. I think they have a right to [their] feelings, and we also have a right to our feelings. . . . I believe that it's about time we put all those [bad things] behind us and think about what we can do to make our future better. So why do we have to remind ourselves of sad issues all the time? I want to think of better times; that is all we should do now.[40]

Such tensions between locals and tourists result in a delicate balancing act for tourism authorities and site managers. If they downplay the slave trade, they risk alienating foreign roots tourists for whom Ghana's place in the slave trade is their primary reason for visiting. If they put too much emphasis on the slave trade, they risk alienating Ghanaians, who constitute the majority of visitors to the sites and form the electorate to whom government officials must answer.[41] Likewise, the Ghanaian government faces the challenge of making diaspora tourists feel like "returnees" while encouraging them to open their wallets like deep-pocketed tourists and foreign investors. But every time diaspora tourists are reminded that they are, in fact, outsiders—paying guests or potential investors rather than far-flung kin—they may feel less attachment to their imagined homeland and be less likely to make a financial commitment toward its betterment.

IMAGINED HOMES

There are some striking similarities between the goals and operations of roots tourism in Ireland and Ghana, but also some telling differences. It is clear, for instance, that diasporans in both locations come in search of imagined homes—the soil that nurtured the ancestors, the landscapes that met their eyes, the sounds and smells and tastes that we imagine still dwell deep in our primordial memories. They seek a sense of belonging, of connection to those who came before them. But, of course, ultimately such "homelands" are largely constructions of the tourist's imagination. Tourists themselves have often never visited these "homes" before. They may have little information on where their ancestors actually lived (or, indeed, *whether* or *how long* their ancestors resided there—because all ancestors migrated from somewhere to what we now think of as their "homelands"). And in any case, the places roots tourists visit have not remained frozen in time awaiting their return. In many ways, these lands have been utterly transformed by the same forces of modernization and globalization that have shaped the nations where roots tourists now reside.

One notable difference between roots tourists in Ireland and Ghana is that while Irish roots tourists are often seeking connections with specific ancestors and living kin—by tracking down church and civil records or visiting an ancestral village—roots tourists to Ghana are often not able to trace their actual ancestry to specific people or locations, or even to Ghana itself. Indeed, because so few written records exist for most African Americans before Emancipation, DNA evidence may be the only way to establish even a loose connection to certain regions or ethnic groups within Africa. This may go some way toward explaining why the pilgrimage and ritual aspects of roots tourism in Ghana are often more elaborate than in Ireland. For anyone with an Irish surname in their family tree, for instance, feeling a sense of connection, of rootedness, in Ireland is easy. As a descendant of the Hogan, Gorman, Leyne, and Crowley families, I happened upon countless pubs, shops, laneways, and grave markers bearing my ancestral names. In every tourist gift shop, I had my choice of surname souvenirs. And surname-based "family reunions" organized for "The Gathering" promised to link me with "kin" from all over the world. For many African American roots tourists in Ghana, however, there are no known surnames, no known villages, so the easy and everyday markers of belonging—street signs and surname T-shirts, for instance—are not an option. Instead, there are what Reed has called "rituals of incorporation." Beginning in the 1990s, various rituals, "including naming ceremonies, wedding rites, chief or queenmother enstoolments, and pilgrimage tours—were devised as a means of integrating diasporans into the African family."[42] The granting of honorary "chief" or "queenmother" titles, in particular, was seen as a way of tying affluent diasporans to particular communities and lineages with the hopes that they would make ongoing material contributions to their new "kin." Arguably because African Americans' direct kinship ties in Africa are not as readily apparent as they are for Irish roots tourists, the means of incorporating them back into the "family" must be more dramatic.

Another notable difference between roots tourism in Ireland and Ghana is the visitors' emotional intensity and seriousness of purpose. Irish roots tourism promotions often characterize their roots excursions as both enlightening and fun. One company promises that visitors will "enjoy the benefits of a guided genealogical tour aimed principally at discovering more about their Irish roots while enjoying the 'craic' [the fun, pleasurable diversions] and soaking up some real Irish culture and hospitality."[43] And, as we saw above, visitors to key Irish roots sites often remark positively on the "fun" and "entertainment" to be found there.

Likewise, some Irish roots tourists arrive with a level of preparation that suggests either a casual approach to, or a general lack of understanding of, genealogical research. At one genealogical library in Ireland, for instance, I observed two American women approach an archivist. "I wonder if you can show us where we can find information on our ancestors," one woman inquired. When the archivist asked for some basic information—such as names, dates of birth, or possible regions of residence—the woman said she was sorry, but she had "left that paper at home." When he then probed further about any research she had already done, she replied, "We've done Ancestry.com. But since we're here, we thought we'd check." The archivist directed them to some possible resources, but they quickly gave up and left. Later I asked the archivist whether he fielded many such inquiries. "Loads!" he responded. Every day such casual ancestor seekers walk in, he said. Most from overseas.

Roots tourists to Ghana, however, often approach their roots quests with the serious existential goals—healing the wounds of the past, helping the spirits of their ancestors rest in peace, affirming their African identities, finding pride in a deep history, and finding a sense of belonging. With this sense of purpose, it is not surprising that so many African American tourists have intensely cathartic experiences when visiting slave heritage sites. After all, they are feeling not only the pain of their distant ancestors, but also the pain of living memories and experiences—of Jim Crow segregation, of civil rights–era struggles, of ongoing discrimination and marginalization within the nation of their citizenship. Unlike those of Irish descent, who have now fully integrated into their respective settler nations and even reached the highest levels of society, people of African descent in predominantly white nations are reminded daily of their otherness. And Mother Africa holds the promise of healing and wholeness. As Hartman has written of African American roots tourists,

It is only when you are stranded in a hostile country that you need a romance of origins; it is only when you *lose your mother* that she becomes a myth; it is only when you fear the dislocation of the new that the old ways become precious, imperiled, and what your great-great-grandchildren will one day wistfully describe as African.[44]

What is clear is that roots tourists in both Ireland and Ghana are pilgrims—separating themselves from the Familiar, journeying to a Far Place (often at great expense), seeking connections with something larger than themselves—the ancestors, history—something authentic and primordial. And eventually, these pilgrims return to their everyday lives transformed—enlightened, healed, restored, or simply with a satisfying array of snapshots and anecdotes to share with friends and family. Likewise, roots journeys in both locations often include elements of "dark tourism"—that is, tourism focused on sites of death, terror, and atrocity—Holocaust concentration camps, the dome at Hiroshima, and sites of battles and massacres, for instance. We can include Ghana's slave castles and Ireland's Great Famine sites on this list.

While dark tourism is not new, scholars have noted the increased popularity of such sites in recent decades. Some have argued that because we have increasingly insulated ourselves from death in the modern era—confining the dying to hospitals, giving over the dead to a cadre of mortuary and legal professionals, and sequestering corpses in sprawling park-like cemeteries on the outskirts of our cities—dark tourism is a way of "domesticating" death, making it seem more immediate, more visible, more understandable. Research suggests that visitors to dark tourist sites are not motivated by an unhealthy fascination with the macabre, but rather are principally motivated by a desire to commemorate and connect with the dead, and perhaps to reflect on their own mortality in an age that generally discourages them from looking too closely at death.[45]

Home Is Where the Self Is

When President Barack Obama visited Ghana with his family in July of 2009, he proclaimed, "I have the blood of Africa within me, and my family's own story encompasses both the tragedies and triumphs of the larger African story." After the First Family toured Cape Coast Castle, he reflected on the visit.

It's a powerful moment for not just myself, but I think for Michelle and the girls. You know, I'm reminded of the same feeling I got when I went to Buchenwald with Elie Wiesel. You know, you almost feel as if the walls can speak and that, you know, you try to project yourself into these incredibly harrowing moments that people go through. . . . On the one hand, you know, it's through this door that the journey of the African American experience begins, and you know, Michelle and her family, like me, draw incredible inspiration and strength from that African American journey.

Cape Coast Castle, he said, served as a painful but necessary reminder of "the capacity of human beings to commit great evil," and a reminder of the need to fight oppression and cruelty in all its forms.

When the First Family visited Ireland two years later, the tone of his remarks was very different. "My name is Barack Obama—of the Moneygall Obamas," he began. "And I've come home to find the apostrophe that we lost somewhere along the way." As the crowd laughed and cheered, he thanked the Irish for their warm welcome. "We feel very much at home," he said. "I feel even more at home after that pint that I had." He proceeded to tell the story of how his great-great-great-grandfather Falmouth Kearney left Ireland during the Great Famine to make a new life in the New World. He celebrated all the contributions people of Irish descent have made to the United States, he reaffirmed the strong ties of friendship and kinship between the United States and Ireland, and he thanked the genealogists who had documented his Irish heritage.

In both places, he noted the struggles of the past—experiences of slavery and colonialism in Ghana, and experiences of famine, religious oppression, and civil strife in Ireland. He spoke of the lessons that have been learned from these sad episodes in history, and of the progress the world has made through the courage of people to stand against tyranny. But there are also striking differences between the speeches—differences that capture the nature of roots quests in Ghana and Ireland. His comments in Ghana referenced Nazi concentration camps, genocide, and all the "evils that sadly still exist in our world." In Ireland, he joked about the "lost" apostrophe in his family name, a welcome pint of beer, and a novelty song that proclaimed "There's No One as Irish as Barack Obama." His comments reflect the different ways roots tourists engage with history and ancestry in the two locations. For American descendants of African slaves, a roots tour to Ghana is a pilgrimage, a somber quest for the deep origins that were stolen from them by the brutalities of slavery. It is a path to pride for peoples long marginalized. And it is a moral duty—to the ancestors, to oneself and one's descendants, and to the world, which can never be allowed to forget "man's inhumanity to man."[46] For Americans of Irish descent, whose ancestors were once denigrated but were eventually "whitened" and integrated into the American mainstream,[47] tracing one's Irish roots is less a solemn duty than a pleasant journey into a land and a history dotted with familiar surnames, familiar food and drink, familiar tunes floating on the air, and familiar, seemingly timeless scenes of rolling green hills, stone cottages, and rugged coastlines.

Despite differences between the experiences of roots tourists in Ireland, Ghana, and elsewhere, and despite the varied ways roots tourism providers structure those experiences through their goods, services, and promotional materials, twenty-first-century roots quests are, above all else, journeys into the self. And like the heroic Hobbit, Frodo Baggins, roots tourists seek "the gold that does not glitter . . . the old that . . . does not wither," and "deep roots [that] are not reached by the frost." They seek the ancestors, they seek a place in history, they seek a home, and they seek the self.

9

OUR ANCESTORS, OURSELVES

Roots and Identity in an Age of Rootlessness

The roots pilgrimages described in the previous chapter neatly capture some of the key features of our current era—what we might call our "age of rootlessness." We can see, for instance, the many ways accelerated *globalization* has shaped our twenty-first-century roots quests. Globalization has entailed mass migrations (including forcible removals) of people from one region to another. And whether these movements were voluntary or coerced, this has resulted in a general sense of dislocation and disconnection from homelands. Globalization prompts us both to transcend international boundaries—for example, by creating global kinship connections—and to seek rootedness in specific localities. These localities may be the communities or nations of our residence, or our ancestral homelands. Globalization has also given us multiethnic societies, and with increasingly easy and rapid international transport, goods and people and ideas now flow relatively unencumbered to all corners of the globe. One of the many complex effects of such global flows is that some of the distinctive cultural traits that were once preserved by geographical boundaries are now dissolving, as people from Los Angeles to Vienna to Kuala Lumpur to Cape Town consume Big Macs and wear blue jeans and Gap T-shirts. So globalization also leaves us longing for cultural distinctiveness and the "stuff" of cultural belonging—the tastes, sounds, and sights we associate with "heritage." These are some of the social, economic, and demographic changes fueling "homecoming" tourism today.

Genealogists themselves recognize that the changes associated with globalization are driving twenty-first-century roots quests. When asked why so many people are exploring their ancestry today, they responded:

> Historically families . . . lived for generations in the same place and knew their extended family. It gave them a sense of belonging. A lot of

society's problems today stem from the lack of a sense of belonging to the larger group. . . . Genealogical research gives roots to a highly mobile society. (Roberta, 67, Kansas)

Nations and cultures have become more homogenized, and some people desire to discover their cultural identity. (Belinda, 61, Indiana)

I think there is a strong disconnect in society today. People seem to be so lost in so many ways. I think genealogy is a way to get that touchstone—to go outside yourself a bit. (Ramona, 46, New York)

I think it has to do with the lack of memory and flatness of American society and culture. . . . Suddenly people are learning that there is almost a kind of spirituality in being connected to other generations. (Richard, 69, Indiana)

Richard's explanation for the popularity of genealogy today captures the influence of another hallmark of our age: *secularization.* Increasing numbers of people are stepping away from organized religion, and they are seeking other transcendent experiences—that is, experiences that give them a sense of belonging to something larger than themselves, something ancient and timeless, something that will outlive them. And, as faith in an afterlife decreases, people are seeking more certain forms of immortality—by documenting their lives and the lives of their ancestors to ensure that those names and memories live on. Whether visiting the slave forts of Ghana, pouring over baptismal records in Ireland, or logging into Ancestry .com, genealogy provides us with a sense of belonging to "one family that lasts forever" (Lawrence, 56, Tennessee), a sense of "permanence" (Teresa, 60, California), a kind of "immortality" (Glen, 44, Indiana). It reminds us that "the world isn't just about you and your particular time on Earth" (Joy, 64, California). It reminds us of our "place in the circle of life" (William, 52, Utah). And often it provides genealogists with a profound sense of spiritual connection with kin, both living and dead.

Certain technological changes are also fueling roots quests today. With increasing *digitization* of records, genealogical research is easier and faster than ever, allowing us to reach into archives and explore locations halfway around the world from the comfort of our homes. Likewise, advances in ancestral DNA testing are allowing us to locate ourselves in deep time and in faraway places, allowing us to *geneticize* our identities. But even as these technological innovations have allowed us to conceptualize our identities in new ways, the rise of social media and the *virtualization* of social interactions have prompted us to seek out our "real" identities. At the same time, scholars stress that all knowledge (of self, of others, and of the world) is *relative* and socially constructed. Identities once assumed to be stable and "natural" are now seen as fluid and contested. In this context, genealogy seems to promise authenticity, permanence, depth, and connection as antidotes to the changeable, simulated, and superficial "selves" and "friends" we cultivate through Twitter, Instagram, and Facebook. As James (61, Illinois) explained,

> The modern dependency on cell phone, Internet, and electronic technology may on the surface lure us into thinking that we are more connected socially than ever before, while in fact we are more socially inept when physically interacting with people face-to-face. I want my children to know and connect with the people that preceded them. It will give them a better understanding of who they are as people.

So twenty-first-century roots quests, whether on our home computers, in archives and graveyards, or in faraway ancestral homelands, both reflect and are shaped by some of the defining features of our age of rootlessness—globalization, secularization, the relativization of knowledge, and the rise of digital, virtual, and genetic technologies.

But there is one more hallmark of our age that we must consider, and that is the increasing commodification of identity. To conclude this book, I consider the ways twenty-first-century genealogy both reflects and is shaped by powerful consumer forces.

ROOTS QUESTS AND THE COMMODIFICATION OF IDENTITY

We can imagine a time in our preindustrial past when you would become a peasant farmer (or a furniture maker or a member of the nobility), because that's what your parents were; and of course, that's what your children would be too. Many scholars have noted that before the modern era—particularly before industrialization, urbanization, mass education, increased literacy, and expanded suffrage—opportunities for social mobility were relatively limited. People were strongly bound to places and kinship networks; and social ranks, roles, and identities were fairly rigidly defined and stable.

But modernity brought both opportunities and challenges. Large numbers of people began moving, from the farm to the city, from one city to another, from one country to another, ideally acquiring skills and capital along the way to propel them upward in society. And gradually, our identities were no longer anchored in specific places, social roles, or groups. Sociologist Zygmunt Bauman has argued that in our current era, we exist in a state of constant "disembeddedness" and flux. Our present age, he says, is characterized by rapid change, weakened social bonds, mobility, and a distinct lack of fixity.[1]

Our identities, likewise, are in a constant state of construction. We are always inventing, always editing, always improving upon our identities, working toward our optimal selves. In other words, we are engaged in an ongoing "project of self." And one of the principal ways we do that is through our consumption practices. The foods we eat, the clothes we wear, the car we drive, the music we listen to, all *reflect* our sense of self, actively *construct* our sense of self, and *communicate* that constructed self to others. In twenty-first-century America, we are what we eat, what we wear, what we drive, and so on.

So let's consider genealogical consumption practices. As I noted in the introduction to this volume, genealogy in twenty-first-century America is an expensive undertaking. There are subscriptions to online databases like Ancestry.com, memberships to genealogical societies, conference fees, hardware and software products, storage and organizational products. There are DNA tests, roots travel packages, professional research services, and training and certification courses. There are how-to books and family tree cross-stitch kits and bumper stickers (GENEALOGISTS NEVER DIE; THEY JUST LOSE THEIR CENSUS), and much, much more. Indeed, my analysis of products advertised in *Family Tree Magazine* over a ten-year period (2000–2009) found some ten thousand products, ranging in price from less than $1 to $4,195 (for a roots tour to Scotland). Each issue contained more than one hundred advertised products, with the dollar amount of the total advertised goods and services averaging $10,364 per issue. In addition, every genealogical conference I attended included a vendors' area—sometimes a massive trade show–style floor—where genealogists could check out the newest products, ask questions to experts in the field, have their pictures taken with a celebrity genealogist, watch high-energy multimedia sales pitches, and pick up branded "giveaways"—pens, magnifying glasses, even backscratchers with a company logo. In short, genealogists are presented with an almost endless array of products and services that promise to make their roots quests easier, faster, more engaging, more meaningful, and more durable.

The genealogists I surveyed spent an average of $1,500 per year on the pursuit, and much more if they engaged in roots tourism. When asked how much they spend each year tracing their ancestry, their responses were revealing. "[I'm] afraid to add it all up, but it's in the thousands" (Roberta,

67, Kansas). "Oh Lord, that's a question I don't even want to consider!" (Glen, 44, Indiana). "More than I'd like to admit!" (Martin, 38, Michigan). There is an undercurrent of discomfort here, perhaps a fear that their expenditures will be perceived as excessive or unseemly. But some genealogists also offered further justifications for their spending. Luanne (80, Texas) noted that she typically spends between $4,000 and $5,500 per year, including her roots travel. "But the experience, information, and memories cannot be duplicated." Beth (70, Wisconsin) admitted that she's "afraid to add it up," but then added, "It may not be the cheapest hobby, but I cannot think of one that is more fun or rewarding." Similarly, Iris (61, Utah) said, "I know it's in the thousands of dollars. [But] is there anything more important?" And Emily (63, Indiana) noted that while she hasn't added it up, she will "spend as much . . . as I deem necessary to accomplish my goals."

So what is the ultimate goal of twenty-first-century roots quests? Certainly there are specific objectives, like discovering the name of your immigrant ancestors' home village, understanding your family's connection to the Civil War, or connecting with previously unknown living relatives. This is where genealogists often start when asked why they do family history research. But the longer they talk, the more likely they are to get to the motivation at the heart of their roots quest. "[Genealogy] somehow grounds me and helps me to understand myself better" (Deidre, 58, Texas). "I do it for myself, because I find it interesting to discover how I became who I am" (Joy, 64, California). "As I learn more about my family, I always learn more about myself" (Lawrence, 56, Tennessee). "If you know your family, you know yourself" (Teresa, 60, California). "It's a journey of self-discovery. I'm learning a lot about myself" (Roberta, 67, Kansas). So, while on one level, roots quests are focused on finding our ancestors or possibly finding living kin, they are at their core quests for self.

In the course of our family history research, we uncover details that we can use to interpret our own lives, details that we can add to our own identities. If my ancestors were poor Irish farmers who survived famine and oppression and mustered the courage to set out across the oceans for the chance of a better life in an unknown land, then I must carry some of their courage and fortitude within me. If my forebear signed the Declaration of Independence, I have my conversation-starter for the Fourth of July picnic. The ancestors are ornaments decorating our family trees, making our own identities shine all the brighter. And we select our ornaments quite deliberately.

While family history researchers are frequently exhorted to adhere to the Genealogical Proof Standard (which requires comprehensive searches, reliable sources, meticulous documentation, and sound reasoning), geneal-ogy is nonetheless an interpretive pursuit. There are points in every gene-alogist's roots quest when she must make choices. She must decide which family line(s) to research. She must decide which individuals in the family tree deserve extra attention. She must weigh the merits of often incom-plete or contradictory evidence. And each of these decisions, whether big or small, will subtly or drastically reshape her family tree. Likewise, each of these decisions has implications for her own identity, for who she thinks she is. It would be understandable if those decisions were influenced by what one genealogist (Bob, 75, Illinois) called "wishful thinking." We certainly saw ample evidence of such hopeful and charitable (if not clearly justifiable) interpretations by amateur and professional genealogists alike in the roots television shows we examined in chapter 6.

Genealogy is now a multibillion-dollar industry. But what are ge-nealogists really buying? Yes, they are spending money on the goods and services detailed above, but in a larger sense, they are buying little frag-ments of the ancestors, and buying little fragments of identity. It is worth considering whether, in this sense, acquiring a new ancestor or a new detail to add to a family history is like acquiring a new dress or a new car—just another commodity to add to our never-ending "project of self." We should also consider certain inherent inequalities built in to our increasingly commercialized roots quests, because in the genealogical marketplace not everyone has an equal ability to pay. Those with greater resources to devote to the pursuit will likely get better results—pushing their trees back further in time, adding to the number of people on their trees, discovering richer details about their ancestors and the times in which they lived. Those who spend less may struggle to create even the spindliest of family trees. This has implications for whose stories will be passed down. Namely, the stories of people of greater means are more likely to be preserved for generations to come, while the stories of less affluent families sink further into obscurity.

And this has implications for our identities. The reality is that people of greater means can afford "better" ancestries—deeper, more detailed, and better-documented family histories. Those of greater means can assemble more impressive "identity kits." It is often said that you cannot choose your family, but an examination of roots work across cultures and over time dem-onstrates that ancestry and kinship are not simply natural "facts" waiting to be discovered. Ancestry and kinship are actively and creatively constructed. Likewise our true identities—who we *really* are—are not simply waiting to be uncovered; our identities must be actively and constantly created. And in our age of rootlessness, we do this, in part, through our roots quests.

NOTES

CHAPTER 1: ROOTS QUESTS

1. Haley (1977).
2. Certified Genealogist (CG); Fellow of the American Society of Genealogists (FASG); Fellow of the National Genealogical Society (FNGS); Fellow of the Utah Genealogical Association (FUGA).
3. Ancestry.com (2010); Weil (2013: 198); and Ancestry.com (2013a). The terms *genealogy* and *family history* are used interchangeably in this book. Although some practitioners feel that *genealogy* places a greater emphasis on names, dates, and places, while *family history* focuses more on the stories and contexts of ancestors' lives, Drake (2001) found roughly equal preference for the two terms in the genealogical community.
4. Ancestry.com (2013b; 2013c; 2014a; 2015a; 2017); Crunchbase.com (2013); Helft (2017); Weil (2013: 206).
5. Santos and Yan (2010: 58); FamilySearch.org (2011).
6. Irish Press (2011); Baran (2012).
7. Rodriguez (2014).
8. The term *American* is used throughout the volume as a gloss for the United States of America and its Colonial beginnings. While diverse Native American ancestral practices deserve full scholarly attention in their own right, they are not the focus of this book.
9. I draw here on Bauman (1978) and Harvey (1989) in regard to postmodern "identity projects," on Hall's (1992) work on cultural identity, and on Hobsbawm (2007) in regard to the cultural effects of globalization. I engage with this scholarship in the chapters ahead.
10. Huyssen (1995; 2000).
11. Pew Research Center (2012); Pew Forum on Religion and Public Life (2007); Fletcher Stack (2017).

12. Particularly relevant here is the notion of time-space compression (or time-space distantiation) discussed by Harvey (1989), Giddens (1990), and Massey (1994), among others. These scholars suggest that developments in realms such as computing, communications, and transportation have accelerated global exchanges (of people, goods, and ideas) to such a degree that distances now appear to shrink away even as time appears to speed up.

13. Holsey (2004); Brand and Platter (2011); P. Basu (2004; 2005); Young and Light (2016); and De Santana Pinho (2008).

14. Lambert (2002: 124).

15. Duke, Lazarus and Fivush (2008).

16. http://www.funstuffforgenealogists.com/store/contents/en-us/d1.html (accessed August 25, 2015).

17. Results from a web-based survey with 4,109 respondents. Drake (2001).

18. I make no assumptions regarding the lived racial or ethnic identity of conference participants, which, of course, may be very different from phenotypical appearance.

19. Of course such a general measure of ethnicity will invariably undercount individuals whose ethnic backgrounds are not readily apparent from physical markers. It is also important to note that two-thirds of these genealogists attended conferences in the Midwest (two in Indiana, two in Illinois, and two in Missouri), which could have resulted in a higher number of white participants than a more representative national sample would yield.

20. The questionnaire was administered via e-mail to genealogists who responded to written requests for research participants. The sample includes thirty-seven women and twenty men, from twenty-one states, with an average of twenty-two years of experience doing genealogy, some professionally and some as a hobby.

21. The average expenditure reported here excludes expenses reported by professional genealogists with more than $5,000 of annual spending. Some professional researchers report as much as $25,000 in annual expenses.

22. The conference was held in a city where, according to the US Census, African Americans make up more than half of the population (http://quickfacts .census.gov).

23. The group is making concerted efforts to overcome this racist image by addressing the issue on their website (http://www.dar.org/national-society/marian -anderson), and engaging in frank discussions at the local level. For instance, because my grandmother was a card-carrying member of the DAR, I have received several kind invitations to join the organization, always with the reassurance that the group has put its racist past behind them.

24. Di Leonardo (1987).

25. Di Leonardo (1987). According to the Institute for Women's Policy Research (2015), women working full-time earn an average of 78 percent of the wage full-time male workers earn.

26. Based on a survey of registered certified genealogists listed on the websites of the Board for Certification of Genealogists (http://www.bcgcertification.org), and the International Commission for the Accreditation of Professional Genealogists (http://www.icapgen.org).

27. Bureau of Labor Statistics (2012); Sutton (2014).

28. Williams (1995).

29. Bouquet (1996) examines the history of family tree diagrams. She traces tree metaphors to the Bible, which detailed the lineages that established descent from Adam through to Christ, and she notes that so-called Trees of Jesse were once commonly used to teach Bible stories in Europe. The same tree imagery was then used by families in their own family trees (which were often inscribed in family Bibles, thereby "grafting" their own families onto the sacred trees of biblical lineages). Trees of pedigree also came to be used by scholars and museum curators charting links between species, cultures, languages, and even schools of thought. Bouquet calls such mapping of relationships "pedigree thinking."

30. Pseudonyms are used throughout the book in order to protect the privacy of those whom I interviewed.

31. Genealogy conference sessions presented by Lisa Louise Cooke, Thomas Jones, and Daniel Poffenberger.

32. Connor (2014); Rubinstein (2010).

33. Sweeney (2010) calls this notion that our ancestry helps to explain "who we are" and why we have certain traits, interests, and experiences, the "genealogical assumption."

34. *Who Do You Think You Are?*, season 1, episode 5.

35. *Finding Your Roots*, season 1, episode 8.

36. *The Generations Project*, season 1, episode 9.

37. Of course, genealogists are well aware of dominant "vocabularies of motives" (Mills 1940), in other words, the motivations that are considered socially acceptable and valued at a given point in time. And this may have shaped their responses.

38. Church of Jesus Christ of Latter-day Saints (2012).

39. Building on the work of Ferdinand Tönnies (2001), sociologists often make an analytical distinction between small-scale societies, which are organized around personal, affective relationships (*Gemeinschaft* communities) and larger-scale societies, which are characterized by a complex division of labor and more formal and impersonal interactions (*Gesellschaft* societies). Hobsbawm (2007) and others have argued that as globalization transforms most societies into impersonal *Gesellschaft* societies, we increasingly try to re-create personal, affective bonds through new forms of association. Likewise, we may attempt to find more "authentic" personal and collective identities through practices such as genealogy.

40. Interviews with Camille (59, Missouri) and Holly (54, Texas).

41. *Who Do You Think You Are?*, season 1, episode 1.

CHAPTER 2: A GENEALOGY
OF AMERICAN GENEALOGY

1. Sweeney (2010) calls this the "genealogical assumption."

2. Previous research has documented the shifting interest in genealogy over time, and the shifting character of genealogical pursuits. See, especially, Hareven (1978); Bockstruck (1983); Taylor and Crandall (1986); Sweeney (2010); Santos and Yan (2010); and Weil (2013).

3. In conceptualizing this timeline, I am indebted to Weil (2013); Sweeney (2010); and Taylor and Crandall (1986) for their work on the development of American genealogy. In particular, I borrow the terms *aristocratic genealogy* and *democratic genealogy* from Weil (2013).

4. Weil (2013).

5. Weil (2013: 10–11). Of course, Anglo-Saxons were only one of the many European cultures with early genealogical traditions. As Erben (1991) has noted, for example, oral genealogical traditions have been a crucial part of maintaining social cohesion in cultures organized into clans, tribes, and other kinship-based groups.

6. Weil (2013: 12–13).

7. Weil (2013: 15, 19–23).

8. Weil (2013: 32–33).

9. Benedict Anderson (1983) documents the many ways "print capitalism" has changed conceptions of the nation. In his influential work on "imagined communities," he argues that the spread of the printed word was central to projects of nation-building. He suggests that improvements in print technology led to the standardization of national vernaculars, to increased literacy, and to the rise of such early mass commodities as the newspaper and the popular novel. These developments, he says, opened up the possibility of identifying with the nation as an entity, as an "imagined community" to which one belongs. Arguably, print capitalism also reshaped individual and family identities by giving people new frames of reference and new ways of thinking about the self and the Other.

10. Weil (2013: 48).

11. The National Archives hold some eighty thousand Revolutionary War Pension and Bounty-Land Warrant application files. Available at https://www.archives.gov/research/microfilm/m804.pdf, accessed September 29, 2015.

12. Bockstruck (1983).

13. Weil (2013: 43).

14. Taylor and Crandall (1986); Sweeney (2010); Weil (2013). As a measure of the popularity of genealogy in this period, by 1870, some eight thousand books and twenty-six thousand pamphlets devoted to genealogy were in circulation (Taylor and Crandall 1986: 6).

15. Sweeney (2010); Weil (2013).

16. Foner (1990); Richardson (2007); Zinn (2005).

17. Tindall and Shi (2012: 589).

18. Barreyre (2011).

19. Richardson (2007: 131).

20. Some six million African Americans participated in this "Great Migration" (1915–1970). See Wilkerson (2010).

21. Zinn (2005: 266).

22. Sweeney (2010: 37–45).

23. Sweeney (2010: 35).

24. Hartman (2012) notes that as non-English immigration to the United States increased in the late-nineteenth and early-twentieth centuries, there were rising fears among whites that racial pollution would lead to national degeneration and the loss of American power. A so-called "Teutonic thesis" emerged, proposing that white Anglo-Saxon, Nordic, and Teutonic men were superior and uniquely equipped to rule due to a natural toughness, boldness, and resourcefulness that had evolved out of experiences of warfare and harsh climates.

25. For an overview of the principles and applications of eugenics, see Kevles (1998).

26. Sweeney (2010: 103).

27. Sweeney (2010: 208–9).

28. Sweeney (2010: 95–129).

29. Sweeney (2010: 121–22).

30. For a discussion of the impact of Haley's *Roots* when it first came out, see Gerber (1977).

31. The book is part fiction and part fact, inspired by Haley's investigation of his own family history. Haley himself classified the book not as a novel but as "faction" (a combination of fact and fiction).

32. Appleby (2005).

33. The concept of "social construction" was clearly articulated in Berger and Luckmann's (1966) *The Social Construction of Reality: A Treatise in the Sociology of Knowledge*. They argued that all human knowledge, even that which appears "natural," arises out of human interactions and negotiations of meaning, so all human knowledge is an agreed-upon construction.

34. See Best and Kellner (1997) for a discussion of the "postmodern turn."

35. Sweeney (2010: 171).

36. Sweeney (2010: 148, 162–64).

37. Haley (1977).

38. From author's interviews with archivists and historians.

39. Author's collection of promotional pamphlets.

40. Board for Certification of Genealogists (2015).

41. Hilbert and López (2011).

42. Internet usage statistics, available at http://www.internetlivestats.com/one-second, accessed September 19, 2017.

43. Ancestry.com (2017).

44. Ancestry.com (2013b; 2013c).

45. Nash (2004).

46. Ancestry.com (2014b).

47. Ancestry.com (2015b).

48. 23andMe (2018).

49. FamilyTreeDNA (2015). Rees Anderson (2014).

50. Shipman (2003).

51. A national television ad, aired in October of 2015. Available at https://www.ispot.tv/ad/wppp/ancestrydna-testimonial-kylewww.ispot.tv/ad/7c4Y/ancestrydna-lederhosen, accessed October 5, 2015.

52. Waters (1990), building on Gans (1979), notes that while ethnic identity is still significant in America, for whites it has become a largely voluntary ("symbolic" or "optional") category. As members of the "unmarked" racial group, whites can selectively choose their ethnic affiliations at little or no personal cost. Ethnicity thus becomes just one more mark of distinction individuals can add to their personal "identity kits."

53. Questions such as "What are you?" or "Where are you from?" directed at ethnic minorities can be considered *microaggressions*, "the brief and commonplace daily verbal, behavioral, and environmental indignities, whether intentional or unintentional, that communicate hostile, derogatory, or negative racial, gender, and sexual orientation, and religious slights and insults to the target person or group" (Sue 2010: 5). Although these slights may be unintentional, they can nonetheless take a psychological toll on individuals who are repeatedly reminded of their "otherness" or their supposedly essential traits. Repeated often enough, such microaggressions help to create a climate which encourages more extreme acts of bigotry (such as racist or homophobic violence).

54. Nash (2004).

55. Jacobs (2014a).

56. My Irish Connections (2015). Available at http://www.myirishconnections.com/tours.htm, accessed October 9, 2015.

57. Time Travel Tours (2015). Available at https://www.timetraveltours.com/genealogy.html, accessed October 9, 2015.

58. My Irish Connections (2015). Available at http://www.myirishconnections.com/tours.htm, accessed October 9, 2015.

59. Interview with Holly (54, of Texas).

60. The national television ad, which aired in September of 2015. Available at https://www.ispot.tv/ad/7pVw/ancestry-com-guide-throughout-the-past, accessed October 5, 2015.

61. Pew Research Center (2012). Pew Forum on Religion and Public Life (2007).

62. FamilySearch.org (2015a).

63. FamilySearch.org (2015b).

64. Nephi Anderson (1911), "Genealogy's Place in the Plan of Salvation," cited in Sweeney (2012: 73).

CHAPTER 3: ROOTS WORK

1. Kastenbaum (1981).

2. In fact, Kastenbaum (1981: 233) observes that Americans are so uncomfortable with grief, grieving, and the bereaved that one clinician developed what was purported to be a quick and efficient "degriefing intervention" for those considered to be suffering from excessive grief.

3. Scholars have long debated whether such practices should be called "ancestor veneration" or "ancestor worship." Ephirim-Donkor (2013), for instance, argues that West African beliefs in ancestral spirits and the ritual practices associated with those beliefs constitute full-fledged religions and should therefore be considered "ancestor worship." However, the English term *worship* often implies belief in an omniscient, omnipotent god, a belief that is not present in many societies in which ancestors are venerated. Furthermore, recent research suggests that in some cultures today, younger generations continue to observe ancestor rituals without an understanding of, or commitment to, the religious beliefs that originally underpinned them (see Clark 2000). For these reasons, I adopt the broader term *ancestor veneration*.

4. See Sheils (1975; 1980).

5. Dernbach (2005).

6. Abasi (1995).

7. Abasi (1995: 473).

8. Abasi (1995: 473).

9. "Ashes to ashes, dust to dust," commonly recited in Christian funerals today, is taken from the Anglican *Book of Common Prayer*, and is based on Genesis 3:19, "By the sweat of your brow you will eat your food until you return to the ground, since from it you were taken; for dust you are and to dust you will return."

10. Reed and Hufbauer (2005); Ubah (1982); Rasmussen (2000); McCall (1995); Ephirim-Donkor (2013); Van der Geest (2000, 1997); Arhin (1994); De Witte (2001); Calhoun (1980); Kyerematen (1969); Mendonsa (1976); Fiawoo (1976); Noret (2005); Dalfovo (1997); Hasu (2009); Rodgers (2008); and Berg (2003).

11. Berg (2003); De Witte (2001); and Ubah (1982).

12. Rodgers (2008).

13. Hasu (2009).

14. Reed and Hufbauer (2005).

15. Van der Geest (2000, 1997); Arhin (1994); and De Witte (2001).

16. Van der Geest (2000, 1997); Arhin (1994); and De Witte (2001).

17. I use the pronoun *he* because in most cultures, men are more likely than women to be revered as ancestral spirits.

18. Ooms (1976); Hamabata (1990); Klass (1996); Daniels (2012); Leavitt (1995); Dernbach (2005); Lohmann (2005); Vega (1999); and Njemanze (2011).

19. De Witte (2001: 45).

20. "Danielle," "Andrea," and "John" featured on *BYU Generations*, season 1, episodes 11, 8, and 7.

21. Dunbar (2003: 1160–61).

22. Watson (1986). While patrilineal descent and patrilocality were typical features of the family system among the majority of Chinese, there was (and is) a wide diversity of kinship arrangements among China's many ethnic minority groups.

23. This system institutionalized male dominance and the oppression of women, a topic we will examine later in this chapter. Interestingly, as the status of expatriate Chinese women has increased, their place in ancestor veneration has also grown more prominent (Kuah-Pearce 2006).

24. Teather (1999).

25. Wolf (1974).

26. Jordan (1972).

27. Clark (2000); Kuah-Pearce (2006).

28. Similarly, Wadley (1999) suggests that for the Iban of Borneo, people may observe death rituals and taboos more as a signal of respect for the living than out of a fear of retribution from the spirits of the dead.

29. Teather (1999).

30. Kuah-Pearce (2006).

31. Smith (1974).

32. Traditionally, only the "main" family of the lineage, that headed by the eldest son, is responsible for the principal ancestral altar (*butsudan*) of the lineage. And, as Hamabata (1990) has shown, family disputes sometimes arise over who has the right and the obligation to tend to the ancestral spirits.

33. Traphagan (2003); and Hamabata (1990).

34. Hamabata (1990); Klass (1996); and Daniels (2012).

35. Smith (1974).

36. Smith (1974).

37. Ooms (1976). As Hamabata (1990) points out, families have a number of flexible and creative ways to ensure that a family line never dies out. It is almost always possible to name a successor who will carry on the family name and continue to care for the ancestral spirits and their altars.

38. Smith (1974); Takeda (1976); and Nelson (2008).

39. Smith (1974); Takeda (1976); and Nelson (2008).

40. Battaglia (1990, 1992).

41. Battaglia (1992).

42. Hermkens (2007).

43. Lohmann (2005).

44. Similarly, according to some traditional Chinese beliefs, "flesh is inherited from the mother and is thereby of the yin essence. Bones, on the other hand, are passed in the patriline and, when manipulated properly, are primarily yang" (Watson 1988: 114). Therefore bodies were customarily first buried in a "wet" grave where flesh decomposed. Then years later, the purified bones were exhumed and stored (sometimes after cremation) in the family tomb.

45. Lohmann (2005).

46. Lohmann (2005).
47. Lohmann (2005).
48. Dernbach (2005).
49. Dernbach (2005).
50. McAnany (2011) notes, for instance, that residential burials are found in many parts of Mesoamerica, in Mesopotamia, and in Sumba, Indonesia.
51. Dernbach (2005).
52. LeFever (1996).
53. LeFever (1996: 320).
54. Apter (1991: 254) cited in LeFever (1996: 327).
55. Prandi (2000: 654).
56. Desmangles (1992: 2).
57. Desmangles (1992); Benoît (2007); Vonarx (2007).
58. Vonarx (2007).
59. Vonarx (2007: 25).
60. Desmangles (1992: 6).
61. Principally the area including Angola and the Democratic Republic of the Congo today.
62. Vega (1999).
63. Vega (1999).
64. Interviews with Deidre (58, Texas); Gloria (54, Missouri); Camille (59, Missouri); Charlotte (70, Illinois); Roberta (67, Kansas); Cindy (70, Maine); and Joy (64, California).
65. Interviews with Deidre (58, Texas); James (61, Illinois); Jen (45, Massachusetts); and a focus group of genealogists at the Family Research Center in Salt Lake City.
66. Interviews with Madeline (69, Missouri); Glen (44, Indiana); Belinda (61, Indiana); Richard (69, Indiana); and Duane (58, Virginia).
67. See Fiawoo (1976); Daniels (2012); Nelson (2008); and Malinowski (1916), among others.
68. Ephirim-Denkor (2013); Dalfovo (1997); Mendonsa (1976); and Jordan (1972).
69. Ooms (1976); Traphagan (2003); Nelson (2008); and Hamabata (1990).
70. Dernach (2005).
71. Fiawoo (1976); Rasmussen (2000); De Witte (2001); Ooms (1976); Traphagan (2003); Nelson (2008); Hamabata (1990); and Lohmann (2005).
72. I use the masculine pronoun *his* because for most of American history, men's lives have been better documented than women's lives.
73. Erben (1991).
74. Evans-Pritchard (1951); Bohannan (1952); and Blount (1975).
75. Panzacchi (1994); Irvine (1978); H. Basu (2005); and Erben (1991).
76. H. Basu (2005).
77. Panzacchi (1994); Irvine (1978); and H. Basu (2005).

78. Shahar and Weller (1996); and Rawksi (1988).
79. Watson (1988); Shahar and Weller (1996); and Rawksi (1988).
80. Smith (1974); Takeda (1976); and Nelson (2008).
81. Clark (2000).
82. Watson (1986).
83. Reed and Hufbauer (2005).
84. Reed and Hufbauer (2005).
85. Rawski (1988: 32).
86. Rüpke (2006); De Witte (2001); Arhin (1994); Rasmussen (2000); Van der Geest (2000); Rawksi (1988); and James (2002).
87. Dernbach (2005).
88. Scholars are divided, however, on the value of identifying cultural universals (or "human universals"). Some critics suggest that so-called cultural universals are simply abstract constructs imposed by mainly Western scholars on cultures around the world, with little regard for how members of those cultures understand their own beliefs and practices. In anthropological terms, critics claim that cultural universals represent an outsider's (or *etic*) perspective rather than an insider's (or *emic*) perspective. A second criticism of cultural universals is that because specific beliefs and practices vary so significantly from culture to culture, any general categories (e.g., "play" or "family") must be so broad that they are not analytically useful. And a third criticism is that it is functionally impossible for researchers to be equally familiar with all cultures that exist today and have ever existed, and the cultural data we do have is always partial (in both senses of the word), so our data set is inherently incomplete. See discussions in Brown (2004; 1991); Peterson (1996); Wiredu (1995); and Paden (2001).
89. Scholars sometimes make distinctions between absolute universals (occurring in all known cultures), near universals (occurring in almost all known cultures), conditional universals (occurring consistently under certain circumstances), statistical universals (not occurring in all cultures, but in such a significant number that it is unlikely to be by chance), and a universal pool (in which there are a limited set of options exercised in all cultures). See Brown (2004).
90. Brown (1991: 88).
91. See Brown (2004: 50).
92. Indeed, some scholars have argued that "ancestor worship" itself is a cultural universal. See Steadman, Palmer, and Tilley (1996).

CHAPTER 4: MEMORY WORK IN THE AGE OF QUANTUM GENEALOGY

1. Wendt (1987: 79).
2. Watson (2011).

3. My use of the term *memory work* should not be confused with the sociological research methodology of the same name developed by Haug (1987) in her work on the sexualization of women. Haug and subsequent researchers have engaged in collective autobiographical projects in which groups of researchers analyze their own experiences of oppression and objectification to better understand the larger social mechanisms of subordination. I use the term *memory work* to refer, more broadly, to the work of constructing, ordering, and maintaining memories. See Lambert's (2002) discussion of genealogists as "memory workers."

4. See Zerubavel (1996).

5. I draw here on Arjun Appadurai's (1990) explication of five realms of human activity that facilitate interactions and exchanges across national borders. He discusses global "flows" of people, technologies, capital, media content, and ideas, and refers to these five kinds of flows, respectively, as ethnoscapes, technoscapes, finanscapes, mediascapes, and ideoscapes. I add a sixth "-scape" here, *memoryscape*, which I conceptualize as the flow of interrelated and co-constituting personal remembrances and collective memories, located in human minds and bodies, in discourses and symbols, in institutional practices, and in the physical world. Reed (2015: 13) has likewise conceptualized memoryscapes as "the ideas, images, and embodiments associated with the past that are selective in nature and subject to the dialectics of remembering and forgetting over time and space."

6. See, for instance, Huyssen (1995; 2000), Nora (2002), de Groot (2009; 2015), and Lowenthal (2015).

7. Space does not allow for a full discussion of when modernity began or whether we are indeed still modern. For our purposes here, I conceptualize modernity as beginning, roughly, with the emergence of industrialization and the rise of scientific thinking in the eighteenth century, and continuing into the present. While scholars such as Jean-François Lyotard (1984) argue that we have entered into a new historical era, postmodernity, others, including Zygmunt Bauman (2000) and Anthony Giddens (1998), contend that we are currently in a phase of late, "liquid," or "high" modernity.

8. See Trubeck (2016).

9. See De Groot (2015), Wang, Lee, and Hou (2016), and Huyssen (1995; 2000).

10. Landsberg (2004) suggests that the mass media are facilitating the development of "prosthetic memories." That is, immersive exposure to other people's memories allows us to vicariously experience events, to have powerful emotional responses to those events, and to more deeply empathize and identify with others. These memories are still external in that we know these events happened to others and not to us. But, like a prosthetic limb, these memories are both outside us and a part of us. We incorporate them into our understanding of the world, and they shape the ways we move through the world. For a cogent critique of the notion of "prosthetic memory," see Berger (2007).

11. Oren, Levi-Belz, and Turel (2015) raise concerns about links between "false" presentations of the self online and phenomena such as depression and low self-esteem. Likewise, Steers, Wickham, and Acitelli (2014) find that Facebook viewing encourages us to compare our lived experiences with the idealized presentations of others' experiences, prompting depressive symptoms.

12. Rojek (2010).

13. See Rojek (2010) on serious leisure and Bourdieu (1986) on cultural capital.

14. Morgan (2010).

15. Lambert (1996) notes that genealogists are keenly aware of a "vocabulary of motives." In other words, they are aware of which motivations are socially acceptable (and therefore freely expressed), and which motivations are socially unacceptable (and therefore likely suppressed). Such an awareness may shape which motivations genealogists choose to claim.

16. Migration figures are taken from the US Census Bureau (2007), the last time such figures were calculated. Job-change statistics are taken from US Bureau of Labor Statistics (2015) and Meister (2012). Diversity data are taken from US Census Bureau (2012), and travel statistics from Federal Aviation Administration (2012), the International Air Transport Association (2012), and the World Bank (2013). In 2012, US airlines carried 736 million passengers, and that number was projected to increase by about 3.2 percent annually, to reach 1 billion passengers by 2024. Global passenger increases are even greater, growing by 5.3 percent annually. Because some individuals took more than one trip during the period, it would be more accurate to call these "passenger trips" rather than "passengers."

17. For a discussion of the rise of nostalgia, see Huyssen (2000), Holdsworth (2011), and Lowenthal (2015).

18. See Stearns (2003) on the development of the social history approach. See Lowenthal (2015) on the personalization of history, Yakel (2004) on genealogy and the personalization of history, and Huyssen (1995) on the musealization of social life.

19. Lynch (2011: 114).

20. See de Groot (2015).

21. De Groot (2009).

22. Becker (1973: ix, 5, 7).

23. See Dollimore's (2001: 119–27) critique of the "denial of death" thesis and its advocates, whom he takes to task for reducing death to merely a "sign," an intellectual object to be endlessly analyzed and, ultimately, only further obscured.

24. Bauman (1992).

25. Ariès (1977) cited in Bauman (1992: 96–101). See also Baudrillard (1993) on cemeteries as "ghettos" of the dead.

26. Freud (1918: np).

27. For a review of the secularization thesis and varied scholarly perspectives of the changing role of religion in modern societies, see Bruce (1992).

28. Laqueur (2015: 550).

29. Pogue Harrison (2003: ix–x).

30. Pogue Harrison (2003: x); and Palsson (2002). As Zerubavel (2012) observes, within genealogy, there are "norms of remembrance," and not all ancestors are equal. Some "count" more than others.

31. Laqueur (2015: 41).

32. Rome's Church of San Silvestro in Capite; the Umayyad Mosque, in Damascus, Syria; Amiens Cathedral, in Amiens, France; and part of his head and other remains on the Island of Sveti Ivan, in Bulgaria.

33. For indigenous Australians, for instance, the repatriation of remains is such a crucial issue that the federal government has established an official advisory committee to guide repatriation efforts. See "Advisory Committee for Indigenous Repatriation." Available at https://www.arts.gov.au/advisory-committee-indigenous -repatriation, accessed October 4, 2016.

34. Pogue Harrison (2003: xi). Of course, as we have seen, funerary practices vary a great deal from culture to culture, and they change over time. So burial is just one of the ways humans ritually handle our dead. But Pogue Harrison's larger point is that one of things that makes us distinct from other species is our ritual treatment of the human corpse.

35. Jenkins (2000).

36. Laqueur (2015: 183–86); Bauman (1992: 130–34).

37. Lynch (2011: 114).

38. Ancestry.com TV spot, "Emily"; Ancestry.com TV spot, "Remarkable Path"; and Ancestry.com TV spot, "Surveillance Officer." Available at https://www.ispot.tv/brands/dhv/ancestry, accessed October 18, 2016. Emphasis added.

39. See Ewen (1976).

CHAPTER 5: THE NEW BLOOD QUANTUM

1. Howell (2003); Nash (2004); Mason (2008); Kramer (2011); and Carsten (2000b).

2. Marks (2001), for instance, points out that scientists have long attempted to classify human populations based on their supposed similarities, differences, and closeness or distance in evolutionary terms. These classifications have changed drastically over time, often directly contradicting each other. *Anthropometrics* (the measurement of human bodies) guided much thinking in the nineteenth century, just as eugenics shaped classifications in the early twentieth century, and genetics are shaping discussions today. Indeed, we can see increasing confidence that more and better genetic data will allow scientists to more accurately classify groups relative to each other, and reveal people's *real* identities. But the idea that DNA data can tell us who we "really" are ignores our own perceptions and experiences of identity. Marks argues, therefore, that we must remember that understandings of genetic data are culturally structured—not just objective facts.

3. Green (2006/2007: 98).

4. Hollinger (2005: 20–21).

5. In a ruling that would help to sustain Jim Crow segregation for the next half-century, *Plessy v. Ferguson* established the legitimacy of "separate but equal" facilities for blacks and whites. This ruling held until *Brown v. Board of Education* (1954) ruled segregation in public schools unconstitutional.

6. Hollinger (2005: 21). Such laws against mixed-race marriages were ruled unconstitutional by the Supreme Court in *Loving v. Virginia* (1967).

7. Green (2006/2007: 100).

8. Carlson (1978: 274).

9. See Spruhan (2006). "Blood quantum" referred to the number of documented "full-blooded" Native Americans in one's family tree. So the child of one "full-blood" and one non-Indian was said to have a blood quantum of one-half.

10. Green (2006/2007: 104).

11. Johnston (2003); Glaberson (2001).

12. Simpson (2000) points out that the increasing attention being given to ancestral DNA has the potential to re-essentialize race and ethnicity, by making them appear to be natural, biological categories. Part of the problem, Simpson explains, is the limited "genetic literacy" of the public, who inaccurately assume that genetic science can neatly sort humans into subgroups. He warns against what he calls the "geneticization" of ethnicity. See also Tutton (2004) and Brodwin (2002), who discuss some of the pitfalls of geneticizing our identities.

13. The cost of having one's full DNA—all three billion base pairs—sequenced has recently decreased to around $1,000. Such sequencing is primarily used to identify predispositions toward certain medical conditions, and is not yet widely used by genetic genealogists. See the National Human Genome Institute (2016).

14. Based on an analysis of promotional materials on the websites of eleven leading ancestral DNA test providers (23andMe, AncestryDNA, Family Tree DNA, African Ancestry, Oxford Ancestors, MyHeritageDNA, myDNA.global, AncestryByDNA, GeneBase, the Genographic Project of the National Geographic Society, and Roots for Real) (see figure 5.2).

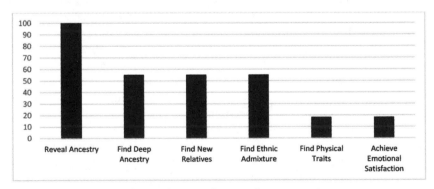

Figure 5.2.   Promises of Genetic Genealogy Testing Companies

15. Brodwin (2002: 329).

16. Greely (2008: 225).

17. For a discussion of the limitations of genetic genealogy, see Wailoo et al. (2012), Klitzman (2013), Duster (2015), and Soo-Jin Lee et al. (2009).

18. See TallBear (2003; 2008) and Kolopenuk (2014) for a discussion of the implications of genetic genealogy for Native American groups.

19. See Duster (2015) and Kahn (2015).

20. Simpson (2000); Day (2004); and TallBear (2008).

21. Duster (2015).

22. Gabriel (2012: 59).

23. Available at https://www.ancestry.com/dna, accessed January 10, 2017.

24. *Faces of America*, episode 4.

25. Native American author Louise Erdrich declined to take a DNA test, saying that her tribe and her family make her who she is. Her DNA is their DNA, so it is not hers to give over for testing.

26. Figures on "false positives" were stated by a representative of AncestryDNA at the 2014 National Genealogical Society in Richmond, Virginia.

27. *Faces of America*, episode 1.

28. See, for instance, Jacobs (2014a; 2014b; 2014c; 2015; 2016).

29. See Kahn (2015), Nash (2013), Koenig et al. (2008), Wailoo et al. (2012), and Duster (2015) for discussions of the problematic potential of DNA tests to re-essentialize race. Gates quote from *Finding Your Roots*, season 1, episode 1.

30. Duster (1990).

31. Nash (2013); Palsson (2002); and Simpson (2000).

32. Sommer (2012: 237); Nash (2013).

33. Panofsky and Donovan (2017).

34. Kelly (2013).

35. Kelly (2013); Palsson (2002); and Simpson (2000).

36. Palsson (2002).

37. Nash (2006: 20).

38. In addition, some scholars argue that the increasing emphasis on the genetic bases of disease can actually have negative effects on health. For example, an overfocus on genetic predispositions toward diseases such as asthma or diabetes can lead researchers to underfocus on highly significant social factors such as poverty that contribute to the development of these diseases. See Marks (2008). Other scholars point out that poor understanding of genetic test results by the public may also lead to people making decisions that harm their health. Indeed, in 2013 the US Food and Drug Administration barred the genetic testing company 23andMe from selling certain tests due to concerns that customers' health could potentially be compromised because they were not being given adequate information to understand their test results (Barajas 2013).

39. Kolopenuk (2014: 18)

40. Mason (2008) cautions us not to take this social isolation thesis too far. She points to a number of studies that suggest that people in modern industrialized

societies remain connected to kin and community in meaningful ways, even though the means of engagement may differ from those in the past.

41. See https://www.bcgcertification.org.

42. Certified Genealogist (CG), Certified Genealogical Lecturer (CGL), Fellow of the American Society of Genealogists (FASG), Fellow of the National Genealogical Society (FNGS), among many others.

43. These "clans," or ancient populations distinguished by certain gene mutations in their mitochondrial DNA, were so named by geneticist Bryan Sykes in his influential (2001) book, *The Seven Daughters of Eve*. The names do not refer to actual individuals (Tara, Jasmine, etc.), but are used as an evocative shorthand for these populations.

44. Available at https://dna-explained.com/2013/01/24/what-is-a-haplogroup, accessed August 7, 2016.

45. Gieryn (1983).

46. While the Genetic Information Nondiscrimination Act (GINA) of 2008 made it illegal for health insurance companies and employers to discriminate against people based on their genetics, broader social attitudes are not easily legislated. Furthermore, the April 2018 arrest of the so-called Golden State Killer has raised serious privacy concerns among genetic genealogists. Investigators used genetic family tree information on the genealogy website GEDmatch to track down a suspect whose violent crimes dated back to at least 1976. Such use of ancestral genetics by law enforcement has prompted some genealogists to remove their information from more publicly accessible sites (Zhang 2018).

47. Hirschman and Panther-Yates (2008: 51) observe that "it is the paradox of DNA testing that it may simultaneously act to disrupt and solidify ethnic identities." That is, consumers may undertake ancestral DNA testing to confirm their link to a desired ethnic or racial group. And if they receive that confirmation, this may bolster their ethnic identity, or even a sense of ethnic purity or superiority. (One DNA testing company even offered to issue consumers with a certificate of "Viking stock" if they proved to have Viking DNA—itself a scientifically problematic construction.) However, consumers may also be forced to confront the notion that they carry the "Other within," if testing reveals previously unknown ethnic or racial origins. On the one hand, it might challenge a consumer's identification with a supposedly superior white elite. On the other hand, it might force a person of color to confront evidence of the oppressor's DNA still colonizing their cells.

48. Ancestral DNA tests are typically quite different from genetic tests used to prove parentage.

49. See Weston (1991) for a groundbreaking discussion of gay and lesbian families of choice.

50. See Nordqvist (2014) on the kinship work of lesbian couples; Almeling (2007) on the market for "ethnic" egg and sperm donors; Carsten (2000b), Howell (2003), and Traver (2007) on kinship work in adoptive families; and Davies (2011) and Finch (2008) on the use of family names as markers of kinship identity.

51. For a brief overview of mitochondrial replacement, see Pritchard (2014).

CHAPTER 6: WHO DO WE THINK WE ARE?

1. Based on a qualitative analysis of ninety-eight roots television episodes from *Who Do You Think You Are?*, *Finding Your Roots*, *Faces of America*, and *The Generations Project*.

2. *Who Do You Think You Are?*, season 1, episode 6; season 2, episode 4; season 3, episode 2; *Finding Your Roots*, episode 4.

3. *Who Do You Think You Are?*, season 2, episode 2; season 2, episode 1; season 2, episode 8; season 3, episode 1; season 3, episode 5.

4. *Who Do You Think You Are?*, season 2, episode 2; season 2, episode 1; season 2, episode 8; season 3, episode 1; season 3, episode 5; *Finding Your Roots*, episode 5.

5. *Who Do You Think You Are?*, season 2, episode 6; season 2, episode 2; season 1, episode 4; season 1, episode 5; *Faces of America*, episode 4; episode 3; *BYU Generations Project*, season 1, episode 3; season 1, episode 8.

6. Such emotional dilemmas are particularly prominent in BYU-TV's *The Generations Project*. *The Generations Project*, season 1, episode 11; season 1, episode 8; season 3, episode 13; season 3, episode 11.

7. *Finding Your Roots*, episode 1.

8. *Who Do Think You Are?*, season 3, episode 3.

9. *The Generations Project*, season 1, episode 10.

10. *The Generations Project*, season 1.

11. *Who Do Think You Are?*, season 2, episode 2; *Finding your Roots*, episode 2.

12. *Who Do Think You Are?*, season 3, episode 8.

13. *Faces of America*, episode 1; *Who Do You Think you Are?*, season 2, episode 5; season 2, episode 3.

14. *Faces of America*, episode 1; episode 3; *Who Do You Think You Are?*, season 2, episode 7; *Finding Your Roots*, episode 5.

15. Figure 6.1 is based on an analysis of *Who Do You Think You Are?*, the PBS shows *Finding Your Roots* and *Faces of America*, and the BYU-TV *Generations Project*. The PBS shows, hosted by an African American scholar, are notable for their inclusion of people of color and their more focused exploration of American racial politics and racial injustices.

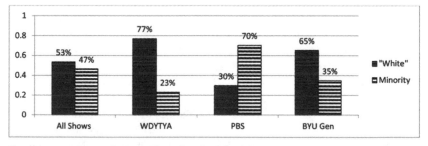

Figure 6.1. Featured Guests by Ethnoracial Status

16. *Who Do You Think You Are?*, season 3, episode 7; season 3, episode 4; *Finding Your Roots*, episode 2. According to research by Mishel et al. (2012), the United States actually lags well behind other wealthy nations in Western Europe, as well as Australia, New Zealand, Canada, and Japan in terms of intergenerational mobility—that is, the ability of families to move up the social ladder over time. So the notion that "only in America" is upward mobility possible, or that America is unparalleled in the opportunities it offers for upward mobility, is not supported by the data.

17. *Finding Your Roots*, episode 5. Notions that the United States is the most generous, loving, and humane nation on Earth are not well supported by the data. For instance, in terms of foreign aid, the United States lags substantially behind other wealthy nations in the percentage of gross national income it devotes to foreign assistance programs. Sweden, for instance, devotes almost ten times more of its income than the United States does in foreign aid (available at http://www.oecd .org/dac/stats/documentupload/ODA%202014%20Tables%20and%20Charts.pdf, accessed June 22, 2017). On this measure, at least, the United States is clearly not the most "generous" nation on Earth. While it is more difficult to compare how "loving" and humane nations are, one issue we can look at is incarceration. While the United States has only 5 percent of the world's population, we have almost 25 percent of the world's total prison population. We imprison a higher percentage of our population than any other nation. And this isn't because we have more crime. Researchers found a strikingly higher prison population rate in the United States compared to countries with similar crime rates (Lee 2015). On this measure, at least, the United States is not the most humane or loving nation in the world.

18. By this logic, disadvantaged groups are blamed for their own disadvantage, and public programs designed to mitigate that disadvantage are portrayed as a waste of taxpayer money. For an incisive discussion of institutionalized inequalities, see Bonilla-Silva (2006).

19. *Who Do You Think You Are?*, season 2, episode 8; *Finding Your Roots*, episode 5.

20. *The Generations Project*, season 1, episode 12; season 1, episode 13; season 2, episode 6.

21. *Who Do You Think You Are?*, season 3, episode 7; season 2, episode 1; season 1, episode 2.

22. *Who Do You Think You Are?*, season 1, episode 3; season 1, episode 1; season 2, episode 5; season 3, episode 5; *Finding Your Roots*, episode 4; episode 10.

23. *The Generations Project*, season 3, episode 6.

24. Interviews with Viola (56, Texas), Delia (50, Maryland), Emily (63, Indiana), Luanne (80, Texas), Joan (51, Illinois), Sharon (55, Missouri), Celia (60, California), Joy (64, California), Charlotte (70, Illinois), Martin (38, Michigan), Ramona (46, New York), Serena (50, New York), Diane (66, Minnesota), Rachel (60, Indiana), Bob (75, Illinois), and a group of fifteen amateur and professional genealogists on a research trip to the Family History Library in Salt Lake City.

25. For instance, futurist Ray Kurzweil predicted that by 2010, humans would spend most of our time inhabiting virtual environments, and would become, in effect, "virtual humans." http://www.kurzweilai.net/foreword-to-virtual-humans, accessed June 23, 2017.

26. See Koblin (2016); Asano (2017); Wallace (2015); Moran (2013); Kiss (2014); and Benwell (2013).

27. For classic formulations of the ideological power of advertisements, see Ewen (1976), Williamson (1978), and Schudson (1984).

CHAPTER 7: IN SEARCH OF THE "LIVING DEAD"

1. Based on a nonscientific survey of electronic sources, figure 7.1 reveals that the number of zombie movies has increased significantly in recent decades. (My thanks to Dr. Bradford Brown for these numbers.)

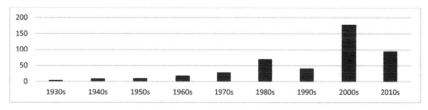

Figure 7.1. Zombie Films by Decade

The phenomenally successful television series *The Walking Dead* (AMC 2010–17) is based on a comic book of the same title (2003–17) by Robert Kirkman, and *World War Z* (2013), the highest-grossing zombie film ever, was based on Max Brooks's (2006) novel of the same title.

2. Dalfovo (1997).

3. Malinowski (1948); Poggie and Gersuny (1972); and Gmelch (1971).

4. "Religious Landscape Study." Available at http://www.pewforum.org/religious-landscape-study/attendance-at-religious-services, accessed September 26, 2017; "Americans' Faith in God May Be Eroding." Available at http://www.pewresearch.org/fact-tank/2015/11/04/americans-faith-in-god-may-be-eroding, accessed September 26, 2017.

5. As Eastwood and Prevalakis (2010) point out, as nations modernize and industrialize, life becomes more predictable. People's "existential uncertainty" decreases, so they have less need for religion. At the same time, modern industrialized societies are characterized by a complex division of labor and highly specialized institutions. In this context, religion becomes just another specialized institution—responsible for spiritual matters, but no longer at the center of economic, political, and broader social processes. So secularization tends to increase

with modernization. It is important to recognize, however, that while scholars have long predicted that religion would become increasingly irrelevant in modern societies, secularization has by no means been uniform or complete. Periods of secularization often spark a resurgence in religiosity, and older forms of religious observance often give way to spiritual innovations.

6. Bauman (1992).

7. As Church founder Joseph Smith wrote in 1842, "The earth will be smitten with a curse unless there is a welding link of some kind or other between the fathers and the children. . . . Let us, therefore, as a church and a people, and as Latter-day Saints, offer unto the Lord an offering in righteousness; and let us present in this holy temple . . . a book containing the records of our dead" (Allen, Embry, and Mehr 1994–95: 20).

8. Allen, Embry, and Mehr (1994–95: 13–14, 19); and Sweeney (2010).

9. Allen, Embry, and Mehr (1994–95: 20–22).

10. Allen, Embry, and Mehr (1994–95: 23, 39–40, 43).

11. Allen, Embry, and Mehr (1994–95: 45–49, 60).

12. Allen, Embry, and Mehr (1994–95: 53).

13. Allen, Embry, and Mehr (1994–95: 215, 239–40).

14. https://familysearch.org/about; https://familysearch.org/archives/; and https://familysearch.org/blog/en/familysearch-2016-year-review.

15. https://familysearch.org/archives/services.

16. https://familysearch.org/archives/faq/; https://familysearch.org/blog/en/mormon-family-history-library-connecting-generations-families-30-years-2.

17. https://familysearch.org/archives/faq.

18. https://familysearch.org/blog/en/familysearch-2016-year-review.

19. Akenson (2007: 52).

20. While recent discussions of this practice often refer to it as "polygamy," *polygamy* technically means "multiple spouses," which might include *polygyny* (multiple wives) or *polyandry* (multiple husbands). The Mormon Church only endorsed polygyny.

21. Hardy and Erickson (2001).

22. Akenson (2007: 55–61). Polygyny persisted unofficially and was tolerated by the Church into the early twentieth century, when a court case forced the issue. And the practice continues today among followers of the Fundamentalist Church of Jesus Christ of Latter-day Saints.

23. Akenson (2007: 63).

24. Allen, Embry, and Mehr (1994–95: 43, 53). As Akenson (2007: 100–101) points out, ironically, despite the Mormons' extraordinary contributions to expanding genealogical research in the United States and around the world, the genealogical records for people of Mormon descent are often highly inaccurate due to these widespread lineage adoptions and factual errors in early records.

25. Akenson (2007: 42–44); Mauss (2003: 36). There are no professional clergy in the Mormon Church. Rather, "priesthood" is a broader concept that generally

includes all men of good standing in the Church who take on certain leadership duties and serve as moral examples for their families and communities.

26. Toone (2017).

27. Church of Jesus Christ of Latter-day Saints (2017); Pew Research Center (2009).

28. Weisenfeld (2013); National Public Radio (2012); and National Public Radio (2017).

29. Johnson (2016).

30. Akenson (2007: 119).

31. Weiser (2015: 442).

32. Ogg (2011).

33. Bishop (2009); Comaroff and Comaroff (2002); Davis and Carne (2015); Dziemanowicz (2009); Morrisette (2014); Saunders (2012); Stratton (2011); Webb and Byrnand (2008); Weiser (2015); and Wonser (2016).

34. Saunders (2012: 80).

35. While early-twentieth-century zombie stories generally featured an evil sorcerer reanimating and enslaving the dead, in twenty-first-century stories, zombies usually result from viruses, contaminants, or mutations that spread rapidly across the globe. See Saunders (2012).

36. Browne (2009); Morton (2008); McIntosh (2008); Palwick (2008); and Cheek (2008).

37. Indeed, many zombie stories include heart-rending scenes in which protagonists must decide whether to kill a zombified loved one.

CHAPTER 8: IMAGINED HOMES

1. Tolkien (1994: 167).

2. Roots tourism is the fastest-growing sector of the "heritage tourism" industry. Heritage tourism includes a vast range of cultural and historical sites, such as museums, historic homes, monuments, and even natural sites that have been given "World Heritage" status (Santos and Yan 2010: 56).

3. Tourism Ireland (2017); Irish Press (2011); Baran (2012); and Elder (2005).

4. Ghana Tourism Authority (2016); World Travel and Tourism Council (2016).

5. De Groot (2009: 113).

6. See Walter Benjamin's (1969) conceptualization of "aura" in works of art. He argued that in the age of mechanically reproduced artworks, art loses its authenticity and authority, its ability to provoke awe and contemplation. Instead, it is reduced to spectacle, a pleasant distraction, a commodity. I would argue that ancestral sites exude the kind of "aura" Benjamin discusses. They concretize authenticity and authority, and therefore provoke a sense of wonder in roots travelers.

7. Turner and Turner (1978); Turner (1973).

8. P. Basu (2004; 2005).
9. P. Basu (2004; 2005).
10. P. Basu (2004; 2005).
11. I draw here on John Urry's (1990) explication of the "tourist gaze," which is characterized by three primary components: difference, pleasure, and power. In other words, objects of the tourist gaze must be sufficiently removed from the ordinary and everyday to be considered different; this difference must be perceived as pleasurable to experience; and tourists must maintain sufficient power over the objects of their gaze to sustain that pleasure. Part of the pleasure of the touristic experience is to contain or capture the spectacle, often through snapshots. Whether one is encountering other places or other people, snapping photos can be seen as managing difference and desire, fear and fascination in encounters with the Other. See also Rojek and Urry (1997).
12. https://myirelandheritage.com; http://www.lynotttours.com/i-gen.htm; http://www.timetraveltours.com/genealogy.html; https://myirelandheritage.com.
13. Campbell (1994); Barrett (2012: 1).
14. The term *diaspora capital* requires explanation here. The word *diaspora*—from the Greek *dia* ("across") and *speirein* ("scatter")—has increasingly been used to refer to any large-scale migrations or dispersions of people. In its more restricted sense, it refers to those people (and their descendants) who have been dispersed from a "homeland" to foreign lands; who still retain at least affective ties to that homeland; and who imagine the "homeland" as an ideal home to which they belong and might one day return. In addition, diasporic peoples may feel alienated to some degree from their host society, which heightens a longing for "home" (see Reed 2015: 8–11). *Diaspora capital* refers to the money that diasporic peoples can bring back to their imagined "homelands," usually in the form of tourist spending and foreign investment. The governments of both Ireland and Ghana have explicitly targeted diaspora capital as one pathway toward economic development.
15. Irish Department of Foreign Affairs and Trade (2011).
16. Irish Department of Foreign Affairs and Trade (2015).
17. Based on author's analysis of all displays at the Dunbrody Famine Ship in New Ross, the Cobh Heritage Centre in Cobh, the Skibbereen Heritage Centre in far southwest County Cork, and Strokestown Park House and Famine Museum in County Roscommon.
18. Strokestown House and Famine Museum display.
19. Levin (2007a; 2007b).
20. https://www.dunbrody.com; http://www.cobhheritage.com; http://www.strokestownlearningzone.com; https://skibbheritage.com/home/about-us. All accessed August 24, 2017.
21. For an incisive discussion of the Great Famine, see Poirteir (1997).
22. Reed (2015: 20).
23. Reviews available at https://www.tripadvisor.com/Attraction_Review-g211925-d318971-Reviews-Cobh_Heritage_Centre-Cobh_County_Cork.html;

https://www.tripadvisor.com/Attraction_Review-g186641-d1720902-Reviews
-Dunbrody_Famine_Ship_Experience-New_Ross_County_Wexford.html;
https://www.tripadvisor.com/Attraction_Review-g211921-d269009-Reviews
-Skibbereen_Heritage_Centre-Skibbereen_County_Cork.html; https://www
.tripadvisor.com/Attraction_Review-g659918-d2037095-Reviews-Strokestown
_Park_National_Famine_Museum-Strokestown_County_Roscommon_Western
_Irel.html, accessed August 31, 2017.

24. Reed (2004; 2012; 2013; 2015); Ohrt Fehler (2014); Yankholmes and Akyeampong (2010); Holsey (2004); Hartman (2002; 2007); Hasty (2002); Pascal (2001); Bruner (1996; 2005).

25. Speech delivered at PANAFEST 2001, reported by Reed (2015: 191).

26. Holsey (2004); Reed (2015); Ohrt Fehler (2014); Hasty (2002); and Bruner (1996).

27. Reed (2015: 18).

28. Reed (2015); Hartman (2002).

29. Online reviews available at https://www.tripadvisor.com/Attraction _Review-g303867-d325039-Reviews-Elmina_Castle-Elmina_Central_Region.html.

30. Reed (2015); Holsey (2004); Hasty (2002); Pascal (2001); and Bruner (1996).

31. Online reviews available at https://www.tripadvisor.com/Attraction _Review-g303867-d325039-Reviews-Elmina_Castle-Elmina_Central_Region .html; https://www.tripadvisor.com/Attraction_Review-g303866-d478868 -Reviews-or20-Cape_Coast_Castle-Cape_Coast_Central_Region.html. Accessed September 7, 2017.

32. Reed (2015); Ohrt Fehler (2014).

33. Reed (2015: 83).

34. Reed (2015: 153); Holsey (2004); Hasty (2002); Pascal (2001); Bruner (1996).

35. Reed (2015: 102).

36. 40 GH¢ converts to about US$8. The usual admission fee to the Castle is 5 GH¢ for Ghanaians, and 10 GH¢ for foreign visitors. This reviewer asserts that the clerk at the gate tried to charge their party of three people 40 GH¢ rather than 30 GH¢. And she further asserts that since she is from the African diaspora, she should only have to pay the lower rate that locals pay.

37. Online review available at https://www.tripadvisor.com/Attraction _Review-g303867-d325039-Reviews-Elmina_Castle-Elmina_Central_Region .html, accessed September 7, 2017.

38. Online review available at https://www.tripadvisor.com/Attraction _Review-g303866-d478868-Reviews-or20-Cape_Coast_Castle-Cape_Coast _Central_Region.html, accessed September 7, 2017.

39. Reed (2015: 109); Bruner (1996). Recent online reviews of the sites indicate that commercial activity has returned to the sites, however. For instance, visitors report being ushered through multiple gift shops within Elmina Castle and complain of being set upon by aggressive street vendors at the entrance to the site.

40. Reed (2015: 188).

41. Reed (2015: 66) notes, for instance, that Ghanaians make up roughly three-quarters of visitors to Cape Coast Castle.

42. Reed (2015: 134). "Enstoolment" is the process of installing a leader (like a chief, king, or queenmother) in office.

43. Available at http://www.myirishconnections.com/tours.htm. Accessed September 7, 2017.

44. Hartman (2007: 98)

45. Young and Light (2016).

46. From Robert Burns (1784), "Man Was Made to Mourn: A Dirge": Many and sharp the num'rous ills / Inwoven with our frame! / More pointed still we make ourselves / Regret, remorse, and shame! / And man, whose heav'n-erected face / The smiles of love adorn, — / Man's inhumanity to man / Makes countless thousands mourn!

47. Ignatiev (1997).

CHAPTER 9: OUR ANCESTORS, OURSELVES

1. Bauman (2000; 2005; 2007). Bauman characterizes our current era as "liquid modernity." That is, an era characterized by the fluidity of identities, institutions, and processes, and one which lacks the certainty and stability of the preindustrial era or the era of "solid modernity."

BIBLIOGRAPHY

23andMe. 2018. "Ancestry Composition." https://permalinks.23andme.com/pdf/samplereport_ancestrycomp.pdf. Accessed July 9, 2018.

Abasi, Augustine Kututera. 1995. "Lua-Lia, the Fresh Funeral: Founding a House for the Deceased among the Kasena of North-East Ghana." *Africa: Journal of the International African Institute* 65, no. 3: 448–75.

Akenson, Donald Harman. 2007. *Some Family: The Mormons and How Humanity Keeps Track of Itself*. Montreal: McGill-Queen's University Press.

Allen, James B., Jessie L. Embry, and Kahlile B. Mehr. 1994–95. "Hearts Turned to the Fathers: A History of the Genealogical Society of Utah, 1894–1994." *BYU Studies* 34: 5–392.

Almeling, Rene. 2007. "Selling Genes, Selling Gender: Egg Agencies, Sperm Banks, and the Medical Market in Genetic Material." *American Sociological Review* 72, no. 3: 319–40.

Ancestry.com. 2010. "Starting Your Family History." http://corporate.ancestry.com/library/media/Getting%20Started%20OneSheet%202.19.10.pdf. Accessed October 1, 2013.

———. 2013a. http://corporate.ancestry.com/library/media/Getting%20Started%20One-Sheet%202.19.10.pdf. Accessed August 16, 2013.

———. 2013b. "Message from Our CEO: Tim Sullivan." http://corporate.ancestry.com/about-ancestry. Accessed August 16, 2013.

———. 2013c. "Ancestry.com LLC Reports Q2 2013 Financial Results." http://corporate.ancestry.com/press/press-releases/2013/07/ancestrycom-llc-reports-q2-2013-financial-results. Accessed August 16, 2013.

———. 2014a. "Company Facts." http://corporate.ancestry.com/press/company-facts. Accessed September 9, 2014.

———. 2014b. http://dna.ancestry.com. Accessed February 27, 2014.

———. 2015a. "Company Facts." http://corporate.ancestry.com/press/company-facts. Accessed October 2, 2015.

————. 2015b. "Ancestry DNA Insights." https://www.ancestry.com/dna. Accessed October 5, 2015.

————. 2017. "Company Facts." https://www.ancestry.com/corporate/about-ancestry/company-facts. Accessed September 19, 2017.

Anderson, Benedict. 1983. *Imagined Communities*. London and New York: Verso.

Appadurai, Arjun. 1990. "Disjuncture and Difference in the Global Cultural Economy." In *Global Culture: Nationalism, Globalization and Modernity*, edited by Mike Featherstone, 295–310. London: Sage Publications.

Appleby, Joyce. 2005. *A Restless Past: History and the American Public*. Lanham, MD: Rowman & Littlefield.

Arhin, Kwame. 1994. "The Economic Implications of Transformations in Akan Funeral Rites." *Africa: Journal of the International African Institute* 64, no. 3: 307–22.

Asano, Evan. 2017. "How Much Time Do People Spend on Social Media?" http://www.socialmediatoday.com/marketing/how-much-time-do-people-spend-lsocial-media-infographic. Accessed March 14, 2017.

Barajas, Joshua. 2015. "23andMe Returns with Modified, FDA-Approved Genetic Tests." http://www.pbs.org/newshour/rundown/23andme-returns-modified-fda-approved-genetic-tests. Accessed May 23, 2016.

Baran, Michelle. 2012. "Visitors of Irish Descent Targeted in Ireland's Gathering Effort." *Travel Weekly*. http://www.travelweekly.com/Europe-Travel/Visitors-of-Irish-descent-targeted-in-Irelands-Gathering-effort. Accessed January 3, 2013.

Barrett, James R. 2012. *The Irish Way: Becoming American in the Multiethnic City*. New York: Penguin Books.

Barreyre, Nicolas. 2011. "The Politics of Economic Crises: The Panic of 1873, the End of Reconstruction, and the Realignment of American Politics." *Journal of the Gilded Age and Progressive Era* 10, no. 4: 403–23.

Basu, Helene. 2005. "Practices of Praise and Social Constructions of Identity: The Bards of North-West India." *Archives de Sciences Sociales des Religions*, no. 130: 81–105.

Basu, Paul. 2004. "My Own Island Home: The Orkney Homecoming." *Journal of Material Culture* 9, no. 27: 27–42.

————. 2005. "Macpherson Country: Genealogical Identities, Spatial Histories and the Scottish Diasporic Clanscape." *Cultural Geographies* 12: 123–50.

Battaglia, Debbora. 1990. *On the Bones of the Serpent, Person, Memory, and Mortality in Sabarl Island Society*. Chicago: University of Chicago Press.

————. 1992. "The Body in the Gift: Memory and Forgetting in Sabarl Mortuary Exchange." *American Ethnologist* 19, no. 1: 3–18.

Baudrillard, Jean. 1993. *Symbolic Exchange and Death*. Translated by Iain Hamilton Grant. London: Sage.

Bauman, Zygmunt. 1978. *Hermeneutics and Social Science*. New York: Columbia University Press.

———. 1992. *Mortality, Immortality and Other Life Strategies*. Cambridge, UK: Polity Press.

———. 2000. *Liquid Modernity*. Cambridge, UK: Polity Press.

———. 2005. *Liquid Life*. Cambridge, UK: Polity Press.

———. 2007. *Consuming Life*. Cambridge, UK: Polity Press.

Becker, Ernest. 1973. *The Denial of Death*. New York: Free Press.

Benjamin, Walter. 1969. "The Work of Art in the Age of Mechanical Reproduction." In *Illuminations*, edited by Hannah Arendt. Translated by Harry Zohn. New York: Schocken Books.

Benoît, Catherine. 2007. "The Politics of Vodou: Aids, Access to Health Care and the Use of Culture in Haiti." *Anthropology in Action* 14, no. 3: 59–68.

Benwell, Max. 2013. "What We Can Learn from the Numbers Twitter and Facebook Don't Want Us to See." *The Independent*. http://www.independent.co.uk/voices/comment/what-we-can-learn-from-the-numbers-twitter-and-facebook-dont-want-us-to-see-9029152.html. Accessed March 13, 2014.

Berg, Astrid. 2003. "Ancestor Reverence and Mental Health in South Africa." *Transcultural Psychiatry* 40, no. 2: 194–207.

Berger, James. 2007. "Which Prosthetic? Mass Media, Narrative, Empathy, and Progressive Politics." *Rethinking History* 11, no. 4: 597–612.

Berger, Peter L., and Thomas Luckmann. 1966. *The Social Construction of Reality: A Treatise in the Sociology of Knowledge*. Garden City, NY: Anchor Books.

Best, Steven, and Douglas Kellner. 1997. *The Postmodern Turn (Critical Perspectives)*. New York: Guilford Press.

Bishop, Kyle. 2009. "Dead Man Still Walking: Explaining the Zombie Renaissance." *Journal of Popular Film and Television* 37, no. 1: 16–25.

Blount, Ben G. 1975. "Agreeing to Agree on Genealogy: A Luo Sociology of Knowledge." In *Sociocultural Dimensions of Language Use*, edited by M. Sanchez and B. Blount, 117–36. New York: Academic Press.

Board for Certification of Genealogists. 2015. "Genealogical Proof Standard." http://www.bcgcertification.org/resources/standard.html. Accessed October 6, 2015.

Bockstruck, Lloyd DeWitt. 1983. "Four Centuries of Genealogy." *A Historical Overview, RQ* 23: 162–70.

Bohannan, Laura. 1952. "A Genealogical Charter." *Africa* 22: 301–15.

Bonilla-Silva, Eduardo. 2006. *Racism without Racists: Color-Blind Racism and the Persistence of Racial Inequality in America*. Lanham, MD: Rowman & Littlefield.

Bouquet, Mary. 1996. "Family Trees and Their Affinities: The Visual Imperative of the Genealogical Diagram." *Journal of the Royal Anthropological Institute* 2, no. 1: 43–60.

Bourdieu, Pierre. 1986. "The Forms of Capital." In *Handbook of Theory and Research for the Sociology of Education*, edited by John Richardson, 241–58. New York: Greenwood.

Bradbury, Ray. 1951. "The Veldt." In *The Illustrated Man*. New York: Doubleday & Company.

Brand, Sondra, and Nina Platter. 2011. "Dark Tourism: The Commoditisation of Suffering and Death." In *The Long Tail of Tourism: Holiday Niches and Their Impact on Mainstream Tourism*, edited by Alexis Papathanassis. Wiesbaden, Germany: Gabler Verlag.

Brodwin, Paul. 2002. "Genetics, Identity and the Anthropology of Essentialism." *Anthropological Quarterly* 75, no. 2: 323–30.

Brooks, Max. 2006. *World War Z: An Oral History of the Zombie War*. New York: Random House.

Brown, Donald. 1991. *Human Universals*. Philadelphia: Temple University Press.

———. 2004. "Human Universals, Human Nature and Human Culture." *Daedalus* 133, no. 4: 47–54.

Browne, S. G. 2009. *Breathers: A Zombie's Lament*. New York: Broadway Books.

Bruce, Steve, ed. 1992. *Religion and Modernization: Sociologists and Historians Debate the Secularization Thesis*. Oxford, UK: Clarendon Press.

Bruner, Edward M. 1996. "Tourism in Ghana: The Representation of Slavery and the Return of the Black Diaspora." *American Anthropologist, New Series* 98, no. 2: 290–304.

———. 2005. *Culture on Tour: Ethnographies of Travel*. Chicago: University of Chicago Press.

Bureau of Labor Statistics. 2012. "American Time Use Survey." http://www.bls .gov/tus/charts/household.htm. Accessed September 10, 2015.

Calhoun, C. J. 1980. "The Authority of Ancestors: A Sociological Reconsideration of Fortes's Tallensi in Response to Fortes's Critics." *Man* 15, no. 2: 304–19.

Campbell, Stephen J. 1994. *The Great Irish Famine: Words and Images from the Famine Museum Strokestown Park, County Roscommon*. Roscommon, Ireland: The Famine Museum.

Carlson, Leonard A. 1978. "The Dawes Act and the Decline of Indian Farming." *The Journal of Economic History* 38, no. 1: 274–76.

Carsten, Janet, ed. 2000a. *Cultures of Relatedness: New Approaches to the Study of Kinship*. Cambridge, UK: Cambridge University Press.

———. 2000b. "Knowing Where You've Come From: Ruptures and Continuities of Time and Kinship in Narratives of Adoption Reunions." *Royal Anthropological Institute* 6: 687–703.

Cheek, Catherine. 2008. "She's Taking Her Tits to the Grave." In *The Living Dead*, edited by John Joseph Adams, 360–68. New York: Night Shade Books.

Church of Jesus Christ of Latter-day Saints. 2012. "Genealogy Volunteers Index 1940 U.S. Census in Record Time." http://www.mormonnewsroom.org/ article/genealogy-volunteers-index-mammouth-1940-census-in-record-time. Accessed September 14, 2015.

———. 2017. "Facts and Statistics." http://www.mormonnewsroom.org/facts-and -statistics#. Accessed July 20, 2017.

Clark, Ian. 2000. "Ancestor Worship and Identity: Ritual, Interpretation, and Social Normalization in the Malaysian Chinese Community." *Sojourn* 15, no. 2: 273–95.

Comaroff, Jean, and John L. Comaroff. 2002. "Alien Nation: Zombies, Immigrants, and Millennial Capitalism." *South Atlantic Quarterly* 101, no. 4: 779–805.

Connor, Alan. 2014. *The Crossword Century: 100 Years of Witty Wordplay, Ingenious Puzzles, and Linguistic Mischief*. New York: Gotham.

Crunchbase.com. 2013. "Ancestry.com Overview." http://www.crunchbase.com/company/ancestry-com. Accessed August 16, 2013.

Dalfovo, Albert Titus. 1997. "The Lugbara Ancestors." *Anthropos* 92, no. 4/6: 485–500.

Daniels, Inge. 2012. "Beneficial Bonds: Luck and the Lived Experience of Relatedness in Contemporary Japan." *Social Analysis* 56, no. 1: 148–64.

Davies, Hayley. 2011. "Sharing Surnames: Children, Family and Kinship." *Sociology* 45, no. 4: 554–69.

Davis, Christine S., and Jonathan L. Carne. 2015. "Dialogue with (Un)Death: Horror Films as a Discursive Attempt to Construct a Relationship with the Dead." *Journal of Loss and Trauma* 20: 417–29.

Day, Elizabeth. 2004. "God Gene Discovered by Scientist behind Gay DNA Theory." *Daily Telegraph*, November 14, 2004. https://www.telegraph.co.uk/news/uknews/1476575/God-gene-discovered-by-scientist-behind-gay-DNA-theory.html. Accessed June 11, 2017.

De Groot, Jerome. 2009. *Consuming History: Historians and Heritage in Contemporary Popular Culture*. New York: Routledge.

———. 2015. "On Genealogy." *The Public Historian* 37, no. 3: 102–27.

Dernbach, Katherine Boris. 2005. "Spirits of the Hereafter: Death, Funerary Possession, and the Afterlife in Chuuk, Micronesia." *Ethnology* 44, no. 2: 99–123.

De Santana Pinho, Patricia. 2008. "African-American Roots Tourism in Brazil." *Latin American Perspectives* 35, no. 3: 70–86.

Desmangles, Leslie Gérald. 1992. *The Faces of the Gods: Vodou and Roman Catholicism in Haiti*. Chapel Hill: University of North Carolina Press.

De Witte, Marleen. 2001. *Long Live the Dead! Changing Funeral Celebrations in Asante, Ghana*. Amsterdam: Aksant Academic Publishers.

Dick, Philip K. 1966. "We Can Remember It for You Wholesale." *Magazine of Fantasy and Science Fiction*. New York: Mercury Press.

Di Leonardo, Micaela. 1987. "The Female World of Cards and Holidays: Women, Families, and the Work of Kinship." *Signs* 12, no. 3: 440–53.

Dollimore, Jonathan. 2001. *Death, Desire and Loss in Western Culture*. New York: Routledge.

Drake, Pamela J. 2001. "Fullerton Genealogy Study." http://psych.fullerton.edu/genealogy/#INTRO. Accessed August 26, 2015.

Duke, Marshall P., Amber Lazarus, and Robyn Fivush. 2008. "Knowledge of Family History as a Clinically Useful Index of Psychological Well-Being and Prognosis: A Brief Report." *Psychotherapy Theory, Research, Practice, Training* 45: 268–72.

Dunbar, Robin. 2003. "Evolution of the Social Brain." *Science* 302, no. 5648: 1160–61.

Duster, Troy. 1990. *Backdoor to Eugenics*. New York: Routledge.

———. 2015. "A Post-Genomic Surprise: The Molecular Reinscription of Race in Science, Law, and Medicine." *British Journal of Sociology* 66, no. 1: 1–27.

Dziemianowicz, Stefan. 2009. "Might of the Living Dead." *Publishers Weekly* 256, no. 28: 20–24.

Eastwood, Jonathan, and Nikolas Prevalakis. 2010. "Nationalism, Religion, and Secularization: An Opportune Moment for Research." *Review of Religious Research* 52, no. 1: 90–111.

Elder, Robert K. 2005. "Lost in Ireland: Where Are My Roots?" *Chicago Tribune*, October 16, 2005. http://articles.chicagotribune.com/2005-10-16/travel/ 0510160193_1_family-historian-great-famine-montana/2.

Ephirim-Donkor, Anthony. 2013. *African Religion Defined: A Systematic Study of Ancestor Worship among the Akan*. Lanham, MD: University Press of America.

Erben, Michael. 1991. "Genealogy and Sociology: A Preliminary Set of Statements and Speculations." *Sociology* 25, no. 2: 275–95.

Evans-Pritchard, E. E. 1951. *Kinship and Marriage among the Nuer*. Oxford, UK: Clarendon Press.

Ewen, Stuart. 1976. *Captains of Consciousness: Advertising and the Social Roots of the Consumer Culture*. New York: McGraw-Hill.

FamilySearch.org. 2011. "Library Background." https://www.familysearch.org/ locations/saltlakecity-library. Accessed September 5, 2011.

———. 2015a. "Collection." https://familysearch.org/locations/saltlakecity-library. Accessed October 9, 2015.

———. 2015b. "Introduction to LDS Family History Centers." https://familysearch .org/learn/wiki/en/Introduction_to_LDS_Family_History_Centers. Accessed October 9, 2015.

FamilyTreeDNA. 2015. "DNA Tests." https://www.familytreedna.com/products .aspx. Accessed September 21, 2017.

Federal Aviation Administration. 2012. "Airline Travel to Nearly Double in Two Decades." http://www.faa.gov/news/press_releases/news_story.cfm ?newsId=13394. Accessed March 12, 2014.

Fiawoo, D. K. 1976. "Characteristic Features of Ewe Ancestor Worship." In *Ancestors*, edited by William H. Newell, 263–81. The Hague and Paris: Mouton Publishers.

Finch, Janet. 2008. "Naming Names: Kinship, Individuality and Personal Names." *Sociology* 42, no. 4: 709–25.

Fletcher Stack, Peggy (2017) "Mormon Growth Rate Falls to Lowest Level in 80 Years, but Ups and Downs Vary by Region." *Salt Lake Tribune,* July 7, 2017. http://archive.sltrib.com/article.php?id=5381411&itype=CMSID.

Foner, Eric. 1990. *A Short History of Reconstruction, 1863–1877*. New York: Harper & Row.

Freud, Sigmund. 1918. *Reflections on War and Death*. Translated by A. A. Brill and Alfred B. Kuttner. New York: Moffat, Yard and Co.

Friedman, Jonathan. 1992. "The Past in the Future: History and the Politics of Identity." *American Anthropologist* 94, no. 4: 837–59.

Gabriel, Abram. 2012. "A Biologist's Perspective on DNA and Race in the Genomics Era." In *Genetics and the Unsettled Past: The Collision of DNA, Race, and History*, edited by Keith Wailoo, Alondra Nelson, and Catherine Lee, 43–66. New Brunswick, NJ: Rutgers University Press.

Gans, Herbert J. 1979. "Symbolic Ethnicity: The Future of Ethnic Groups and Cultures in America." *Ethnic and Racial Studies* 2, no. 1: 1–20.

Gerber, David A. 1977. "Haley's Roots and Our Own: An Inquiry into the Nature of a Popular Phenomenon." *Journal of Ethnic Studies* 5, no. 3: 87–111.

Ghana Tourism Authority. 2016. "Tourism Information on Ghana." http://www
.ghana.travel/wp-content/uploads/2016/11/Tourism-Statistics.docx. Accessed August 16, 2017.

Giddens, Anthony. 1990. *The Consequences of Modernity*. Stanford, CA: Stanford University Press.

———. 1998. *Conversations with Anthony Giddens: Making Sense of Modernity*. Stanford, CA: Stanford University Press.

Gieryn, Thomas F. 1983. "Boundary-Work and the Demarcation of Science from Non-Science: Strains and Interests in Professional Ideologies of Scientists." *American Sociological Review* 48, no. 6: 781–95.

Glaberson, William. 2001. "Who Is a Seminole, and Who Gets to Decide?" *New York Times*, January 29, 2001. https://www.nytimes.com/2001/01/29/us/who
-is-a-seminole-and-who-gets-to-decide.html. Accessed March 13, 2017.

Gmelch, George. 1971. "Superstition and Ritual in American Baseball." *Society* 8, no. 8: 39–41.

Greely, Henry T. 2008. "Genetic Genealogy: Genetics Meets the Marketplace." In *Revisiting Race in a Genomic Age*, edited by Barbara A. Koenig, Sandra Soo-Jin Lee, and Sarah S. Richardson, 215–34. New Brunswick, NJ: Rutgers University Press.

Green, Keneisha M. 2006/2007. "Who's Who: Exploring the Discrepancy between the Methods of Defining African Americans and Native Americans." *American Indian Law Review* 31, no. 1: 93–110.

Haley, Alex. 1976. *Roots: The Saga of an American Family*. New York: Doubleday.

———. 1977. "My Search for Roots: A Black American's Story." *Reader's Digest*, April: 148–52.

Hall, Stuart. 1992. "The Question of Cultural Identity." In *Modernity and Its Futures*, edited by Stuart Hall, David Held, and Anthony McGrew, 274–316. Cambridge, UK: Polity Press.

Hamabata, M. M. 1990. *Crested Kimono: Power and Love in the Japanese Business Family*. Ithaca, NY: Cornell University Press.

Hardy, Carmon, and Dan Erickson. 2001. "Regeneration—Now and Evermore!": Mormon Polygamy and the Physical Rehabilitation of Humankind." *Journal of the History of Sexuality* 10, no. 1: 40–61.

Hareven, Tamara K. 1978. "The Search for Generational Memory: Tribal Rites in Industrial Society." *Daedalus* 107, no. 4: 137–49.

Hartman, Ian C. 2012. "Appalachian Anxiety: Race, Gender, and the Paradox of Purity in an Age of Empire, 1873–1901." *American Nineteenth Century History* 13, no. 2: 229–55.

Hartman, Saidiya V. 2002. "The Time of Slavery." *South Atlantic Quarterly* 101, no. 4: 757–77.

———. 2007. *Lose Your Mother: A Journey along the Atlantic Slave Route.* New York: Farrar, Straus and Giroux.

Harvey, David. 1989. *The Condition of Postmodernity.* Oxford, UK: Basil Blackwell.

Hasty, Jennifer. 2002. "Rites of Passage, Routes of Redemption: Emancipation Tourism and the Wealth of Culture." *Africa Today* 49: 47–76.

Hasu, Päivi. 2009. "For Ancestors and God: Rituals of Sacrifice among the Chagga of Tanzania." *Ethnology* 48, no. 3: 195–213.

Haug, Frigga. 1987. *Female Sexualization: A Collective Work of Memory.* Translated by E. Carter. London: Verso.

Helft, Miguel. 2017. "Ancestry.com DNA Database Tops 3M, Sales Rise to $850M Ahead of Likely 2017 IPO." https://www.forbes.com/sites/miguel helft/2017/01/10/ancestry-com-dna-database-tops-3m-sales-rise-to-850m -ahead-of-likely-2017-ipo/#14708c8f13b3. Accessed September 19, 2017.

Hermkens, Anna-Karina. 2007. "Church Festivals and the Visualization of Identity in Collingwood Bay, Papua New Guinea." *Visual Anthropology* 20: 347–64.

Hilbert, Martin, and Priscila López. 2011. "The World's Technological Capacity to Store, Communicate, and Compute Information." *Science* 332, no. 6025: 60–65.

Hirschman, Elizabeth C., and Donald Panther-Yates. 2008. "Peering Inward for Ethnic Identity: Consumer Interpretation of DNA Test Results." *Identity: An International Journal of Theory and Research* 8: 47–66.

Hobsbawm, Eric. 2007. *Globalisation, Democracy and Terrorism.* London: Little, Brown.

Holdsworth, Amy. 2011. *Television, Memory and Nostalgia.* New York: Palgrave Macmillan.

Hollinger, David A. 2005. "The One Drop Rule and the One Hate Rule." *Daedalus* 134, no. 1: 18–28.

Holsey, Bayo. 2004. "Transatlantic Dreaming: Slavery, Tourism, and Diasporic Encounters." In *Homecomings: Unsettling Paths of Return*, edited by Fran Markowitz and Anders Stefansson. Lanham, MD: Lexington Books.

Howell, Signe. 2003. "Kinning: The Creation of Life Trajectories in Transnational Adoptive Families." *Journal of the Royal Anthropological Institute* 9: 465–84.

Huyssen, Andreas. 1995. *Twilight Memories: Marking Time in a Culture of Amnesia.* New York and London: Routledge.

———. 2000. "Present Pasts: Media, Politics, Amnesia." *Public Culture* 12, no. 1: 21–38.

Ignatiev, Noel. 1997. *How the Irish Became White*. New York and London: Routledge.

Institute for Women's Policy Research. 2015. "Pay Equity and Discrimination." http://www.iwpr.org/initiatives/pay-equity-and-discrimination. Accessed September 10, 2015.

International Air Transport Association. 2012. "Airlines to Welcome 3.6 Billion Passengers in 2016." http://www.iata.org/pressroom/pr/pages/2012-12-06-01 .aspx. Accessed March 12, 2014.

Irish Department of Foreign Affairs and Trade. 2011. "Certificates of Irish Heritage." http://www.heritagecertificate.ie. Accessed December 19, 2011.

———. 2015. "Certificate of Irish Heritage Scheme to Be Discontinued." https:// www.dfa.ie/news-and-media/press-releases/press-release-archive/2015/august/ certs-of-irish-heritage-scheme-discontinued. Accessed September 3, 2015.

Irish Press. 2011. "Tourism Ireland Steps Up United States Marketing Drive to Capitalise on Presidential Visit." http://www.irishpressreleases.ie/2011/05/20/ tourism-ireland-steps-up-united-states-marketing-drive-to-capitalise-on -presidential-visit. Accessed August 30, 2011.

Irvine, Judith T. 1978. "When Is Genealogy History? Wolof Genealogies in Comparative Perspective." *American Ethnologist* 5, no. 4: 651–74.

Jacobs, A. J. 2014a. "The World's Largest Family Reunion, and You're Invited!" (TED Talk) http://ajjacobs.com. Accessed October 6, 2015.

———. 2014b. "Are You My Cousin?" https://www.nytimes.com/2014/02/01/ opinion/sunday/are-you-my-cousin.html. Accessed January 10, 2017.

———. 2014c. "You're Probably Related to Ryan Gosling." https://www .buzzfeed.com/jessicamisener/youre-probably-related-to-ryan-gosling.

———. 2015. "The Global Family Reunion." http://globalfamilyreunion.com/ about. Accessed January 10, 2017.

———. 2016. *Twice Removed*. https://gimletmedia.com/twiceremoved. Accessed January 10, 2017.

James, Kerry. 2002. "The Cost of Custom: A Recent Funeral in Tonga." *Journal of the Polynesian Society* 111: 223–38.

Jenkins, Richard. 2000. "Disenchantment, Enchantment and Re-Enchantment: Max Weber at the Millennium." *Max Weber Studies* 1, no. 1: 11–32.

Johnson, Frances. 2016. "Choosing Love or the Mormon Church." https://www .theatlantic.com/national/archive/2016/03/lgbt-mormons/475035. Accessed July 21, 2017.

Johnston, Josephine. 2003. "Resisting a Genetic Identity: The Black Seminoles and Genetic Tests of Ancestry." *Journal of Law, Medicine and Ethics* 31: 262–71.

Jordan, David K. 1972. *Gods, Ghosts and Ancestors: The Folk Religion of a Taiwanese Village*. Berkeley: University of California Press.

Kahn, Jonathan. 2015. "When Are You From? Time, Space, and Capital in the Molecular Reinscription of Race." *British Journal of Sociology* 66, no. 1: 68–75.

Kastenbaum, Robert J. 1981. *Death, Society and the Human Experience*. St. Louis, MO: The C. V. Mosby Company.

Kelly, Spencer. 2013. "Icelandic Phone App Stops You Dating Close Relatives." https://www.bbc.com/news/av/technology-24304415/icelandic-phone-app -stops-you-dating-close-relatives. Accessed May 23, 2016.

Kevles, Daniel J. 1998. *In the Name of Eugenics: Genetics and the Uses of Human Heredity*. Cambridge, MA: Harvard University Press.

Kirkman, Richard. 2011. *The Walking Dead*. Berkeley, CA: Image Comics.

Kiss, Jemima. 2014. "Facebook's 10th Birthday: From College Dorm to 1.23 Billion Users." *The Guardian*, February 4, 2014. https://www.theguardian.com/ technology/2014/feb/04/facebook-10-years-mark-zuckerberg. Accessed October 10, 2015.

Klass, Dennis. 1996. "Ancestor Worship in Japan: Dependence and the Resolution of Grief." *Omega: An International Journal for the Study of Dying, Death, Bereavement, Suicide, and Other Lethal Behaviors* 33, no. 4: 279–302.

Klitzman, Robert. 2013. "The Failed Promise of 23andMe." https://www .bloomberg.com/view/articles/2013-12-03/the-failed-promise-of-23andme. Accessed May 23, 2016.

Koblin, John. 2016. "How Much Do We Love TV? Let Us Count the Ways." *New York Times*, June 30, 2016. https://www.nytimes.com/2016/07/01/business/ media/nielsen-survey-media-viewing.html. Accessed June 3, 2017.

Koenig, Barbara A., Sandra Soo-Jin Lee, and Sarah S. Richardson, eds. 2008. *Revisiting Race in a Genomic Age*. New Brunswick, NJ: Rutgers University Press.

Kolopenuk, Jessica. 2014. "Wiindigo Incarnate: Consuming Native American DNA." *GeneWatch* 27, no. 2: 18–20.

Kramer, Anne-Marie. 2011. "Kinship, Affinity and Connectedness: Exploring the Role of Genealogy in Personal Lives." *Sociology* 45, no. 3: 379–95.

Kuah-Pearce, Khun Eng. 2006. "Moralising Ancestors as Socio-Moral Capital: A Study of a Transnational Chinese Lineage." *Asian Journal of Social Science* 34, no. 2: 243–63.

Kyerematen, Alex. 1969. "The Royal Stools of Ashanti." *Africa: Journal of the International African Institute* 39, no. 1: 1–10.

Lambert, Ronald D. 1996. "The Family Historian and Temporal Orientations towards the Ancestral Past." *Time and Society* 5, no. 2: 115–43.

———. 2002. "Reclaiming the Ancestral Past: Narrative, Rhetoric and the Convict Stain." *Journal of Sociology* 38, no. 2: 111–27.

Landsberg, Alison. 2004. *Prosthetic Memory: The Transformation of American Remembrance in the Age of Mass Culture*. New York: Columbia University Press.

Laqueur, Thomas W. 2015. *The Work of the Dead*. Princeton, NJ: Princeton University Press.

Leavitt, Stephen C. 1995. "Seeking Gifts from the Dead: Long-Term Mourning in a Bumbita Arapesh Cargo Narrative." *Ethos* 23, no. 4: 453–73.

Lee, Michelle Ye Hee. 2015. "Yes, U.S. Locks People Up at a Higher Rate than Any Other Country." https://www.washingtonpost.com/news/fact-checker/wp/2015/07/07/yes-u-s-locks-people-up-at-a-higher-rate-than-any-other-country/?utm_term=.c51b17550442. Accessed June 22, 2017.

LeFever, Harry G. 1996. "When the Saints Go Riding In: Santeria in Cuba and the United States." *Journal for the Scientific Study of Religion* 35, no. 3: 318–30.

Levin, Amy, ed. 2007a. *Defining Memory: Local Museums and the Construction of History in America's Changing Communities*. Lanham, MD: Alta Mira Press.

———. 2007b. "Business as Usual: Can Museums Be Bought?" In *Defining Memory: Local Museums and the Construction of History in America's Changing Communities*, edited by Amy Levin, 235–51. Lanham, MD: Alta Mira Press.

Lohmann, Roger Ivar. 2005. "The Afterlife of Asabano Corpses: Relationships with the Deceased in Papua New Guinea." *Ethnology* 44, no. 2: 189–206.

Lowenthal, David. 2015. *The Past Is a Foreign Country, Revisited*. New York: Cambridge University Press.

Lynch, Claire. 2011. "Who Do You Think You Are? Intimate Pasts Made Public." *Biography* 34, no. 1: 108–18.

Lyotard, Jean-François. 1984. *The Postmodern Condition: A Report on Knowledge*. Translated by Geoff Bennington. Minneapolis: University of Minnesota Press.

Malinowski, Bronisław. 1916. "Baloma: The Spirits of the Dead in the Trobriand Islands." *Journal of the Royal Anthropological Institute of Great Britain and Ireland* 46: 353–430.

———. 1948. *Magic, Science and Religion*. Garden City, NY: Doubleday.

Marks, Jonathan. 2001. "We're Going to Tell These People Who They Really Are: Science and Relatedness." In *Relative Values: Reconfiguring Kinship Studies*, edited by Sarah Franklin and Susan McKinnon, 355–83. Durham, NC: Duke University Press.

———. 2008. "Past, Present, and Future." In *Revisiting Race in a Genomic Age*, edited by Barbara A. Koenig, Sandra Soo-Jin Lee, and Sarah S. Richardson, 21–38. New Brunswick, NJ: Rutgers University Press.

Mason, Jennifer. 2008. "Tangible Affinities and the Real Life Fascination of Kinship." *Sociology* 42, no. 1: 29–45.

Massey, Doreen. 1994. *Space, Place, and Gender*. Minneapolis: University of Minnesota Press.

Mauss, Armand L. 2003. *Abraham's Children: Changing Mormon Conceptions of Race and Lineage*. Champaign: University of Illinois Press.

McAnany, Patricia A. 2011. "Practices of Place-Making, Ancestralizing, and Reanimation within Memory Communities." *Archeological Papers of the American Anthropological Association* 20, no. 1: 136–42.

McCall, John C. 1995. "Rethinking Ancestors in Africa." *Africa: Journal of the International African Institute* 65, no. 2: 256–70.

McIntosh, Will. 2008. "Followed." In *The Living Dead*, edited by John Joseph Adams, 405–11. New York: Night Shade Books.

Meister, Jeanne. 2012. "Job Hopping Is the New Normal for Millennials: Three Ways to Prevent a Human Resource Nightmare." *Forbes*, August 14, 2012. https://www.forbes.com/sites/jeannemeister/2012/08/14/job-hopping-is-the-new-normal-for-millennials-three-ways-to-prevent-a-human-resource-nightmare/#560d017f5508. Accessed July 10, 2017.

Mendonsa, Eugene L. 1976. "Elders, Office-Holders and Ancestors among the Sisala of Northern Ghana." *Africa: Journal of the International African Institute* 46, no. 1: 57–65.

Mills, C. Wright. 1940. "Situated Actions and Vocabularies of Motives." *American Sociological Review* 5, no 6: 904–13.

Mishel, Lawrence R., Josh Bivens, Elise Gould, and Heidi Shierholz. 2012. *The State of Working America*, 12th ed. Ithaca, NY: Cornell University Press.

Moran, Andrew. 2013. "Online Gaming Industry Growing, Players Transitioning to Mobile Devices." http://www.examiner.com/article/online-gaming-industry-growing-players-transitioning-to-mobile-gaming. Accessed March 13, 2014.

Morgan, Francesca. 2010. "Lineage as Capital: Genealogy in Antebellum New England." *New England Quarterly* 83, no. 2: 250–82.

Morrissette, Jason J. 2014. "Zombies, International Relations, and the Production of Danger: Critical Security Studies versus the Living Dead." *Studies in Popular Culture* 36, no. 2: 1–27.

Morton, Lisa. 2008. "Sparks Fly Upward." In *The Living Dead*, edited by John Joseph Adams, 268–76. New York: Night Shade Books.

Nash, Catherine. 2004. "Genetic Kinship." *Cultural Studies* 18, no. 1: 1–33.

———. 2006. "Irish Origins, Celtic Origins." *Irish Studies Review* 14, no. 1: 11–37.

———. 2013. "Genome Geographies: Mapping National Ancestry and Diversity in Human Population Genetics." *Transactions of the Institute of British Geographers* 38: 193–206.

National Human Genome Institute. 2016. "The Cost of Sequencing a Human Genome." https://www.genome.gov/sequencingcosts. Accessed January 2, 2016.

National Public Radio. 2012. "Mormon Baptism of Wiesenthal Kin Sparks Jewish Outrage." http://www.npr.org/sections/thetwo-way/2012/02/14/146854645/mormon-baptism-of-wiesenthal-kin-sparks-jewish-outrage. Accessed July 21, 2017.

———. 2017. "Mormon Church Limits Access to Controversial Baptism Records." http://www.npr.org/sections/thetwo-way/2012/03/09/148318491/mormon-church-limits-access-to-controversial-baptism-records. Accessed July 21, 2017.

Nelson, John. 2008. "Household Altars in Contemporary Japan: Rectifying Buddhist Ancestor Worship with Home Decor and Consumer Choice." *Japanese Journal of Religious Studies* 35, no. 2: 305–30.

Njemanze, Paul Obiyo Mbanaso. 2011. "Pan-Africanism: Africa in the Minds and Deeds of Her Children in the Caribbean." *Journal of the Historical Society of Nigeria* 20: 152–65.

Nora, Pierre. 2002. "Reasons for the Current Upsurge in Memory." http://www.eurozine.com/pdf/2002-04-19-nora-en.pdf. Accessed September 3, 2016.

Nordqvist, Petra. 2014. "Bringing Kinship into Being: Connectedness, Donor Conception and Lesbian Parenthood." *Sociology* 48, no. 2: 268–83.

Noret, Joel. 2005. "Between Authenticity and Nostalgia: The Making of a Yoruba Tradition in Southern Benin." *African Arts* 41, no. 4: 26–31.

Ogg, J. C. 2011. "Zombies Worth over $5 Billion to Economy." *24/7 WallStreet*, October 25, 2011. http://247wallst.com/investing/2011/10/25/zombies-worth-over-5-billion-to-economy. Accessed July 21, 2017.

Ohrt Fehler, Benedicte. 2014. "(Re)Constructing Roots: Genetics and the Return of African Americans to Ghana." In *Links to the Diasporic Homeland: Second Generation and Ancestral "Return" Mobilities*, edited by Russell King, Anastasia Christou, and Peggy Levitt. London and New York: Routledge.

Ooms, Herman. 1976. "A Structural Analysis of Japanese Ancestral Rites and Beliefs." In *Ancestors*, edited by William H. Newell, 61–90. The Hague and Paris: Mouton Publishers.

Oren, Gil-Or, Yossi Levi-Belz, and Ofir Turel. 2015. "The Facebook-Self: Characteristics and Psychological Predictors of False Self-Presentation on Facebook." *Frontiers in Psychology* 6, no. 99. Web. doi: 10.3389/fpsyg.2015.00099.

Paden, William E. 2001. "Universals Revisited: Human Behaviors and Cultural Variations." *Numen* 48, no. 3: 276–89.

Palsson, G. 2002. "The Life of Family Trees and the Book of Icelanders." *Medical Anthropology* 21: 337–67.

Palwick, Susan. 2008. "Beautiful Stuff." In *The Living Dead*, edited by John Joseph Adams, 137–47. New York: Night Shade Books.

Panofsky, Aaron, and Joan M. Donovan. 2017. "When Genetics Challenges a Racist's Identity: Genetic Ancestry Testing among White Nationalists." Presentation at the annual meeting of the American Sociological Association in Montreal, Canada, August 12–15, 2017.

Panzacchi, Cornelia. 1994. "The Livelihoods of Traditional Griots in Modern Senegal." *Africa* 64, no. 2: 190–210.

Pascal, G. Zachary. 2001. "Tangled Roots: For African-Americans in Ghana, the Grass Isn't Always Greener." *Wall Street Journal*, March 14, 2001. https://www.wsj.com/articles/SB984521987681892576. Accessed August 1, 2017.

Peterson, Philip L. 1996. "Do Significant Cultural Universals Exist?" *American Philosophical Quarterly* 33, no. 2: 183–96.

Pew Forum on Religion and Public Life. 2007. "U.S. Religious Landscape Survey." http://religions.pewforum.org/pdf/report-religious-landscape-study-chapter-2.pdf. Accessed March 14, 2014.

Pew Research Center. 2009. "A Portrait of Mormons in the US." http://www
.pewforum.org/2009/07/24/a-portrait-of-mormons-in-the-us/#3. Accessed
July 21, 2017.

———. 2012. "'Nones' on the Rise." http://www.pewforum.org/2012/10/09/
nones-on-the-rise. Accessed March 14, 2014.

Poggie, John J., Jr., and Carl Gersuny. 1972. "Risk and Ritual: An Interpretation
of Fishermen's Folklore in a New England Community." *Journal of American
Folklore* 85, no. 335: 66–72.

Pogue Harrison, Robert. 2003. *The Dominion of the Dead*. Chicago: University of
Chicago Press.

Póirtéir, Cathal. 1997. *The Great Irish Famine*. Chester Springs, PA: Dufour Edi-
tions.

Prandi, Reginaldo. 2000. "African Gods in Contemporary Brazil: A Sociological
Introduction to Candomblé Today." *International Sociology* 15, no. 4: 641–63.

Pritchard, Charlotte. 2014. "The Girl with Three Biological Parents." http://
www.bbc.com/news/magazine-28986843. Accessed January 12, 2017.

Rasmussen, Susan J. 2000. "Alms, Elders, and Ancestors: The Spirit of the Gift
among the Tuareg." *Ethnology* 39, no. 1: 15–38.

Rawski, Evelyn S. 1988. "A Historian's Approach to Chinese Death Ritual." In
Death Ritual in Late Imperial and Modern China, edited by James L. Watson and
Evelyn S. Rawski, 20–34. Berkeley: University of California Press.

Reed, Ann. 2004. "Sankɔfa Site: Cape Coast Castle and Its Museum as Markers of
Memory." *Museum Anthropology* 27, no. 1–2: 13–23.

———. 2012. "The Commemoration of Slavery Heritage: Tourism and the Rei-
fication of Meaning." In *The Cultural Moment in Tourism*, edited by Laurajane
Smith, Emma Waterton, and Steve Watson. London: Routledge.

———. 2013. "Diaspora Tourism: The Heritage of Slavery in Ghana." In *A
Companion to Diaspora and Transnationalism*, edited by Ato Quayson and Girish
Daswani. Oxford, UK: Blackwell Publishing.

———. 2015. *Pilgrimage Tourism of Diaspora Africans to Ghana*. New York: Routledge.

Reed, Bess, and Benjamin Hufbauer. 2005. "Ancestors and Commemoration in
Igbo Odo Masquerades." *RES: Anthropology and Aesthetics*, no. 47: 135–52.

Rees Anderson, Amy. 2014. "Opportunity Is About to Knock, so Get Ready to
Open Your Door." https://www.forbes.com/sites/amyanderson/2014/11/23/
opportunity-is-about-to-knock-so-get-ready-to-open-your-door/#7e96064
ddaf6. Accessed September 15, 2017.

Richardson, Heather Cox. 2007. *West from Appomattox: The Reconstruction of America after the Civil War*. New Haven, CT: Yale University Press.

Rodgers, Graeme. 2008. "Everyday Life and the Political Economy of Displacement on the Mozambique–South Africa Borderland." *Journal of Contemporary
African Studies* 26, no. 4: 385–99.

Rodriguez, Gregory. 2014. "How Genealogy Became Almost as Popular as Porn." *Time.* http://time.com/133811/how-genealogy-became-almost-as-popular-as -porn. Accessed August 25, 2015.

Rojek, Chris. 2010. *The Labour of Leisure: The Culture of Free Time.* Los Angeles and London: Sage.

Rojek, Chris, and John Urry, eds. 1997. *Touring Cultures: Transformations of Travel and Theory.* New York and London: Routledge.

Rubinstein, William D. 2010. "A Very British Crime Wave." *History Today* 60, no. 12: 43–48.

Rüpke, Jörg. 2006. "Triumphator and Ancestor Rituals between Symbolic Anthropology and Magic." *Numen* 53: 251–89.

Santos, Carla Almeida, and Grace Yan. 2010. "Genealogical Tourism: A Phenomenological Examination." *Journal of Travel Research* 49, no. 1: 56–67.

Saunders, Robert A. 2012. "Undead Spaces: Fear, Globalisation, and the Popular Geopolitics of Zombiism." *Geopolitics* 17: 80–104.

Schudson, Michael. 1984. *Advertising, the Uneasy Persuasion: Its Dubious Impact on American Society.* New York: Basic Books.

Shahar, Meir, and Robert P. Weller. 1996. "Introduction: Gods and Society in China." In *Unruly Gods: Divinity and Society in China,* edited by Meir Shahar and Robert P. Weller, 1–36. Honolulu: University of Hawaii Press.

Sheils, Dean. 1975. "Toward a Unified Theory of Ancestor Worship: A Cross-Cultural Study." *Social Forces* 54, No. 2: 427–40.

———. 1980. "The Great Ancestors Are Watching: A Cross-Cultural Study of Superior Ancestral Religion." *Sociological Analysis* 41, no. 3: 247–57.

Shipman, Pat. 2003. "Marginalia: We Are All Africans." *American Scientist* 91, no. 6: 496–99.

Simpson, Bob. 2000. "Imagined Genetic Communities, Ethnicity and Essentialism in the 21st Century." *Anthropology Today* 16, no. 3: 3–6.

Smith, Robert J. 1974. *Ancestor Worship in Contemporary Japan.* Stanford, CA: Stanford University Press.

Sommer, Marianne. 2012. "It's a Living History, Told by the Real Survivors of the Times—DNA: Anthropological Genetics in the Tradition of Biology as Applied History." In *Genetics and the Unsettled Past: The Collision of DNA, Race, and History,* edited by Keith Wailoo, Alondra Nelson, and Catherine Lee, 225–46. New Brunswick, NJ: Rutgers University Press.

Soo-Jin Lee, Sandra, Deborah A. Bolnick, Troy Duster, Pilar Ossorio, and Kimberly TallBear. 2009. "The Illusive Gold Standard in Genetic Ancestry Testing." *Science* 325: 38–39. http://www.sciencemag.org. Accessed May 12, 2016.

Spruhan, Paul. 2006. "A Legal History of Blood Quantum in Federal Indian Law to 1935." *South Dakota Law Review* 51, no. 1: 1–50.

Steadman, Lyle B., Craig T. Palmer, and Christopher F. Tilley. 1996. "The Universality of Ancestor Worship." *Ethnology* 35, no. 1: 63–76.

Stearns, Peter N. 2003. "Social History Present and Future." *Journal of Social History* 37, no. 1: 9–19.

Steers, Mai-Ly N., Robert E. Wickham, and Linda K. Acitelli. 2014. "Seeing Everyone Else's Highlight Reels: How Facebook Usage Is Linked to Depressive Symptoms." *Journal of Social and Clinical Psychology* 33, no. 8: 701–31.

Stratton. Jon. 2011. "Zombie Trouble: Zombie Texts, Bare Life and Displaced People." *European Journal of Cultural Studies* 1, no. 3: 265–81.

Sue, Derald Wing. 2010. *Microaggressions in Everyday Life: Race, Gender, and Sexual Orientation*. Hoboken, NJ: John Wiley and Sons.

Sutton, Ryan. 2014. "Women Everywhere in Food Empires but No Head Chefs." http://www.bloomberg.com/news/articles/2014-03-06/women-everywhere in chang colicchio empires-but-no-head-chefs. Accessed September 10, 2015.

Sweeney, Michael S. 2010. "Ancestors, Avotaynu, Roots: An Inquiry into American Genealogy Discourse." PhD dissertation, University of Kansas.

Sykes, Bryan. 2001. *The Seven Daughters of Eve*. New York: Norton.

Takeda, Choshu. 1976. "Recent Trends in Studies of Ancestor Worship in Japan." In *Ancestors*, edited by William H. Newell, 129–40. The Hague and Paris: Mouton Publishers.

TallBear, Kimberly. 2003. "DNA, Blood, and Racializing the Tribe." *Wicazo Sa Review* 18, no. 1: 81–107.

———. 2008. "Native-American-DNA.com: In Search of Native American Race and Tribe." In *Revisiting Race in a Genomic Age*, edited by Barbara A. Koenig, Sandra Soo-Jin Lee, and Sarah S. Richardson, 235–52. New Brunswick, NJ: Rutgers University Press.

Taylor, Robert M., Jr., and Ralph J. Crandall, eds. 1986. *Generations and Change, Genealogical Perspectives in Social History*. Macon, GA: Mercer University Press.

Teather, Elizabeth K. 1999. "High-Rise Homes for the Ancestors: Cremation in Hong Kong." *Geographical Review* 89, no. 3: 409–30.

Tindall, George Brown, and David E. Shi. 2012. *America: A Narrative History* (brief 9th ed., vol. 2). New York: Norton.

Tolkien, J. R. R. 1994. *The Lord of the Rings*. New York: HarperCollins and Houghton Mifflin.

Tönnies, Ferdinand. 2001. *Community and Civil Society*, edited by Jose Harris. Cambridge, UK: Cambridge University Press.

Toone, Trent. 2017. "How Technology Revolutionized Family History Work in Recent Decades." http://www.deseretnews.com/article/865676564/How -technology-revolutionized-family-history-work-in-recent-decades.html. Accessed July 20, 2017.

Tourism Ireland. 2017. "Mid-Year Review of Overseas Tourism 2017." https:// www.tourismireland.com/Press-Releases/2017/August/Mid-year-review-of -overseas-tourism-2017. Accessed August 16, 2017.

Traphagan, John. 2003. "Older Women as Caregivers and Ancestral Protection in Rural Japan." *Ethnology* 42, no. 2: 127–39.

Traver, Amy. 2007. "(Ap)Parent Boundaries: Parents' Boundary Work at Cultural Events for Families with Children Adopted from China." *Sociological Focus* 40, no. 2: 221–41.

Trubeck, Anne. 2016. *The History and Uncertain Future of Handwriting.* New York: Bloomsbury.

Turner, Victor. 1973. "The Center Out There: Pilgrim's Goal." *History of Religions* 12, no. 3: 191–230.

Turner, Victor, and Edith Turner. 1978. *Image and Pilgrimage in Christian Culture.* New York: Columbia University Press.

Tutton, Richard. 2004. "They Want to Know Where They Came From: Population Genetics, Identity, and Family Genealogy." *New Genetics and Society* 23, no. 1: 105–20.

Ubah, C. N. 1982. "The Supreme Being, Divinities and Ancestors in Igbo Traditional Religion: Evidence from the Otanchara and Otanzu." *Africa* 52, no. 2: 90–105.

Urry, John. 1990. *The Tourist Gaze: Leisure and Travel in Contemporary Societies.* London: Sage.

US Bureau of Labor Statistics. 2015. "Number of Jobs Held, Labor Market Activity, and Earnings Growth among the Youngest Baby Boomers: Results from a Longitudinal Survey." http://www.bls.gov/news.release/pdf/nlsoy.pdf. Accessed September 13, 2016.

US Census Bureau. 2007. "Calculating Migration Expectancy Using ACS Data." https://www.census.gov/hhes/migration/about/cal-mig-exp.html. Accessed September 13, 2016.

———. 2012. "US Census Bureau Projections Show a Slower Growing, Older, More Diverse Nation a Half Century from Now." https://www.census.gov/newsroom/releases/archives/population/cb12-243.html. Accessed September 13, 2016.

Van der Geest, Sjaak. 1997. "The Changing Value of Old Age in Rural Ghana." *Africa: Journal of the International African Institute* 67, no. 4: 534–59.

———. 2000. "Funerals for the Living: Conversations with Elderly People in Kwahu, Ghana." *African Studies Review* 43, no. 3: 103–29.

Vega, Marta Moreno. 1999. "Espiritismo in the Puerto Rican Community: A New World Recreation with the Elements of Kongo Ancestor Worship." *Journal of Black Studies* 29, no. 3: 325–53.

Vonarx, Nicolas. 2007. "Vodou, Illness and Models in Haiti: From Local Meanings to Broader Relations of Domination." *Anthropology in Action* 14, no. 3: 18–29.

Wachowski, Lana, and Lilly Wachowski. 1999. *The Matrix.* Warner Brothers.

Wadley, Reed L. 1999. "Disrespecting the Dead and the Living: Iban Ancestor Worship and the Violation of Mourning Taboos." *Journal of the Royal Anthropological Institute*, no. 5: 595–610.

Wailoo, Keith, Alondra Nelson, and Catherine Lee, eds. 2012. *Genetics and the Unsettled Past: The Collision of DNA, Race, and History.* New Brunswick, NJ: Rutgers University Press.

Wallace, Kelly. 2015. "Teens Spend a 'Mind-Boggling' 9 Hours a Day Using Media, Report Says." *CNN*, November 3, 2015. https://www.cnn.com/2015/11/03/health/teens-tweens-media-screen-use-report. Accessed June 3, 2017.

Wang, Qi, Dasom Lee, and Yubo Hou. 2016. "Externalising the Autobiographical Self: Sharing Personal Memories Online Facilitated Memory Retention." *Memory* 25, no. 6: 772–76.

Waters, Mary C. 1990. *Ethnic Options: Choosing Identities in America*. Berkeley: University of California Press.

Watson, James. 1988. "Funeral Specialists in Cantonese Society: Pollution, Performance and Social Hierarchy." In *Death Ritual in Late Imperial and Modern China*, edited by J. L. Watson and E. S. Rawski, 109–34. Berkeley and Los Angeles: University of California Press.

Watson, Rubie S. 1986. "The Named and the Nameless: Gender and Person in Chinese Society." *American Ethnologist* 13, no. 4: 619–631.

Watson, S. J. 2011. *Before I Go to Sleep*. New York: HarperCollins.

Webb, Jen, and Sam Byrnand. 2008. "Some Kind of Virus: The Zombie as Body and as Trope." *Body and Society* 14, no. 2: 83–98.

Weil, François. 2013. *Family Trees: A History of Genealogy in America*. Cambridge, MA: Harvard University Press.

Weisenfeld, Judith. 2013. "On Not Being Jewish . . . and Other Lies: Reflections on *Racial Fever*." *Soundings: An Interdisciplinary Journal* 96, no. 1: 9–11.

Weiser, Lee. 2015. "The Zombie Archetype: Living in a Viral Culture." *Psychological Perspectives* 58: 442–54.

Wendt, Albert. 1987. "Novelists and Historians and the Art of Remembering." In A. Hooper et al. (eds.), *Class and Culture in the South Pacific*, Centre for Pacific Studies, University of Auckland, and Institute of Pacific Studies, University of the South Pacific, Suva.

Weston, Kath. 1991. *Families We Choose: Lesbians, Gays, Kinship*. New York: Columbia University Press.

Wilkerson, Isabel. 2010. *The Warmth of Other Suns: The Epic Story of America's Great Migration*. New York: Vintage Books.

Williams, Christine L. 1995. *Still a Man's World: Men Who Do Women's Work*. Berkeley: University of California Press.

Williamson, Judith. 1978. *Decoding Advertisements: Ideology and Meaning in Advertising*. London: Marion Boyars.

Wiredu, Kwasi. 1995. "Are There Cultural Universals?" *The Monist* 78, no 1: 52–64.

Wolf, A. P. 1974. "Gods, Ghosts and Ancestors." In *Religion and Ritual in Chinese Society*, edited by A. P. Wolf, 131–82. Stanford, CA: Stanford University Press.

Wonser, Robert. 2016. "Between the Living and the Undead: How Zombie Cinema Reflects the Social Construction of Risk, the Anxious Self, and Disease Pandemic." *Sociological Quarterly* 57: 628–53.

World Bank. 2013. "Air Transport, Passengers Carried." http://data.worldbank .org/indicator/IS.AIR.PSGR. Accessed March 12, 2014.

World Travel and Tourism Council. 2016. "Travel and Tourism Economic Impact 2016 Ghana." https://www.wttc.org/-/media/files/reports/economic%20impact %20research/countries%202016/ghana2016.pdf. Accessed August 16, 2017.

Yakel, Elizabeth. 2004. "Seeking Information, Seeking Connections, Seeking Meaning: Genealogists and Family Historians." *Information Research* 10, no. 1, paper 205.

Yankholmes, Aaron K. B., and Oheneba A. Akyeampong. 2010. "Tourists' Perceptions of Heritage Tourism Development in Danish-Osu, Ghana," *International Journal of Tourism Research* 12: 603–16.

Young, Craig, and Duncan Light. 2016. "Interrogating Spaces Of and For the Dead as 'Alternative Space': Cemeteries, Corpses and Sites of Dark Tourism." *International Review of Social Research* 6, no. 2: 61–72.

Zerubavel, Eviatar. 1996. "Social Memories: Steps to a Sociology of the Past," *Qualitative Sociology* 19, no. 3: 283–99.

———. 2012. *Ancestors and Relatives: Genealogy, Identity, and Community.* New York: Oxford University Press.

Zhang, Sarah. 2018. "How a Genealogy Website Led to the Alleged Golden State Killer." *The Atlantic.* https://www.theatlantic.com/science/archive/2018/04/ golden-state-killer-east-area-rapist-dna-genealogy/559070. Accessed May 8, 2018.

Zinn, Howard. 2005. *A People's History of the United States.* New York: Harper Perennial Modern Classics.

INDEX

Note: Italicized page numbers indicate illustrations.

adoption and kinship, 50, 83, 98, 99,
100, 108, 130, 188n50, 192n24
advertisements, genealogical, 6, 33, 36,
80, 82, 119–20, *149*, 170, 191n27
AIDS epidemic and Chagga ancestor
beliefs, 46
Allen County Public Library, 2
American Dream, the, 5, 109, 110–12,
116, 117
American exceptionalism, 111–13
American genealogical eras: American
democratic genealogy, *22*, 23–24,
176n3; eugenic, nationalistic and
aspirational genealogy, *22*, 24–28;
multicultural, self-revelatory
genealogy, *22*, 28–31; old
world and American aristocratic
genealogy, *22*, 21–23, 176n3;
quantum genealogy, *22*, 31–39
American genealogists, demographic
traits of, 9–10
ancestor veneration (or worship), 4,
42, 44–48, 51, 55, 121, 179n3,
182n92: in China, Taiwan and
Malaysia, 48–51, 59, 61–62;
in Japan, 51–53, 59, 61–62;
in Melanesia, 53–54, 59; in

Micronesia, 54–55, 59, 62; in sub-
Saharan Africa, 45–47, 59, 61–62;
in the New World, 55–58, 59
Ancestry.com, 2, 32, 33, 36–37,
73, 80–81, 116, 119, 129, 163,
168, 170, 173n3, 173n4, 177n44,
178n46, 178n47, 185n38, 187n23
AncestryDNA, 83, 88, 91, 178n51,
186n14, 187n26
Anderson, Benedict, 176n9
Anderson, Nephi, 38, 127–28, 178n64
anthropometrics, 185n2
anti-miscegenation laws, 27, 84,
85–86, 186n6
Appadurai, Arjun, 183n5
Ariès, Philippe, 75, 184n25
Asabano mourning rituals, 53–54
assisted reproduction and kinship, 83,
99–100
aura of authenticity, 142, 193n6
autosomal DNA tests, 34, 87, 88

Baudrillard, Jean, 184n25
Bauman, Zygmunt, 74, 75, 125,
170, 173n9, 183n7, 184n24, 185
n24–25, 185n36, 192n6, 196n1
Benjamin, Walter, 193n6